24 15

The Hellenistic Stoa

The Hellenistic Stoa

Political Thought and Action

Andrew Erskine

Cornell University Press

Ithaca, New York

First published 1990 Cornell University Press.

Library of Congress Cataloging-in-Publication Data

Erskine, Andrew.
    The Helllenistic stoa : political thought and action / Andrew
Erskine.
        p.   cm.
    Includes bibliographical references.
    ISBN 0-8014-2463-1 (alk. paper)
    1. Political science—History.   2. Stoics.   I. Title.
JC51.E77   1990
320′.0938—dc20   89-37091

Printed in Great Britain

Contents

5. Property and Justice

6. The Spartan Revolution

7. The Gracchi

8. The Justification of the Roman Empire

Abbreviations

1. Collections of evidence and works of reference

DK	*Fragmente der Vorsokratiker*, H. Diels and W. Kranz
EK	*Posidonius 1: the fragments*, L. Edelstein and I.G. Kidd (Cambridge 1972)
FGH	*Fragmente der griechischen Historiker*, F. Jacoby
FIRA	*Fontes Iuris Romani Anteiustiniani*, vol. 1^2, S. Riccobono (Florence 1941)
GGM	*Geographici Graeci Minores*, C. Müller (Paris 1855-61)
HRR	*Historicorum Romanorum Reliquiae*, vol. 1^2, H. Peter (1914)
IG	*Inscriptiones Graecae*
IGRR	*Inscriptiones Graecae ad res Romanas pertinentes*, R. Cagnat
ILLRP	*Inscriptiones Latinae Liberae Rei Publicae*, A. Degrassi
Kock	*Comicorum Atticorum Fragmenta*, T. Kock (Leipzig 1880-88)
Moretti	*Iscrizioni Storiche Ellenistiche*, L. Moretti (Florence 1965)
OGIS	*Orientis Graeci Inscriptiones Selectae*, W. Dittenberger (Leipzig 1903-5)
ORF	*Oratorum Romanorum Fragmenta*[2], H. Malcovati (Turin 1955)
Panaetius	*Panaetii Rhodii Fragmenta*[3], M. Van Straaten (Leiden 1962)
PG	*Patrologiae Cursus, Series Graeca*, J.P. Migne
RE	*Realencyclopädie der classischen Altertumswissenschaft*, Pauly-Wissowa
SIG	*Sylloge Inscriptionum Graecarum*[3], W. Dittenberger (Leipzig 1915-24)
SVA	*Die Staatsverträge des Altertums*, vol. 3, H.H. Schmitt (Munich 1969)
SVF	*Stoicorum Veterum Fragmenta*, H. von Arnim (Stuttgart 1903-5)

Theiler   *Posidonius: Die Fragmente*, W. Theiler (Berlin/
                                     New York 1982)

2. Sources

The evidence for the Stoa and Stoic political thought is given by
reference to H. von Arnim's collection of Stoic fragments, *Stoicorum
Veterum Fragmenta* (SVF). In most cases this reference is
supplemented by the full reference to the original work from which the
fragment is taken (e.g. Plut. *St. Rep.* 1034c, SVF 1.200). In some cases I
have only cited the name of the author, for instance when the work is
not easily accessible. Occasionally no reference to SVF is given,
because the relevant passage has been broken up among too many
fragments and thus much of the sense of the original has been lost. A
fairly extensive collection of sources in translation is provided by A.A.
Long and D.N. Sedley, *The Hellenistic Philosophers*, vol. 1:
Translations of the principal sources with philosophical commentary
(Cambridge 1987).

Aelian *VH*	Aelian (c. AD 170-235), *Varia Historia*
Agis	Plutarch, *Life of Agis*
Alex. Aphrod.	Alexander of Aphrodisias, Peripatetic, c. AD 200
Ambrose *De Off.*	Ambrose, *De Officiis Ministrorum*, bishop, fourth century AD
Appian *BC*	Appian (early second century AD), *Bella Civilia* (Civil Wars)
Lib.	*Libukê, Roman History*, bk 8
Arist.	Aristotle (384-322 BC)
Ath. Pol.	*Athenaion Politeia* (Constitution of Athens)
NE	*Nicomachean Ethics*
Pol.	*Politics*
Protrept.	*Protrepticus*, ed. I. Düring (1961)
Rhet.	*Rhetorica*
Arius Didymus	Alexandrian doxographer, first century BC, see Fortenbaugh 1983
Athen.	Athenaeus (c. AD 200), *Deipnosophistai*, learned conversation at dinner
Aug.	Augustine (AD 354-430)
De Civ	*De Civitate Dei* (City of God)
Con. Iul.	*Contra Julianum*
Cic.	Cicero (106-43 BC)
Acad. Pr/Post.	*Academica Priora/Posteriora*
Ad Att.	*Ad Atticum* (Letters to Atticus)
Ad Fam.	*Ad Familiares* (Letters to Friends)
Ad Q. F.	*Ad Quintum Fratrem* (Letters to Quintus)

De Div.	*De Divinatione* (On Divination)
De Fin.	*De Finibus Bonorum et Malorum* (On Ends)
De Har. Resp.	*De Haruspicum Responso*
De Leg.	*De Legibus* (On Laws)
De Leg. Ag.	*De Lege Agraria contra Rullum*
De Nat. Deo.	*De Natura Deorum* (On the Nature of the Gods)
De Off.	*De Officiis* (On Duties)
De Orat.	*De Oratore*
De Rep.	*De Republica* (On the State)
De Sen.	*Cato Maior de Senectute* (On Old Age)
Laelius	*Laelius de Amicitia* (On Friendship)
Pro Mur.	*Pro Murena*
Tusc. Disp.	*Tusculan Disputations*
Clem. Al. *Strom.*	Clement of Alexandria, *Stromateis* (Miscellanies), bishop and philosopher, c. AD 200
Cleom.	Plutarch, *Life of Cleomenes*
Comp.	Plutarch, *Comparison of Agis and Cleomenes and the Gracchi*
Dem.	Demosthenes (384-322 BC)
D.H. *AR*	Dionysius of Halicarnassus (late first century BC), *Roman Antiquities*
Dio Cass.	Dio Cassius (c. AD 200), *Roman History*
Dio Chrys.	Dio Chrysostom, Greek orator influenced by Stoic-Cynic philosophy, c. AD 100
Diod.	Diodorus Siculus (first century BC), a world history
D.L.	Diogenes Laertius (early third century AD?), *The Lives and Opinions of the Philosophers*
Epict.	Epictetus, *Dissertations*, Stoic philosopher, c. AD 55-135
Euseb. *Praep.*	Eusebius of Caesarea, *Praeparatio Evangelica*, bishop and church historian c. AD 260-340
Galen *HP*	Galen, *De Placitis Hippocratis et Platonis* (On the Doctrines of Hippocrates and Plato), Greek medical writer and philosopher, late second century AD.
Gell.	Aulus Gellius (second century AD), *Noctes Atticae*
Isid. *Orig.*	Isidorus Hispalensis, *Origines* or *Etymologiae*, seventh century AD
Isoc.	Isocrates (436-338 BC)
Archid.	*Archidamus*
Paneg.	*Panegyricus*
Panath.	*Panathenaicus*
Lact. *Inst.*	Lactantius, *Divinae Institutiones*, Christian, c. AD 240-320

Livy	Livy (late first century BC – early first century AD), *History of Rome*
Per.	*Periochae*
Oxy. Epit.	*Oxyrhynchus Epitome*
Marcianus	Roman jurist, third century AD
Origen	Christian theologian/philosopher, third century AD
Paus.	Pausanias (second century AD), *Description of Greece*
Philod.	Philodemus, *Peri Stoikôn* (On the Stoics), Epicurean, first century BC
Vol. Rhet.	*Volumina Rhetorica* (ed. S. Sudhaus)
Plato *Alc.*	Plato (c. 429-347 BC), *Alcibiades* 1 (spurious)
Def.	*Definitions* (spurious)
Rep.	*Republic*
Theat.	*Theatetus*
Tim.	*Timaeus*
Pliny *NH*	Pliny (c. AD 61 – c. 112), *Natural History*
Plut.	Plutarch, Platonist philosopher and biographer, c. AD 100
Al. Fort.	*De Alexandri Fortuna* = *Mor.* 326d
Arat.	*Life of Aratus*
CG	*Life of Gaius Gracchus*
Comm. Not.	*De Communibus Notitiis adversus Stoicos* (Against the Stoics on common conceptions) = *Mor.* 1058e
Demet.	*Life of Demetrius*
De Mus.	*De Musica* = *Mor.* 1131a
Lyc.	*Life of Lycurgus*
Marc.	*Life of Marcellus*
Mor.	*Moralia*
Per.	*Life of Pericles*
St. Rep.	*De Stoicorum Repugnantiis* (On Stoic Self-contradictions) = *Mor.* 1033a
TG	*Life of Tiberius Gracchus*
Tranq. An.	*De Tranquillitate Animi* = *Mor.* 464e
Polyb.	Polybius, *Histories*, see Chapter 8.2
Quintilian, *Inst.*	Quintilian (first century AD), *Institutio Oratoria*
Sall. *Jug.*	Sallust (c. 86-35 BC), *Jugurtha*
Sen.	Seneca (c. AD 1-65), Roman Stoic, adviser to Nero
Ad Helv.	*Ad Helviam Matrem de Consulatione*
Cons. Marc.	*Ad Marciam de Consulatione*
De Ben.	*De Beneficiis*
Ep.	*Epistulae Morales* (Moral letters)
Sext. Emp.	Sextus Empiricus, *Adversus Mathematicos*

	(Against the Professors), Sceptical philosopher, c. AD 200
Stob. *Ecl.*	Stobaeus, *Eclogae* (ed. C. Wachsmuth), Greek anthologist, c. fifth century AD, see Fortenbaugh 1983
Strabo	Stoic influenced writer of *Geography*, 64/3 BC – after AD 21
Suet. *Gram.*	Suetonius, *De Grammaticis*
Thuc.	Thucydides
Val. Max.	Valerius Maximus, early first century AD
Vel. Pat.	Velleius Paterculus, *Historiae Romanae*, early first century AD
Xen.	Xenophon (early fourth century BC)
Ages.	*Agesilaus*
Hel.	*Hellenica*
Lac. Pol.	*Lakedaimoniôn Politeia* (The Spartan Constitution)
Mem.	*Memorabilia*

Acknowledgments

In writing this book I am indebted to many people for their assistance. It began as a D.Phil. thesis and especial thanks are due to my two supervisors: George Forrest gave me invaluable criticism, in particular on Sparta, while Peter Derow patiently taught me much about billiards and, in between, about Roman history. Many others have helped me with criticism or advice at different stages, notably my two examiners, Professor F.W. Walbank and Dr John Briscoe, along with Julia Annas, Christian Habicht, Stephen Halliwell, Brad Inwood, John Rist and, moreover, Theresa Urbainczyk. My parents also deserve a place here for their encouragement over the years.

Introduction

Hellenistic philosophy often used to be dismissed as the product of second-rate philosophers, an attitude made easier by the loss of most of their writings. Their work could not stand comparison with the great achievements of Plato and Aristotle.[1] In recent years much has been done to rehabilitate the Hellenistic schools and to disinter their philosophy from the often misleading accounts of later writers.

Although Stoicism has been the subject of much valuable research, the field of Stoic political thought in this period has been relatively neglected.[2] Often it is only subjected to brief treatment in the course of a survey of Stoic philosophy or Hellenistic political thought, although Zeno's *Politeia* has always attracted more detailed attention.[3] Elsewhere Stoic political thought has been introduced into the study of particular ideas, personalities or events, for instance, the unity of mankind,[4] Antigonus Gonatas[5] or the Spartan revolution.[6] In such cases Stoicism is only peripheral to the main subject of enquiry. Consequently claims about specific aspects of Stoic thought are sometimes taken for granted without ensuring that they are intelligible within the context of Stoic political thought or Stoic philosophy as a whole. When a coherent picture of their political thought is established, it may be that such assumptions have to be revised or even rejected.

It is in response to these shortcomings that I am reconstructing and examining the course of the political thought of the Stoa from Zeno, its founder, through to its emergence in Rome. In doing so I aim to reassess certain assumptions that have been made and identify those issues which particularly concerned them. The Hellenistic period was a time of considerable change in the Greek world, and Stoic political thought itself was far from static. I intend to examine it in its historical context and so explore the interaction between thought and events. I am concerned to trace how what began as a radical doctrine came to be

[1] For instance Zeller 1923: 12-15, Cornford 1932: 108-9. Bevan 1913: 32 can describe Stoicism as 'a system put together hastily, violently to meet a desperate emergency'.

[2] The most recent study to concentrate on Stoic political thought in the Hellenistic period is the brief survey by Reesor.

[3] Sinclair 1951, Aalders 1975 contain sections on Stoic political thought.

[4] Baldry 1970, Tarn 1933, 1948.

[5] Tarn 1913.

[6] Ollier 1936, 1943.

so closely identified with the Roman establishment. The book concentrates on the political thought of the Stoa, but other aspects of their philosophy are introduced where they are relevant.

Scholars have adopted different approaches to the study of political thought. It is proposed here to examine the ideas of the Stoa in their historical context. Some, however, believe that political thought can be satisfactorily studied in abstraction from the environment in which it was developed. What is important is the coherency and validity of the arguments.[7] Yet political thought is intimately connected to its social and political environment and it is this environment which is the subject of its inquiry. Philosophers are not separate from society but part of it and consequently, whether they are analysing or rejecting contemporary society, the nature of their analysis or rejection is conditioned by the form of that society, its values and its beliefs. An examination of the arguments in isolation may show that they are coherent and valid as arguments, but, if the context is to be ignored, it becomes hard to see how it is possible to understand what the arguments are actually about.

The philosopher is engaged in constant interaction with the society in which he lives. Whether he is writing, lecturing or debating, he intends to communicate with his contemporaries. The early Stoics, for instance, taught in public in the Stoa Poikile. Such communication will involve shared values and beliefs which often may be presupposed in argument. The philosopher will seek to change and develop man's understanding of his environment, but he will at the same time be constrained both in his own thoughts and in the expression of those thoughts by existing linguistic conventions and conceptual patterns. His originality can only be understood by an awareness of those constraints. Thus an understanding of his work must involve an understanding of both his intellectual and social environment, that is to say his relationship to the ideas of his predecessors and contemporaries, both philosophers and non-philosophers.

Different societies will pose different problems for the philosopher and the nature of that society will affect the way that he seeks to resolve those problems. Not to take account of these conditions which will embrace both the philosopher and his audience is to fail to appreciate much of what the philosopher is saying. This is not to suggest that one should put oneself in the position of a Greek listening to Zeno, but that one should seek to understand both the work and the relationship between philosophy and society and that these two objectives are interrelated. Such considerations of context make it possible to see that, while some of the ideas of the early Stoa were

---

[7] The claim that 'the *text* itself should form the self-sufficient object of inquiry and understanding' is subjected to a vigorous critique by Skinner 1969: 4-39.

thought to be outrageous in Rome, they would not necessarily have been considered so extreme in Athens. Here they had developed out of a long tradition of debate which was related to the social, intellectual and political environment, whereas in Rome they were not only divorced from this context but presented to an alien culture.[8]

So far I have considered the importance of context in understanding what a philosopher said, but from the point of view of a historical inquiry the context also helps to explain why it was said. In commenting on society the philosopher will be influenced by his political and social environment. An analysis of his response to circumstances can serve to explain some of the changes that take place within political thought and at the same time assist in the understanding of the thought itself. This book is concerned with change in Stoic thought, changes that occur in a period of considerable social and political upheaval. I am seeking to consider whether these changes are related and, if so, the nature of the relationship.

The evidence

An important consideration to be taken into account in the study of Stoic political thought in the Hellenistic period is the nature of the evidence. There is virtually no extant writing by any Stoic writer of this period, except for a few verses of Cleanthes.[9] Instead their arguments have to be reconstructed from later accounts, such as those of Cicero, Plutarch and Diogenes Laertius. In the process of transmission the arguments may have become distorted. In order to assess the meaning and value of these later reports of early Stoic thought,[10] several factors need to be taken into account. It is necessary to consider the context of the reference to the Stoa in the later work and the purpose of the writer, both in writing the work and in making the citation. For instance, Plutarch in *De Stoicorum Repugnantiis* (On Stoic Self-contradiction) is clearly hostile to the Stoa and seeking to prove that the Stoic philosophers contradicted themselves. Nor should one only guard against a writer whose intention is hostile. Writers, such as Christians, will use and adapt a Stoic argument, but as they are making a different point from the Stoics they may change the emphasis of the argument to produce one that is consistent with their own ideas; in this case it would be consistent with a Christian rather

---

[8] Valuable contributions to the methodology of the study of political thought are made by Skinner 1969: 3-53, Dunn 1972: 158-73, cf. also Rorty 1984: 49-75 on the problems of discussing the history of philosophy.

[9] The longest and most well-known of the verses of Cleanthes is the *Hymn to Zeus*, Stobaeus SVF 1.537, cf. also Epict. SVF 1.527, Clement SVF 1.557, 559.

[10] Calling these reports 'fragments', although convenient, can be misleading in so far as it implies that these are quotations from Stoic writers and free from later interpretation. This is rarely the case.

than a Stoic context. Even a later Stoic, such as Seneca, cannot be assumed to be a neutral reporter of early Stoic arguments.[11] Such writers are not trying to publicise the early Stoa but to support their own case. Even ostensibly impartial doxographical accounts will not be free from interpretation, misunderstanding and selectiveness.

The assessment of a later report of Stoic thought cannot be limited only to consideration of the work in which it appears and the views and intentions of the author. The period in which the work is written is also relevant. For it may reflect not merely the ideas of the author but also those of the age. Indeed what a later writer feels to be important and interesting about the early Stoa need not coincide with what the early Stoics themselves thought important and interesting. The later writer will be affected by the preoccupations of his own age and select and omit accordingly. In the period of the Roman Empire there was an increased interest in monarchy, but the issue of different types of constitution was of far less relevance than it had been in the third century BC. Consequently our conception of Stoic political thought could be distorted by what those in later periods, both writers and their audiences, felt interesting and significant.

Owing to the wide variety of later writers who do provide evidence for early Stoic theory, such points will be considered in connection with particular sources as they arise. Although the Stoa in Greece is examined first and then its relationship with Rome, the presence of Rome will be felt throughout. As almost all the sources come from the period of Roman predominance, it will be constantly necessary to take account of the Roman context. Such an examination is also valuable because it helps to reveal the way in which the early Stoa was perceived by later generations.

The nature of the sources for Stoicism in the Hellenistic period requires any attempt at reconstruction to be undertaken with caution, giving due consideration to the points mentioned above. The historian should be wary of attributing ideas that may be anachronistic. Fortunately it is possible to have some form of control. This can to a certain extent be achieved by establishing the relationship between Stoic ideas in this period and the ideas present in the extant writings of their predecessors and successors. Similarly any reconstruction should be compatible with contemporary currents of thought, at least in so far as they can be determined. Thus any attempt to recover the main ideas of Stoic political thought should not attribute to the Stoa ideas which are inappropriate to the intellectual, social and political context.

Further assistance can be gained from the nature of Stoic philosophy

---

[11] Cf. for instance Kidd 1985: 3-5, who writes on Posidonian fragments in the work of Seneca: 'Ideally one has to read the whole of Seneca to be armed for a single Senecan 'fragment', because the basic question is how is Seneca using Posidonius?'

itself, because in the Stoic system all the fields of philosophy were interrelated. Understanding of one required the understanding of the rest (on which see especially D.L. 7.40). Thus not only should their political thought be internally consistent, but it should be consistent with the rest of their philosophical views. Where there is an absence of consistency, it may be that their thought has been misunderstood, although at the same time allowance must be made for unintentional or unresolved inconsistencies within their system. This intimate relationship between the parts of their system helps to compensate for some of the deficiencies in the evidence. For changes in other areas of their philosophy may illuminate changes in their political thought which are less well-documented.

The school

In the fourth century the leading schools of philosophy had been Plato's Academy and that of his pupil, Aristotle, at the Lyceum. At the beginning of the third century, under the leadership of Polemo and Theophrastus respectively, both these schools continued, but in this century they were to be eclipsed by two new schools, the Epicureans and the Stoics. In about 306 Epicurus, an Athenian citizen from Samos, came to Athens and began to teach there. Known as the Garden because it was located in some property Epicurus had bought, this new school emphasised friendship and sought to live as a community separate from the city. Of the other schools Cynicism attracted much attention. Cynics rejected convention and caused considerable shock by following their founder Diogenes in the practical application of their theories.

Zeno, the founder of Stoicism, had come from Citium in Cyprus to Athens in the late 310s, aged twenty-two. After a period as a pupil of the Cynic Crates he spent time listening to the Megarian philosopher Stilpo and the Academic Polemo. At some point he himself began to talk about philosophical problems, walking up and down the Stoa Poikile as he did so. Consequently his followers became known as Stoics, just as the Academy gave its name to the pupils of Plato. The Stoa Poikile, meaning Painted Stoa, was a colonnade, known for its series of paintings depicting the battle of Marathon; it was on the north side of the agora and so in the centre of Athens among the main public buildings.[12] Philosophers often taught in public places, where they could find an audience, for instance gymnasia such as the Lyceum, the Academy or the Cynosarges.[13] Despite their name Stoics also taught in other locations in Athens; Chrysippus, head of the school

[12] For a collection of literary and epigraphic evidence on the Stoa Poikile, see Wycherley 1957: 31-45, cf. also 1953: 20-35.
[13] Lynch 1972: 38-41, 130-4. The Cynosarges was used by the Stoic Aristo, D.L. 7.161.

(scholarch) in the last quarter of the third century, is reported to have taught in both the Lyceum and the Odeion.[14]

The Stoic school was less formally organised than some of its competitors, such as the Peripatetics and the Epicureans.[15] The only clear element of organisation for which there is evidence is the existence of the head of the school, whose succession would have assisted its continuity, but it is not known how he was chosen or indeed how formal his appointment was. Zeno was followed by Cleanthes of Assos, who led the school from 261 until about 230, and then came Chrysippus of Soli who is of particular importance in the history of Stoicism. Chrysippus, who had already set up himself up as a teacher even before the death of Cleanthes, was described as the second founder of the school; it was said about him, 'Without Chrysippus there would have been no Stoa' (D.L. 7.183). It is noticeable that none of these leading Stoics was Athenian, and this trend was to continue. It was to be about two hundred years before there was an Athenian scholarch; indeed even Athenian pupils are rarely named. If the sources provide little information on organisation in the third century, they provide even less about the second. The scholarchs are said to have been Zeno of Tarsus, who succeeded Chrysippus in about 206, Diogenes of Babylon who was followed by Antipater of Tarsus in about 152 and Panaetius of Rhodes who took up the position in about 129. By this time philosophers tended to be mentioned because they went to Rome rather than because of anything they may have done in Athens.

At this point it may be useful to outline the structure of this book. The first three chapters concentrate on early Stoic views about society; throughout, their ideas are compared and contrasted with those of Plato and Aristotle. First the ideal society of the wise is examined in its philosophical and political context. Their ideal was linked to their criticisms of the present and in the second chapter it will be seen that Zeno and Chrysippus analysed contemporary society, arguing that it was in effect a hierarchy of slavery incompatible with harmony and unity. Chapter 3 considers Stoic attitudes to political participation and constitutional forms; here democratic tendencies in Stoic thought are noted.

Their political thought is consistent with their sympathy for the policy of leading Athenian democrats. Chapter 4 reassesses Stoic involvement in third-century Athenian politics, particularly Zeno's 'friendship' with Antigonus Gonatas. Chapters 5 and 6 examine Stoic arguments on property and justice and their relation to the ideology of the Spartan revolution. In the latter particular attention is paid to the role of Sphaerus.

---

[14] D.L. 7.184, 187.
[15] Peripatetics: Lynch 1972; Epicureans: De Witt 1954.

Chapters 7 and 8 and the Conclusion are concerned with the way that the Stoic political outlook changed during the second century and the impact of Roman predominance. A division emerges between those sympathetic to the ideas of their predecessors and those who wish to distance themselves from this heritage. This division is seen in the differing attitudes to the tribunate of Tiberius Gracchus. An increased acceptance of contemporary society is apparent in the development of a Stoic justification of empire: slavery is in the interests of those who are incapable of governing themselves.

For Theresa

1

Zeno's *Politeia*

The Hellenistic Stoa displayed a consistent interest in political theory, beginning with the founder of the School, Zeno of Citium. Zeno wrote a short work called the *Politeia* (*Republic*); it was a philosophical inquiry which speculated about the nature of a society of wise men. No other work by Zeno, or indeed any Stoic, attracted as much attention or as much abuse as this one. There are more references to this book by Zeno than to any of his other writings. This highly controversial work was central to the political thought of the early Stoa and so it provides a suitable starting point for this present study.

Nevertheless from antiquity onwards there has been a reluctance to accord the *Politeia* this central role. This reluctance stems from the persistent belief that the *Politeia* was a very early work, written under the influence of Cynicism, and so incompatible with Zeno's later ideas. It will be argued here that the belief that it was an early work is mistaken. Further, its Cynic character has been greatly exaggerated. An examination of the evidence for the *Politeia* will show that there were substantial differences between it and Cynicism, differences which arose from Zeno's reaction to and progression from Plato, while absorbing influences from the contemporary political situation. Consequently it will be found that the *Politeia* is perfectly compatible with early Stoic theory in general.

1. An early or mature work?

A discussion of Zeno's *Politeia* needs to begin by asking where approximately in the development of Zeno's thought it comes. It is commonly claimed to have been written very early in his career, either while he was a pupil of the Cynic, Crates, or shortly after he finished his Cynic education.[1] The evidence for this is meagre and unreliable. The claim is partly the result of a general view that the *Politeia* exhibited such strong traces of Cynicism that it must be early; the validity of this argument will be examined later. More important, however, is the evidence of two ancient writers, both of whom refer to

[1] Pupil of Crates: Rist 1969: 64, Pohlenz 1970: 137. Early work: Sandbach 1975: 20, Baldry 1965: 154.

9

the *Politeia* as early, Philodemus, *On the Stoics (Peri Stôikôn)*[2] 9.1-6, and Diogenes Laertius (D.L.) 7.4.

To evaluate these two passages adequately the context in which they were written needs to be examined. Both stem from the period after 100 BC, by which time there was a strong reaction against the more extreme, indeed scandalous, views of Zeno, as represented by the *Politeia*. Those who wished to attack the Stoic school found such views suitable material for polemic. The fullest evidence of such an attack is provided by Philodemus, an Epicurean of the first century BC; his book, *On the Stoics*, is a vigorous polemic against the Stoics, characterising the views of their founder as 'without shame' and 'impious' (Philod. 11.10-11, 14.23-4) and his work as extreme impiety (Philod. 12.16-18). Further assaults on the *Politeia* by Cassius the Sceptic and Isidorus of Pergamum are recorded in Diogenes Laertius, a passage that contains much of our evidence for the contents of the *Politeia* (D.L. 7.32-4). Plutarch suggests that the references to homosexuality in the *Politeia* are more appropriate to a drinking party than a serious work (*Mor.* 653e, SVF 1.252).

These attacks elicited various responses from the Stoics themselves. From about the mid second century BC onwards they clearly found the *Politeia* a deep embarrassment and generally sought to minimise its importance as much as possible. Their arguments on this subject are an interesting indicator of the attitude of the later Stoics to their founder and his ideas. The most extreme response to such criticisms was to deny the authenticity of the *Politeia* altogether. Diogenes Laertius concludes his discussion of it by noting that the passages which he has just mentioned are regarded as spurious (D.L. 7.34). Earlier, however, he seeks the authority of Chrysippus to testify to its authenticity, again implying that some had denied that Zeno was the author (D.L. 7.34). Nobody but a Stoic would have an interest in making such a denial. Not all Stoics went as far as this in their desire to rid themselves of the *Politeia*. Athenodorus, a Stoic who was in charge of the library at Pergamum in the early first century BC, decided to remove all offending passages from the *Politeia*, although they were later replaced (D.L. 7.34). Philodemus in *On the Stoics* sets

---

[2] Philodemus *Peri Stôikôn* is cited as 'Philod.', the first figure is the column number, the second the line. The edition used here is that of T. Dorandi, *Cronache Ercolanesi* 12 (1982), 91-133. Since the numbering of the columns differs from the earlier edition of W. Crönert, the following conversion table may be useful:

Dorandi	= Crönert	Dorandi	= Crönert	Dorandi	= Crönert
I	–	IX	XV	XVI	XIV
II	–	X	XVI	XVII	VII
III	II	XI	XVII	XVIII	VIII
IV	III	XII	XVIII	XIX	IX
V	IV	XIII	XI	XX	X
VI	V	XIV	XII	XXI	XIX
VII	–	XV	XIII	XXII	XX
VIII	VI				

out several contemporary Stoic defences of their position and then proceeds to prove that they are all invalid. Some Stoics deny that Zeno was the founder of the school at all and instead trace their origins back to Socrates via Antisthenes and Diogenes the Cynic (Philod. 12.20-13.4). Another group accept him only in so far as he was the discoverer of the *telos* (end or goal of human life) and reject the rest of his ideas (Philod. 14.4-9). A third argument, perhaps used alongside the others, holds that he was not really a significant person and points out that he himself admitted this (Philod. 10.7-13). All these seek in varying degrees to minimise the importance of Zeno to the Stoic school and by implication accept that his more radical and unacceptable ideas, as presented in the *Politeia*, were central to his thought.

If there were any later Stoics who wished to retain Zeno as their founder and avoid diminishing his importance, there were two other lines of argument that they could follow, both of which are reported by Philodemus. One was simply to accept the *Politeia* and say that nothing in it needed justification, although Philodemus notes that homosexuality is felt to need a justification (Philod. 15.1-12). An alternative would be to agree that Zeno did write it and admit that there are mistakes in it, but at the same time argue that he should be excused because he wrote it when he was 'young and foolish', before he became established as a philosopher (Philod. 9.1-6). Yet it is the very passage which contains this argument which is used by modern scholars as evidence for an early dating of the *Politeia*.

There must be serious doubts about the reliability of such a passage as evidence for an early date. It contains one of a series of arguments used by various Stoics to minimise the significance of the *Politeia*. This argument is in fact the most attractive solution to their problems; it trivialises the *Politeia* and dismisses it as a minor work of his youth, yet at the same time preserves Zeno's (and their own) integrity. If they could deny its authenticity, censor it, deny that Zeno was the founder of the school, deny that he was an important figure, they would surely have no scruples about back-dating it and saying that it was the work of a young and foolish man, especially when it was so manifestly in their interests to do so. In the first and late second centuries BC it would have been difficult to come to any firm conclusions about a work written so long before. We have no records of the date of composition of any other work of Zeno, and this is because no other work was as controversial or shocking as this one. In the case of the *Politeia* an early date was an essential part of the apology for it, and as such ought to be treated with caution. The early Stoics were not embarrassed by it and as a result, even if it was an early work, they had no reason to bother to record that it was. This only became worth claiming when the attitude of the Stoa to it changed, by which time the date may only have been a matter of conjecture. The chronologers such as

Apollodorus recorded dates such as when philosophers were born, died and headed schools, but there is no evidence that they were concerned with the chronology of their writings or had any interest in these at all.[3] If the argument in defence of Zeno had claimed that it was his first published work, that might have given it more credibility, because his first published work would have been worth recording. This claim is not made. Indeed it is rare to find the first work of any philosopher recorded and even when it is recorded it is likely to be on the basis of deductions from the content and the style. For instance some ancient writers said that the *Phaedrus* was Plato's first work, a claim which is clearly incorrect.[4]

An argument which dates the *Politeia* early and as a result close to Zeno's Cynic education is useful material for Philodemus. For he is engaged in a polemic against the Stoics and thus it is in his interests to associate the Stoics and the Cynics as much as possible, given the contemporary disapproval of Cynic shamelessness. In Cicero's *De Officiis*, also written in the first century BC, the Cynics are attacked for their disregard of modesty, *verecundia*:[5] 'The whole philosophy of the Cynics must be rejected; for it is inimical to modesty, without which nothing can be right (*rectum*), nothing morally good (*honestum*).' By choosing such a Stoic argument about the date of the *Politeia* Philodemus has the added bonus of having the Stoics themselves conceding that the *Politeia* was shocking and unsavoury even to them. It is significant that Philodemus answers this apology for Zeno by pointing out that he never retracted it and even maintained the same point of view in other writings (Philod. 9.7-11). This is confirmed by Diogenes Laertius who notes that the same treatment of erotic subjects appears in two other works (D.L. 7.34). It might be argued that, because Philodemus does not dispute the claim that it was an early work, it must have been. But it is not relevant to his case to dispute this; he merely has to show that the *Politeia* represented the consistent viewpoint of Zeno. Elsewhere in *On the Stoics* he makes it clear that he believed the *Politeia* to be an integral part of Zeno's thought. Against those who gave Zeno credit only for the discovery of the end (*telos*) he argues that they cannot dismiss the rest of his thought, including the *Politeia*, because it is all interrelated (Philod. 14.12-15)

So Philodemus does not help in establishing an early date for the *Politeia*, although he does assist in showing the controversy that surrounded not only the contents but also Zeno himself. Clearly the later Stoics were prepared to go to considerable lengths to rid themselves of this uncomfortable heritage and this could cause

[3] Cf. the fragments of Apollodorus, Jacoby 1902, FGH 244.

[4] D.L. 3.38, Olymp. *Vit. Plat.*, De Vries 1969: 7-11.

[5] Cic. *De Off.* 1.148, cf. 1.128 where Zeno himself is to be included among those hostile to *verecundia*, as Cic. *Ad Fam.* 9.22 makes clear.

confusion over what the actual circumstances of the *Politeia* were. As a result one would be justified in having doubts about evidence in subsequent writers which could show that it was an early work, especially if it occurs in an apologetic context.

There is only one other passage that does attribute the *Politeia* to Zeno's early period, but this presents problems similar to those posed by the passage of Philodemus. This is Diogenes Laertius 7.4: 'For a while then Zeno was a pupil of Crates [a Cynic]. At this time when he had written his *Politeia* some people said as a joke that he had written it on the Cynosoura [a place meaning "the tail of the dog"].'

If Zeno wrote the *Politeia* while or shortly after he was a pupil of Crates, then it belongs to his early career. We have, however, already seen that the controversy generated by the *Politeia* produced arguments in which an early dating was an essential feature of the defence of Zeno. The suspicion that this remark may have originally had an apologetic aim is further supported by the passage which immediately precedes it. This clearly is an apology for Zeno's links with the Cynics;[6] it emphasises how Zeno was too modest for Cynic shamelessness and supplies an anecdote to illustrate this. Thus this section on Zeno and Crates (D.L. 7.3-4) could derive from those Stoics cited by Philodemus who argued that the *Politeia* was written while Zeno was still young and foolish. It is certainly consistent with their arguments. Wilamowitz believed that the passage of Diogenes from 7.2 to the end of the list of Zeno's writings was derived from the Stoic, Apollonius of Tyre.[7] He is mentioned in D.L. 7.2 as a source and he is known to have written a list of Stoic writing (Strabo SVF 1.37). He presented an apologetic view of the relationship between Zeno and Crates: once when Zeno was listening to the philosopher Stilpo, Crates came and dragged him away from Stilpo by his cloak, but Zeno told him that his mind was still with Stilpo, because a philosopher should be taken by persuasion not by force (D.L. 7.24, SVF 1.278). But Wilamowitz was puzzled by the *Politeia* anecdote, because he believes that since Apollonius is trying to defend Zeno he would not mention the *Politeia* and so it is an intrusion. Yet an early dating was used by those who wished to rehabilitate Zeno as Philodemus makes clear. Apollonius was roughly contemporary with Philodemus and was known to him.[8] It was almost impossible to deny that Zeno wrote it (although some tried); Athenodorus limited himself to censoring it. It might have been best to claim that it was from his Cynic days rather than to deny its authenticity altogether, at the same time playing down Zeno's intimacy with the Cynics. Whether or not one accepts that Apollonius of Tyre was one of the propagators of this defence, the

---

[6] D.L. 7.3, Wilamowitz 1881: 338.
[7] Wilamowitz 1881: 106, 338.
[8] Philod. *Ind. St*. 37.1, Wilamowitz 1881: 109f.

passage and context are clearly apologetic in tone and content. As a result it may stem not from a true tradition about Zeno, but from those contemporaries of Philodemus who sought to relieve themselves of the burden of the *Politeia*.

So this passage of Diogenes cannot be relied upon as evidence for the date of the *Politeia*. It might be objected that the joke that the *Politeia* was written 'on the tail of the dog (i.e. Cynicism)' represents a temporal link and provides confirmation of the dating, but this need not be so at all. It is more likely to mean that the *Politeia* showed signs of Cynic influence due to Zeno's early adherence to them. The apologists could even have used this very anecdote as their evidence for the claim that the *Politeia* was an early work, regardless of the original intention or context of the joke, hence its appearance here.

Philodemus and Diogenes Laertius, therefore, provide no grounds for believing that Zeno's *Politeia* was a very early work.[9] Indeed some of the arguments found in Philodemus imply that not all Stoics agreed that it was an aberration of his youth. To reach such a conclusion it would be necessary to argue that what we know of the *Politeia* is closer to Cynicism than to Stoic doctrine. It will later be shown that, although there are similarities between Cynicism and Zeno's *Politeia*, there are also significant differences. The mere presence of controversial ideas, such as those recalling Cynic shamelessness, is not sufficient ground for concluding that the work is early. Not only were such ideas characteristic of Zeno, as Philodemus asserts, but many of them also appear in the work of his successors, Cleanthes and Chrysippus. Community of women appears in the *Politeiai* of both Zeno and Chrysippus (D.L. 7.33, 131, SVF 1.269, 3.728), while the latter in his book permits incest (D.L. 7.188, SVF 3.744). Zeno, probably in his *Politeia*, had also allowed incest (Sext. Emp. SVF 1.585). Cleanthes shows a similar disregard for sexual convention (Sext. Emp. SVF 1.585). All three and Diogenes the Cynic saw nothing intrinsically wrong in eating human flesh (SVF 3.747-50). Zeno, following the Cynics, advocated complete freedom of speech in sexual matters, denying that there was any such thing as obscene language. Chrysippus was heavily criticised for his use of coarse language; his version of the story of Hera and Zeus was too obscene for Diogenes Laertius to relate.[10] Thus these Cynic ideas were a feature of mainstream Stoicism in the third century and cannot be limited to the early career of Zeno.

[9] The only scholar, as far as I am aware, to dispute the early dating has been Tarn 1933: n. 98, who argued that if D.L. 7.4 meant Zeno wrote the *Politeia* while a pupil of Crates, then it would follow (wrongly) that all Zeno's works listed there were written in this period. But in Tarn 1948: 2.418 he changed his mind.

[10] Zeno: Cic. *Ad Fam.* 9.22, SVF 1.77; Chrysippus: D.L. 7.187; for avoidance of euphemism as Cynic trait, Cic. *De Off.* 1.128.

So far little attempt has been made to suggest a date for the composition of the *Politeia*; it could have been written any time from Zeno's arrival in Athens until his death in the late sixties of the third century. It will be seen that it is consistent with the rest of his philosophical ideas, as Philodemus pointed out. Consequently it would be peculiar if it was written long before these ideas were formulated. Thus it must have been written after or at the earliest during his period as a pupil of Polemo, the head of the Academy.[11] This gains support from the arguments to be put forward later in this chapter that the *Politeia* shows strong links with Plato and that its contents are less Cynic than commonly supposed. The *Politeia* is a conscious reaction against Plato and may therefore date from the time of his arguments with the Academic philosopher Arcesilaus in the third century. In the course of these Zeno vigorously attacked Plato. Numenius, who records this, hopes that he never has the time to discuss Zeno's shocking attack on Plato which was shameless and far from noble; such a description would be particularly appropriate to the *Politeia* (*ap.* Euseb. *Praep. Evang.* 14.732c). If the *Politeia* had always been accepted as an early work, why was there so much controversy among later Stoics about how to cope with it? Surely all the arguments recorded by Philodemus and other subterfuges would have been superfluous. Athenodorus' experiments with censorship and the disputes over the authenticity of Diogenes' and Zeno's *Politeiai* show that such literary manipulation was not uncommon and leads to the truth becoming obscured if not altogether absent. The mass of contradictory arguments can only be explained if the early Stoa did accept the *Politeia* as a mature work and part of the main body of Zeno's work.

2. Zeno's philosophy: a summary

At this point it is useful to summarise some of those aspects of Stoic theory which are known to have been held by Zeno. In this way the context into which the *Politeia* fits can be seen. Certain of these elements were clearly present in it, but others are not included in our evidence for it. An argument from silence is scarcely satisfactory for concluding that they were absent.

The Stoics, including Zeno, follow earlier philosophers in seeing the end of life as *eudaimonia* (happiness) and they too emphasise the necessity of *aretê* (excellence/virtue) for achieving this. They agree that *eudaimonia* requires what is good, but differ from philosophers such as Aristotle by making the claim, often criticised in antiquity, that only

---

[11] D.L. 7.1, SVF 1.1, Strabo SVF 1.10, Numenius SVF 1.11, Cic. *Acad. Post.* 1.34, *De Fin.* 4.3, SVF 1.13.

what is morally good is good. Therefore *eudaimonia* is dependent on virtue alone. *Eudaimonia* is defined by them as life in accordance with virtue; living in this way is identified with life in agreement with *phusis* (nature).[12]

The emphasis on *phusis* is present throughout Stoic thought and is fundamental to it. Chrysippus wrote 'there is no other or more appropriate way to approach the subject of good and bad things, the virtues and happiness, than from universal nature and the dispensation of the universe' (Plut. *St. Rep.* 1035c, SVF 3.68). Nature is a creative, rational force, guiding the workings of the world so that it forms one coherent universal system. Because one of the qualities of nature is perfect reason, its manifestations are both right and good. Everything in the universe has its own individual nature, whether it is a cylinder, a plant or an animal, and will act in accordance with it and at the same time with universal nature. Thus it is natural and right for a tulip to produce a tulip flower, not a rose-bud, and for bees to live in colonies. Although it is right and good, it does not make them moral agents; for they are not conscious of the concepts of good and bad and could not act otherwise anyway; rather they are correctly programmed.

The distinctive feature of human beings, however, is that they, like nature, possess reason (*logos*), but at the same time due to this they have it in their power to act not in accordance with nature. It is because they have the power to choose that they are moral agents. Nature is identified not only with right reason (*orthos logos*) but also with law. This law, known variously as natural law, common law and divine law, commands what should be done and forbids what should not be done.[13] For a person to live in accordance with nature their reason must be perfectly developed; only then will they measure up to nature's evaluative standard. The only person who achieves this is the *sophos*, the wise man. Since his reason is in harmony with the reason of the universe, he will comprehend the way in which nature works. As a result he will have knowledge of good and bad and will be able to act on it. Everybody else, on the other hand, is classified as foolish and bad; only the wise man is good. Chrysippus draws an analogy with a man underwater, but only an inch below the surface – he will be just as

---

[12] D.L. 7.87, SVF 1.179, Rist 1977: 167ff.

[13] The most well-known statement on this is by Chrysippus in Marcianus SVF 3.314, cf. also Stob. *Ecl.* 2.96.10-17, 102.4-10 SVF 3.613, 614, but the idea of natural law was also present in Zeno's thought, though probably not as developed, SVF 1.162; on the relationship with Nature, D.L. 7.87-8, 128. Natural law as it appears in the Stoa should be distinguished from the natural justice of Aristotle and Plato, Striker 1987. The actual content of natural law is somewhat obscure, but it is unlikely that the early Stoa conceived of it as a set of fixed rules, rather it was a set of principles which the wise man would know and understand by virtue of his reason, Inwood 1985: 105-11, 205-15, Inwood 1987. Natural law only takes on a degree of rigidity in the writings of the later Stoics and Cicero, cf. Inwood 1987: 97-8, Watson 1971.

much dead as the man ten feet below. Thus it is a straightforward division: if you are not good, you are bad. This means that the wise man will have all the virtues. He cannot have one without the rest; for that is the nature of his knowledge.[14]

Other than the sharp divide between good and bad through the emphasis on reason, there is another such division, that between what is morally good and everything else. Only what is morally good is good, and only that which is morally bad is bad, everything else is indifferent (*adiaphoron*). Thus, much that earlier philosophers such as Aristotle had considered good is now indifferent, such as health, wealth and life itself. It was said earlier that the end of life is *eudaimonia*, defined as life in accordance with *aretê*. Once it is established that nothing is good but what is morally good, it should be clear that nothing which is morally indifferent can in itself be necessary for a life in accordance with virtue. Consequently, moreover, nothing is necessary for *eudaimonia* but what is morally good, over which the wise man has a monopoly. This does not mean that the wise man will ignore indifferents; he cannot do this, because he has to exercise his virtue, but these indifferents (or rather preferred indifferents) are only the material of his virtue (Plut. *Comm. Not.* 1069e, SVF 3.491). Yet none are in themselves essential to the wise man; he would still have a virtuous disposition even if none existed. It is the attitude and intentions of the agent that are important for attaining *eudaimonia*, not the success of the action.

Although all these things are considered to be morally indifferent, this does not place them all on the same level with no distinction between them. For it is only in the moral context that they are indifferent, being irrelevant to the *eudaimonia* of the individual. For these indifferents are divided into the preferred (*proêgmena*) and their opposite (*apoproêgmena*), the former being things in accordance with nature, *ta kata phusin*, and the latter things contrary to nature, *ta para phusin*. In Stobaeus there are examples of *ta kata phusin*, things such as health, strength and having one's senses in order, while examples of *ta para phusin* include disease, weakness and mutilations. Nevertheless they only have value or disvalue relative to other indifferents; alongside virtue they have no value. The wise man in his actions will direct his attention towards *ta kata phusin* rather than towards *ta para phusin*.[15]

Some have argued convincingly that the Stoic view of *phusis* as the laws of the physical universe can be associated with Zeno's move to study with the Academy of Polemo.[16] Even if the idea did not come

[14] Kerferd 1978.
[15] For a fuller account and references, Rist 1969, Long 1986[2]: 149-209, Gould 1970 and the works cited there.
[16] Rist 1977, Brink 1956.

from his study with Polemo, it must follow his break with the Cynics.[17]
This introduction of *phusis* as a standard of evaluation also owes much
to Aristotle, as is apparent from the first book of the *Politics* and the
first book of *De Partibus Animalium*. To achieve an understanding of
phusis it would be necessary to pay some attention to the study of
biology and physics. It might be argued that the introduction of such
studies into Stoic theory is inconsistent with the report that Zeno, in
the *Politeia*, had dismissed the standard educational curriculum as
useless (D.L. 7.32, SVF 1.259). This would be to misunderstand the
nature of such a curriculum (*enkuklios paideia* or *enkuklia
mathêmata*). Various references make it clear that it included the
study of music, geometry and literature, but there is no indication that
it included the study of biology, physics or logic.[18] Indeed at D.L. 6.104
it is treated separately from logic and physics. It is reasonable to
believe that the Stoa held that the knowledge of the wise man
consisted in a fundamental knowledge of causes and principles and
that this bears no relation to the standard educational curriculum.[19]

3. The subject of the *Politeia*

Before examining the *Politeia*'s relation to other philosophical ideas
and the contemporary situation, an attempt must be made to
determine what was expressed in it. Initially only those passages
referring to it will be used, supplemented occasionally by other
evidence which may illuminate subjects known to have been discussed
in it.[20] Since the case for an early date for the *Politeia* is no longer
tenable, it is possible to consider the *Politeia* in the wider context of
Stoic thought, a procedure that should enable the work to be better
understood. Indeed the ease with which it does fit into this wider
context reinforces the argument that it is not an early work.

Zeno's *Politeia* proposed an ideal society, but there is much dispute
as to the nature of this society and its extent. On the one hand, W.W.
Tarn argued that it was a small city-state, containing both wise men
and fools, modelled on the helot-based society of Sparta; on the other
hand, H.C. Baldry and many others see it as a society of the wise alone
and of indeterminate extent.[21] There are strong grounds for believing
that this latter interpretation is largely correct. For two passages
consider *homonoia*, harmony or unity, to be fundamental to this ideal
society (Plut. *Lyc.* 31, Athen. 13.561c). This is not in itself an argument

[17] As pointed out by Rist 1977: 171-2.
[18] D.L. 6.104, Quintilian *Inst.* 1.10, cf. D.L. 4.10; Marrou 1956: 176-7.
[19] Kerferd 1978.
[20] The passages referring to it by name are collected in Baldry 1959.
[21] Tarn 1948: 2.418, Baldry 1959: 6-8, cf. Zeller 1923: 302, Mueller 1984: 304 n. 9,
Reesor 1951: 10, Rist 1969: 64-8.

against the claim that Zeno advocated a class society. Both Plato and Aristotle combined *homonoia* and a class society, but for them the maintenance of this *homonoia* was dependent on the quality of the governing class.[22] For Zeno this is not adequate; those who would form the bottom class in Plato's state are those he brands as fools. These are seen as slaves and enemies to one another (D.L. 7.32-3) and it is hard to conceive of their behaviour as being compatible with *homonoia*, whereas the wise are citizens, friends, kindred and free. The wise, therefore, are perfectly suited to *homonoia*. We are told that the god, Eros, is associated with friendship (*philia*), freedom (*eleutheria*) and *homonoia*. Since friendship and freedom are characteristics of good men but not of bad men, this furnishes stronger proof that *homonoia* is a feature of the relationship of the wise alone.[23] Certainly this was the view of the early Stoa in general, though not explicitly attested for Zeno (Stob. *Ecl.* 2.94.1-6, 108.15-18 SVF 3.625, 630). Eros is supposed to lead to the safety of the city and given the nature of fools or bad men it is improbable that this could be achieved with their presence. For these reasons it is impossible to include them as an inferior class. As the state is further examined it will be seen how they would also be incompatible with such a state in other ways.

Yet Tarn holds the opposite view, that the ideal society was a small class one on the model of the Spartan helot-based state. The main reason for this appears to have been Plutarch, *Lycurgus* 31. Here it is said that Lycurgus thought that a city was like an individual and so would achieve happiness through virtue and internal harmony, *homonoia hê pros hautên*; with this in mind he arranged his city. Plato, Diogenes and Zeno took this as the basis for their own ideal societies. Tarn contends that they took Sparta itself as their model, but Plutarch makes much more sense if he is understood to mean that the philosophers adopted the principle on which Lycurgus based his city; this is what Plutarch is in fact discussing at the time.[24] That Plato did adhere to this principle in his *Republic* (see especially Book 4) would have been commonplace among those familiar with philosophy. What would have been controversial, however, was the proposition that it originated with Lycurgus. It is Plutarch himself who has drawn the analogy in order to contrast, as he says, Lycurgus the man who put his ideas into practice with the philosophers who left only writings, and also to show how Lycurgus anticipated these famous philosophers. The early Stoics, though not specifically Zeno, felt contempt for Lycurgus as

[22] For example, Plato Rep. 4.432a; they did not always use the term *homonoia*, but it is clear that they believed the best *polis* to be a class society that was free from *stasis*.

[23] Athen. 13.561c – on this text see Chapter 2 n. 37; for a discussion of the relationship between *philia, eleutheria* and *homonoia*, see Chapter 2.5.

[24] Tarn 1948: 2.417-23. A succession of scholars have pointed out that Tarn has misrepresented Plutarch, beginning with Fisch 1937: 69, who is followed by Merlan 1950: 161-2, Baldry 1959: 8, Chroust 1965: 177-8.

a law-maker (Cic. *Acad. Pr.* 2.136, SVF 3.599, Plut. *St. Rep.* 1033f). Thus it would be improbable that Zeno would try to copy the Spartan state, but conceivable that he would approve of the underlying principle as presented by Plutarch.

Elsewhere, too, Plutarch compares achievements and philosophy, this time of Alexander and Zeno respectively (Plut. *Al. Fort.* 1.6, SVF 1.262). He writes that Zeno said that 'all men' would be fellow citizens of one another in the ideal society. Some assume that 'all men' must mean that both wise and fools were included.[25] But this need not be so; others have pointed out that it is acceptable to understand it as all wise men.[26] There are two ways in which this may have come about. Plutarch may have adapted the idea to fit in with the contemporary Stoic idea of a world state, which was more suitable with the analogy with Alexander. Yet, on the other hand, the cause may lie with Zeno himself; for once he had established the hypothesis that all inhabitants were to be wise, he presumably did not keep repeating it, but often referred to them simply as men. Thus at D.L. 7.34 we read that the clothes of men and women will be the same, but there is no mention of wise men.

The evidence of Polybius indicates that the conception of a city of wise men was not foreign to him and, therefore, suggests that he was aware that such a society had been proposed. He writes that in Rome superstition and religion are promoted as a means of keeping the lower classes in order. This, he says, might not be necessary in a state composed of wise men (Polyb. 6.56.10), a remark which could have Zeno's *Politeia* in mind.[27] It is unlikely that he is referring to Plato's ideal society. For firstly Plato's ideal was a class society which was not composed exclusively of wise men and secondly Plato did support the use of certain myths to manipulate the population.

So the ideal society of Zeno's *Politeia* contained only the wise, but there might be other grounds for accepting Tarn's contention that the society was only a city-state and not on a larger scale. Apart from the analogy with Sparta Tarn cites various aspects of the society which he believes would be incompatible with anything but a small city-state.[28] First one could travel abroad. But this is only an assumption based on the statement that there was no currency either for the purpose of exchange or for travelling abroad (D.L. 7.33). The statement could also be understood to mean that money was not necessary for this purpose because there was no limitation to the society. Tarn's interpretation requires that no citizen was allowed to travel in the area outside the state. This seems to be a curious restriction on the freedom of the wise

[25] Pöhlmann 1925: 273 n. 2.
[26] As argued by Murray 1966: 369.
[27] Hirzel 1882: 2.878-9 links this passage with the Stoa.
[28] Tarn 1948: 2.418.

man, especially if Zeno held, as seems probable, that the virtue of the wise man could not be lost.[29] Secondly, Tarn argues that because all women were held in common and each citizen was to love all children as if he was their father (D.L. 7.33, 131), this must have been a small community. But this does not imply actual association with all children, merely that the affection which a man feels for each child he comes into contact with will be the same as it would be if it was his own child.

Diogenes Laertius notes that there will be no lawcourts, temples or gymnasia built in the *poleis*, cities (D.L. 7.33). This might seem sufficient to reject any argument that the *Politeia* was limited to a single city. Athenaeus, however, writes that Eros promotes 'the security of the *polis*, city' (Athen. 13.561c, SVF 1.263). Thus, while Diogenes unambiguously describes the society as containing several cities, Athenaeus only refers to a single city. Tarn thought that Athenaeus was referring to the city-state *Politeia* which he had deduced from Plutarch's *Lycurgus*, but was uncertain how to explain the passage in Diogenes. Baldry is hesitant and unwilling to take the passages literally. He dismisses the view that the *polis* of Athenaeus refers to the whole state including the particular cities of D.L. 7.33 and suggests that the inconsistency reflects the indeterminate character of Zeno's approach; that is to say that Zeno is not explicit, but left it open whether he was talking of a city or cities in general.[30] Of course one cannot tell to what extent the sources which we now possess have altered what Zeno originally wrote. Yet it seems curious that Zeno's indeterminacy should cause him to change from *polis* to *poleis* at different parts of his short work, simply because what he was writing was appropriate to both.

It is possible to reconcile these two passages. For Athenaeus is particularly talking of the security of the individual city, which would be threatened with internal discord without Eros. This seems to be the natural way to take the sentence, but, if *'polis'* had been written in the plural, it would have become ambiguous. For it could then be referring either to unity amongst the citizens of a particular city or the relationships between cities. So one case would be referring to civil conflict, the other to war between cities, neither of which, as it happens, could take place in the ideal society, but the passage is only referring to the former. It is purely a point of detail on the previous sentence in Athenaeus and not suggesting that the role of Eros is only confined to one city. There is no contradiction between this and the *poleis* of D.L. 7.33, because both words are deliberately chosen for the function which they perform in the sentence. It is perfectly natural to

[29] Rist 1969: 16-19, 78; D.L. 7.128, SVF 1.569, D.L. 7.127, SVF 1.568, 3.237, Simplicius SVF 3.238.

[30] Tarn 1948: 2.420, Baldry 1959: 8.

say that there will be no lawcourts, gymnasia or temples in the *poleis*, because no confusion can be caused. It is simply a general statement about how matters will be run in the cities of the ideal state.

Baldry rightly argues that Zeno is not concerned with the question of geographical extent.[31] This is not, however, inconsistent with the claim that the ideal society should contain more than one *polis*. For this is an argument not about the size of the society but about its nature. No longer does the independent *polis* represent the ideal as it does in Plato; consequently the importance of the *polis* is diminished. This downgrading of the *polis* is apparent in a passage of Plutarch (Plut. *Al. Fort.* 1.6, SVF 1.262). He states that the main point of Zeno's *Politeia* was the desirability of unity among all wise men, which was incompatible with living in separate *poleis* and demes with their own peculiar concepts of justice. It might be argued that we are faced here with an inconsistency, between the cities referred to earlier and the denial of cities in this passage. Nevertheless it is not saying that men will not live in communities, but that they will not live in cities on the Greek model, each with its own brand of justice; the Stoic city would be totally different from this with no lawcourts and none of the attributes normally associated with a Greek *polis* and will be governed by universal law.

Thus Zeno is outlining an ideal society where all are wise, living in harmonious communities. For *homonoia* is a fundamental feature of the society. Everything in it will be compatible with this harmony and, as such, will be *kata phusin*, in accordance with nature. The wise man's behaviour will be in line with this; he is free to act how he wants, but he is wise and so will only act in accordance with his reason. Such wisdom is not considered as a restriction on his freedom but the essence of it. Yet, when reading the remains of the *Politeia*, it is easy to gain the impression that Zeno wrote down a set of rules for the wise to follow and assume that these requirements were for the maintenance of the community. For the passages referring to the *Politeia* report that Zeno 'legislated', 'ordered' or 'arranged'.[32] This might appear inconsistent with the wise man as free, but in fact is not. These would merely be the various words used by the doxographers to introduce Zeno's ideas, which, owing to his view of the universe, could easily appear to be rules. Rather, as has been said, the wise man lives according to his reason, that is to say he is in harmony with nature. He is not compelled to live in harmony with nature, but because his reason, just as that of nature, is perfectly developed, it is the only rational course to follow. Certain behaviour, irrational behaviour, would be incompatible with nature and thus with the harmony of the

[31] Baldry 1959: 8.

[32] Philod. 12.10, D.L. 7.33, Plutarch SVF 1.252; terms include *nomothetein, dogmatizein, oiesthai dein, keleuein, katatetachthai.*

ideal society. Thus, what Zeno writes are not rules governing the details of life among the wise but how he imagines life would be, basing it on the premise that all are wise.[33] This will not directly promote harmony; for the wise are by nature harmonious already, indeed they are the only ones who can be. At the same time such characteristics of the society will reflect the *homonoia* and emphasise it.

Zeno's society is derived from Stoic principles. He began the *Politeia* by writing that contemporary society is corrupt; it is full of bad men, fools who are enemies and slaves.[34] This is because they lack wisdom and consequently do not live in harmony with nature or right reason. Therefore Zeno is asking what would a society be like in which men did live in harmony with nature. Such a society would represent the natural condition of man. Zeno is not concerned with placing this society in a historical or geographical context, but with examining it in isolation. The assumption is made that there are no other states co-existing with the ideal state. We learn that there is no coinage for the purpose of exchange or travel abroad, so there can be no trade or relations with non-wise communities, unlike in Plato's state.[35] What Zeno put forward in the *Politeia* was not a description of a world state or community as some have supposed but a philosophical inquiry. It is an ideal and natural society not located in any particular time or place. It is not limited to a single *polis*, but nor are its limits clearly defined, because this is irrelevant to the purpose of the inquiry.

This ideal society would be one where there would be no temples, lawcourts, gymnasia nor images of the gods (D.L. 7.33, SVF 1.267; SVF 1.264). There would be no coinage (D.L. 7.33, SVF 1.267). The institution of marriage would be abolished and there would be community of women; men would feel paternal affection for all children (D.L. 7.33, 131, SVF 1.269). There would be no distinction in the dress of men and women; it is also reported that no part of the body would be concealed, presumably meaning that clothes were purely functional, so nobody would have inhibitions about not wearing them if there was no need (D.L. 7.33, SVF 1.257). Finally homosexuality was acceptable in the ideal society (D.L. 7.129, SVF 1.248; Plut. SVF 1.252); just as there was community of women there may also have been community of men.[36] From this brief summary it is clear that many would find these notions objectionable, as Philodemus did, describing them as shameful and impious (Philod. 11.10-11).

For Zeno the ideal society of the *Politeia* represented one of moral

---

[33] This is not to say that there are no general principles which the wise man will follow, cf. Stobaeus SVF 3.613, 614, but the remarks of Zeno are concerned with specific points about the mode of life of the wise which will be in accordance with these general principles, cf. Inwood 1985: 107-11. See also n. 13 above.

[34] D.L. 7.32, SVF 1.226.

[35] D.L. 7.33, SVF 1.268, Plato *Laws* 5.742ab.

[36] I owe this suggestion to John Rist.

perfection; thus it is necessary to consider how he reached conclusions that many ancient writers held to be morally abhorrent. It is not enough to argue that temples, gymnasia, money and institutions for reproduction are indifferent and, therefore, to be omitted from Zeno's society.[37] This is to misunderstand the notion of indifferent; if this view were taken to its logical extreme one could conclude that the wise man should not eat, because food too is indifferent. It is not simply that such things as temples are indifferent; if they are incompatible with the ideal society, they must also be *para phusin*.

In most instances the sources do not say the reason why any particular thing is excluded from the ideal society, although there are a couple of passages which indicate why there would be no temples. They were to be rejected because the product of builders and workmen was neither holy nor worthy of the gods (SVF 1.264). This itself need not represent contempt for such men *qua* workmen. Rather one is prompted to ask: if temples are not worthy of the gods, what is? The answer comes in Epiphanius SVF 1.146, a passage which may derive from the *Politeia*, and it fits neatly with the passages just mentioned. Zeno said that temples should not be built, but men should have the divine within their mind, *nous*, because it is immortal. Thus man should not honour the gods with buildings but with his mind, a natural conclusion for a theory that holds that *logos* is the common possession of men and the gods (Arius Didymus SVF 2.528). Elsewhere Zeno says that a city should be embellished not by offerings to the gods but by virtue (Stobaeus SVF 1.266).

Homonoia provides a reason for the rejection of some aspects of the contemporary Greek *polis*, not because rejection will lead to *homonoia* but because men living in harmony will not need them. There is no need for law-courts in a society where all are friends; it is only the fools who will require them. This also provides a further reason for believing that the society would contain only the wise. Friendship, *philia*, for the Stoics means showing concern for the interests of all; in D.L. 7.124, SVF 3.631, not a passage from the *Politeia*, friendship is said to be the common use of all that relates to life; for we treat our friends as ourselves. *Homonoia* in combination with friendship would lead to everything being held for the common use of all, which explains why there would be no need for coinage. This along with the rejection of the family implies the absence of private property.

Gymnasia were not only or even mainly for bodily welfare, but had a competitive aspect incompatible with *homonoia* and displayed excessive concern for one's body. Baldry suggests that they were rejected because bodily welfare was not relevant for the true happiness of the wise, but this seems to be another way of saying that it was

---

[37] As Devine 1970: 326-7 argues.

indifferent.[38] Indeed it seems as though the wise man will know what
is appropriate and train accordingly, but there is no need for a
gymnasium to do this. It is said, perhaps by Chrysippus, that the wise
man will train in order to increase his powers of bodily endurance (D.L.
7.123, SVF 3.715).

Zeno envisaged that women would be held in common (*koinai*) in the
ideal society of the wise and thus the institution of marriage and the
family would be out of place. Baldry explains this, in conjunction with
the wearing of the same clothes, as being a means to harmony within
the society by getting rid of social divisions and jealousy. John Rist
objects that, since the wise by nature live in harmony anyway, there
would be no need to introduce these practices in order to achieve it.[39]
To maintain the institution of marriage and the family and associated
sexual taboos would be to impose unnecessary restrictions on the
behaviour of the wise man or woman, who should be perfectly capable
of freely making his or her decision on the matter. For there should be
philia to all and mere conventional restrictions should not hinder it
arbitrarily. At the same time Baldry's explanation is not wholly
irrelevant, as Rist's failure to answer the point about wearing the same
clothes might suggest. For children would not, one imagines, be born
wise; they will be influenced by their environment and hence it would
be necessary that this harmony and unity should be as visible as
possible. The Stoics did hold that environment was important in this
way, as they were likely to do as a result of their causal theories.[40]
Although family divisions and sexual ones would be of no importance
to the wise, their children would be aware of these divisions and, not
having full understanding, would be adversely influenced by them. It
is important to realise that it is not just the wise who are concerned but
also the potential wise, for whose development a suitable environment
and training would be necessary. Moreover, the absence of these
divisions would encourage the young to care for all. Only by ensuring
that successive generations are wise can *homonoia* be preserved. In
order that the children are imbued with the right attitudes, therefore,
the wise men would act as fathers to all and indeed, if sexual
relationships are promiscuous, they should have no idea who is their
own child anyway.

So there would be no permanent relationships and if they did occur
they could produce social division. But there is one passage that is
often taken to suggest that marriage might be tolerated. Here Zeno is
said to have written that the wise man would *gamein* and
paidopoieisthai (D.L. 7.121, SVF 1.270). Certainly the wise man will

[38] Baldry 1959: 11.
[39] Ibid. 9, Rist 1969: 66.
[40] Long 1986[2]: 77; Chalcidius SVF 3.229, D.L. 7.89, SVF 3.228, and the influence of
nurses etc., SVF 3.733-7.

produce children, but *'gamein'*, which is normally taken to mean 'marry', seems inconsistent with the account of sexual relationships given above. Various solutions have been proposed: that marriage was allowed in the form of a freely chosen permanent relationship, that it refers only to the wise man's life in the ordinary city or that it results from a later Stoic trying to make Zeno's ideas more palatable.[41] The problem arises from viewing *'gamein'* as the institution of marriage in the modern concrete sense.[42] If there were no families or contemporary forms of marriage in the ideal society, *'gamein'* could be used in this context simply for sexual intercourse. In Plato's *Republic* women are held in common and there the phrase, *'gamoi kai paidopoiiai'*, is used for the mating not only of man and woman but also of animals (Plato *Rep.* 5.459a, d). *'Gamein'* and its noun *'gamos'* do occur in non-marital contexts in other writers, though often later ones; certainly by the Roman period it was just a crude term for sexual intercourse. The very fact that the meaning can change in this way suggests that its precise sense was not fixed in the first place.[43]

There are no references in the relevant passages which discuss how the ideal society would be governed. Possibly such a question is superfluous in a classless society where all are wise. Plato had justified the rule of one class over another by arguing that those with wisdom should impose reason on those who lacked it (Plato *Rep.* 9.590cd). This is irrelevant in a society where there are no degrees of wisdom. Here there would be total cooperation between people who would know what the right course of action was. This implies that equality was a characteristic of Zeno's society; for all are equally wise and, therefore, equally virtuous. Moreover, the outward signs, and perhaps causes, of inequality are removed. There is no money, property or competitiveness. Women were traditionally not seen as the equals of men, but here we are told that men and women will wear the same clothes; Zeno presumably believed, as did other Stoics, that virtue was the same in both men and women (Lactantius SVF 3.253, Clement SVF 3.254). All are friends and, therefore, treat others as themselves, showing concern for common interests. Nevertheless, since even the wise are not omniscient, there may have been some form of official for the purposes of administrative convenience, chosen, for instance, by election or by lot or on the basis of seniority. This is not incompatible

---

[41] Rist 1969: 67, Pohlenz 1970: 1.139, Baldry 1959: 9-10, Merlan 1950: 162-3.

[42] Arist. *Pol.* 1253b9 notes that there is no word for a union, *suzeuxis*, between a man and a woman; *gamikê* is the best he can find. Marriage in classical Greece was not 'a single well-defined legal form', but a confusion of different elements, Vernant 1980: 45ff.

[43] Apart from Plato, there is Eurip. *Troades* 44, Lucian *Asinus* 32, Rufinus 35, *AP* 5.94, Clem. Al. *Strom.* 8.12.78. A curse from the fourth century BC against a certain Aristocydes reads: *mêpot' auton gêmai allên gunai(ka) ê paida*, in Wunsch CIA Appendix, *Defixionum tabellae* (1897) n. 78. On the Roman period, Cameron 1982: 171-2, following Robert 1967: 77-81, both of whom list further examples.

with the stress on equality, as Aristotle recognises in his discussion of democracy. For democratic freedom is such that men both rule and are ruled in turn; this is freedom based on equality, *kata to ison*.[44] Similarly the Stoics say that the wise man will both rule and be ruled (Stob. *Ecl.* 2.102.11-19, SVF 3.615).

4. The philosophical background

Here we have what appear to be the main features of Zeno's ideal society. Some have seen Zeno as appearing in Athens with these ideas, supposedly foreign to Greek thought.[45] Yet much of his writing can be seen as a development from earlier philosophers, and the ancient doxographers place him firmly in the Greek philosophical tradition. Many others have sought to emphasise the connection between Cynicism and the *Politeia*. It has been argued earlier that there are no grounds for imagining that it was written while Zeno was a pupil of Crates or even shortly afterwards; indeed the Cynicism of the *Politeia* has been much exaggerated. For while Cynicism is an essentially negative doctrine, Zeno's *Politeia* is far more positive in many ways, as will be seen, owing more to Plato than to the Cynics. The Cynics were famous for their disregard of convention, but they abandoned convention with nothing to put in its place except the wise man himself. He would be virtuous because virtue is natural, but there is no explanation of what virtue is, although presumably the wise man would know. The Stoics, on the other hand, set virtue and the wise man in the context of a universal system by introducing the study of physics.

There was no Cynic ideal society in the constructive sense that Zeno proposed. Cynic wise men were linked with their fellow wise men and they were citizens not of any particular place but of the world (D.L. 6.72, 63). This does not imply any Cynic state on a world scale; it merely means that Cynics recognised no city as their own, which, given their attitude to convention, is simply being consistent.[46] There is no evidence that Diogenes' *Politeia* (if he ever wrote one) dealt with anything more than the wise man in existing society.[47] Nothing that he

---

[44] Arist. *Pol.* 1317a40-18a10; on seniority: Arist. *Pol.* 1332b32-41

[45] For instance Pohlenz 1970: 22, 28, 164-5 stresses the Semitic background of Zeno and Chrysippus. In his view it is only with Panaetius that the Stoa becomes hellenised, p. 207.

[46] Tarn 1948: 2.404-7.

[47] The ancient evidence on the existence of a *Politeia* by Diogenes is contradictory. Diogenes Laertius 6.80 gives a list of works by Diogenes which includes the *Politeia*, but he adds that Satyrus and Sosicrates claimed that Diogenes left nothing in writing. He also includes a list by Sotion which omits the *Politeia* and claims to be complete. Philodemus knows of Diogenes' *Politeia* and cites Cleanthes and Chrysippus as Stoics who were familiar with it (*Peri St.* 15). He knows that some deny that Diogenes wrote it (17.11-13). Dudley 1937: 25-7, following Von Fritz 1926: 55-7, argues that these

said could refer only to an actual society of wise men in Zeno's sense. Those instances which could be relevant reveal more about Diogenes' attitude to convention than about anything else. Thus all things are the property of the wise (D.L. 6.72), but the argument makes it clear that this need have nothing whatsoever to do with an ideal society; for the initial premise is that everything belongs to the gods. He advocated that women should be held in common, but again this could apply just as much to the wise in present conditions as in an ideal society, similarly with his advocacy of cannibalism (D.L. 6.72-3). When he suggests knucklebones as coinage (Athen. 4.159c), it is significant that he does not propose abolishing coinage. If he is talking of an ideal society, by his own argument there would be no need for coinage, because everything would be the common property of the wise.

On the other hand, Zeno is definitely dealing with a state or total society of some form, not just the way the wise men will behave in existing society. For he advocates the abolition of lawcourts, temples and gymnasia, which would be impossible except in the context of a state; indeed he goes so far as to talk about cities. There is no evidence for anything like this in Diogenes.[48] According to Diogenes there was nothing wrong in stealing from temples (D.L. 6.73), which presupposes temples, but may have nothing to do with his alleged *Politeia*. Ascribed to this work by Philodemus is the statement that women should exercise nude in the gymnasium, which presupposes gymnasia (Philod. 19.17). Diogenes is reported to have thought that gymnastic training was useful for virtue (D.L. 6.70).

The Cynics were abandoning convention, but saying that it did not matter whether these things existed or not; they were unimportant because they were not concerned with morality. Things that were according to convention had no priority over those that were not, if both were morally indifferent. It was up to the wise man at any given moment to decide what was the right course of action and it did not matter that convention opposed this. There could be temples, but one

---

omissions reflect an embarrassed Stoa trying to make their past more respectable. But as Tarn 1948: 2.407-9 points out, Satyrus and Sotion were not Stoics but Peripatetics and anyway in Satyrus' time, the third century BC, Stoic opinion believed the *Politeia* was genuine. Since Satyrus and Sosicrates are concerned with denying that Diogenes wrote anything, they need have no interest in the authenticity of the *Politeia* in particular. Although Sotion omits the *Politeia*, he also omits a good many other works which Diogenes Laertius attributes to Diogenes and even adds some new ones. This all suggests that confusion about what Diogenes actually wrote, if anything, set in at a fairly early date, when the morality of the alleged *Politeia* was unlikely to have been as controversial as it later was. In the light of the existing evidence the question of its attribution to Diogenes must remain open, cf. Baldry 1965: 102-3. But since Cleanthes and Chrysippus accepted the attribution to Diogenes, it is reasonable to believe that, if not the work of Diogenes, it was at least representative of Cynic thought.

[48] Dudley 1937: 99 says Diogenes proposed the abolition of lawcourts, gymnasia and temples, but I can find no evidence for this (cf. Rist 1969: 68)

could steal from them. This was very different from Zeno – temples, lawcourts and gymnasia may be indifferent, but he recommended that there should be none in the ideal society nevertheless. They were undesirable for the reasons outlined above; the fact that he did reject them adds further grounds to the view expressed earlier, that he had already formulated the distinction between the preferred (*proêgmena*) and the rejected (*apoproêgmena*) by the time he wrote the *Politeia*. For if the only standard of evaluation was morality itself and these things were morally indifferent, how could he accept some classes of morally indifferent things and reject others? This is only possible for him once he has made nature the standard of evaluation for such things. The Cynics without this distinction could only ignore these things and display their contempt for them, but their theory did not allow them the grounds for outright rejection. Thus any form of Cynic ideal society could not progress beyond the relationship between wise men in the existing world.

Crates put forward a playful ideal *polis*; it was not an ideal society on a world scale or even a city-state scale, but Pera, the philosopher's bag, which symbolised his self-sufficiency, *autarkeia*, and so makes him independent of communities.[49] Thus the Cynic wise man will live outside society, doing things his own way; he may not approve of the institutions of society, but they will still exist. Zeno proposed the abolition of those institutions; he visualised a society completely different from the present one. This is a major shift and should not be minimised by saying that the Cynics were talking of a few wise men while Zeno was talking about a lot of them. This is a complete change of attitude and the explanation can be found in the Academy and the Lyceum.

The Cynics never made this shift because, although the wise man should not necessarily lead an isolated life, it did not matter if he did. Such things were morally indifferent. He would be neither happier nor more virtuous as a result of being involved in society. Zeno, too, would agree that it would make the wise man no happier. For both the wise man was self-sufficient as a moral agent. How then could Zeno take this step? It has been argued above that it was due to the influence of the Academy and Aristotle that Zeno evolved the notion of nature as a universal system and guiding force. Everything had a place in this system. Nature was the standard of evaluation; therefore to create a society in which the wise man could properly be a part would be preferable. The Stoics held that the wise man would not live in solitude; for he is by nature made for society, *phusei koinônikos* (D.L. 7.123, SVF 3.628). Given that Zeno envisaged an ideal society, it is reasonable to believe that he held this too and that it was one of the

---

[49] Baldry 1959: 14, D.L. 6.85.

premises which enabled him to make the move from the Cynic concentration on the individual wise man to his own view of an ideal society or state.

The most prominent discussion of an ideal society written prior to Zeno was the *Republic* of Plato. Zeno's was a far more radical document, contrasting with Plato's in many ways, but the nature of these differences suggests that he had Plato in mind when he wrote it. For, although different, many ideas can be seen as extensions of those in Plato. The differences would derive in part from the different philosophical contexts. Plutarch reports that Zeno attacked Plato's *Republic* and, although he does not say in which work, it is very probable that it was in the *Politeia*.[50] That is not to say that Zeno wrote it solely to attack Plato, but that by doing so he could develop his own view of an ideal society. Among the references to Zeno's *Politeia* there are three to Plato, indicating that some writers at least connected the two (SVF 1.262, 263, 269). Association with the Academy would have brought him into contact with these ideas; Polemo even complained that Zeno stole his ideas (D.L. 7.25).

Plato's *Republic* could be interpreted as a philosophical justification of aristocratic society which reflects some of the prejudices that would have been held by a man of Plato's social position.[51] Such a criticism cannot be levelled against Zeno in spite of his division of men into wise and foolish, because in the ideal society there were no classes; all were wise. For Plato, on the other hand, the inferiority of one class was an integral element of the ideal. So Zeno differs from Plato in the absence of such a hierarchy and in the egalitarian nature of his ideal society.

Plutarch wrote that Diogenes, Plato and Zeno took the concept of *homonoia* from Lycurgan Sparta (Plut. *Lyc.* 31). The use of this concept by the Cynic Diogenes should not be stressed by those who wish to strengthen the connection between Cynicism and Stoicism; for what is important is not the adoption of it but the context in which it is set. As far as this is concerned Zeno had more in common with Plato and Aristotle, both of whom set it in a state or society. Plato and Aristotle, although realising the need to maintain political stability in the face of the fourth-century political situation, responded to this need in terms of the existing structure, that is to say a *polis*-based class society. For Zeno this is bound to fail when confronted with conflict between the classes and also war, so his solution requires the abandonment of the independent *polis* and classes. It might be argued that Zeno simply sought to solve this problem in a different way and that Plato had no bearing on it.

Close comparison between Plato and Zeno, however, leads to some

---

[50] Plut. *St. Rep.* 1034e, SVF 1.260, cf. Numenius in Eusebius, *Praep. Evang.* 14.732c.
[51] Wood 1978: 119-208, esp. 137-71, cf. Farrington 1939: 26-32, 87-106 and *passim*.

points of contact. Plato had divided his society into three classes: the philosopher rulers, the auxiliaries and the mass of the common people. In spite of this division he considers the society as essentially the wise ruling over those who have no control over their desires, in Zeno's terminology the 'fools' (Plato *Rep.* 4.431cd). *Homonoia* is manifested in the relationship between these classes, a relationship in which each knows his place (Plato *Rep.* 4.432a). Plato's ideal city is a just city analogous in structure to the soul of the just man. Corresponding to the three classes of the city, there are three parts of the soul, reason, which should rule in the soul, spirit and irrational desire. The ideal, justice, is a particular relationship of the classes or parts. In both cases, the city and the soul, *homonoia* is identified with *sôphrosunê*, the control of wayward desires.

Clearly Zeno would disagree with this; the fools are enemies of each other and their existence is incompatible with *homonoia* or any sort of harmony. Thus Zeno could have attacked Plato for false optimism, claiming that, while the causes of disruption were still there, the problem had not been solved. For Zeno *homonoia* was not a relationship between classes which would not work, but a relationship between individual wise men; it was based not on suppression of recalcitrant elements, a potential source of conflict, but on their absence. One might imagine that such a connection between Zeno and Plato is somewhat fanciful. Nevertheless, just as the structure of Plato's ideal society has its parallel in his psychology, so too does that of Zeno. This suggests that what one sees here is a conscious attempt to answer Plato and solve problems which he had overlooked. According to Zeno fools are incompatible with the ideal society and their presence would render it no longer ideal. Similarly a man could not be wise if he had any unsuitable desires, *pathê*, whether or not he acted on them. Unsuitable desires and the immoral action which follows from them are a manifestation of inadequately developed reason and not due to any conflict between rational and irrational parts of the soul which reason loses. Since the reason of the wise man is perfectly developed, he has no such unsuitable desires. All his desires are correct, a reflection of his perfect rationality.[52] So for Zeno there are no fools in the good city and no *pathê* in the soul of the good man.

For Plato, on the other hand, the ideal man or city must have elements hostile to the whole, but he must also have control of them. This is brought out most vividly in the myth of Phaedrus: the soul is compared to a charioteer with two horses, one good and obedient, the other bad and concerned only with pursuing its desires. The charioteer must make the unruly horse conform to his wishes. Persuasion and commands have no effect; instead he must be compelled to obey by

[52] See further on the soul, Chapter 2.5, Chapter 3.2, Chapter 8.4.

sheer brute force. If the better elements force the bad to submit, then the struggle will lead to a life that is happy (*makarios*) and harmonious (*homonoêtikos*).[53] For Zeno such a conception of the ideal would be nonsensical, a contradiction in terms. He answered what he saw as the deficiencies in Plato by positing a society purely of wise men.

Moreover it cannot be argued that earlier Cynic thinkers would have reached the same conclusion as Zeno. For not only was he introducing a more complex psychology not known in Cynicism, but he was also placing greater emphasis than they appear to have done on the fact that the fools were enemies. The Cynics had held that the fools were mad and slaves (cf. D.L. 6.33, 43), but nowhere are they recorded as saying that they were enemies. This is not to suggest that they did not make this claim; indeed it might be implicit in their view that the wise are friends of the wise. The absence of this epithet, while the others (for example, mad, slave) are present, suggests that it had no great importance in their thought, whereas a constructive approach such as Zeno's in the context of his overall system would have required him to consider it.

Zeno's attack on Plato would have been directed primarily at the premises of his *Republic*, as has been shown, and it is not necessary to view every difference as part of this attack, but merely as a consequence of it. Thus while it is correct to point out that Zeno rejected lawcourts, gymnasia and temples, which all had found a place in Plato's *Laws*,[54] this need provide no grounds for assuming that Zeno was directly criticising Plato on these points.

At the same time Zeno did free himself from some of the problems that Plato created for himself. For Plato, both in the *Republic* and the *Laws*, introduced complications by seeking to consider his ideal society in relation to the real world. Zeno, on the other hand, studied a society in isolation and consequently had no need to concern himself with the influence of external factors. Thus Plato banned visiting poets (Plato *Rep.* 3.398a) and forbade foreign travel to all those under forty (Plato *Laws* 12.950ff) in order to avoid the danger of external corruption, something that was irrelevant to Zeno.[55] Similarly the possibility of wars compelled Plato to devote much of the city's resources to defence; indeed the whole class of guardians in the *Republic* is primarily for this purpose. Yet within Zeno's society the communities are at peace. Moreover the concept of community of women (*koinônia gunaikôn*) had occurred in both Plato and Zeno, but the nature of Plato's *Republic* made it almost impossibly complex. For it was nothing like simple promiscuity, but rather a matter of eugenic selection which would be

---

[53] Plato *Phaedrus* 246a-57a, esp. 253c-6c, cf. Plato *Timaeus* 69b-72d.

[54] Dyroff 1897: 210-11, Plato *Laws* 761c, 778cd.

[55] It is true that the wise man could not be corrupted, but those who had not reached the age of reason were presumably vulnerable to corruption even in Zeno's ideal society.

unnecessary in Zeno's ideal society. To say that Zeno could abandon eugenic selection because all would be wise and good is to give only half the reason.[56] It is true that there were no degrees of wisdom for Zeno, but, even if Plato had made all the guardians equally wise, he would still have had eugenic selection because it was designed not only to mate the wisest but also those best in battle in the interests of defence (Plato *Rep.* 5.460b). Only when there is no need for defence is there no need for eugenic selection. So by abstracting his society from the real world of bad men Zeno simplified matters and gave himself the opportunity to concentrate on the essentials of the ideal.

The only case in the references to the *Politeia* where there appears to be direct opposition to a proposal of Plato is at D.L. 7.33 where 'currency is not thought to be necessary for either exchange or foreign travel'. This may be a reference to Plato *Rep.* 2.371b where he allowed 'currency for exchange'. Even so it could be said that it is not a straightforward contradiction, because Plato does not allow money for the guardians (Plato *Rep.* 3.417a) so it is quite consistent with Zeno who only has the wise in his society.[57] Nevertheless, the reasons for the absence of coinage are different; Plato fears it will corrupt the guardians (Plato *Rep.* 3.417ab), whereas for Zeno virtue cannot be lost. Zeno's statement does directly contradict Plato's views in the *Laws*. Here 'currency for daily exchange' is allowed for use by all inhabitants. Moreover there should always be a store of 'Greek currency for military purposes and for foreign travel' (Plato *Laws* 5.742a).

5. The political background

Zeno's *Politeia* can be seen as a conscious rejection of Plato's *Republic*, yet at the same time Plato's work could be said to have worked as a catalyst. It should be clear that both Plato and the Cynics were influential on Zeno's thought in his *Politeia*, but by themselves they do not explain it. Zeno could have progressed from Cynicism to be influenced by other aspects of Plato's or the Academy's thought or not by their thought at all. It may naturally follow on from previous thought but so may many other theories that were never propounded. It is not sufficient to explain this development in Zeno's political thought by a mere quirk in his personality or accident in that he happened to be tutored by Polemo. It was not bound to develop in a certain way, in isolation, as if driven on by its own internal momentum. Political thought is surely susceptible to influence from the political conditions of the time. Moreover, if those ideas gain acceptance, they are successfully appealing to something in society;

[56] As suggested by Baldry 1959: 9.
[57] Chroust 1965: 180.

they are in tune with people's attitudes. To determine what influences are at work is by nature very hard and often only very general observations can be made. To say that certain political conditions may have resulted in some particular aspect of Zeno's thought is not to exclude the possibility that he was also influenced by previous political thought, but rather the prevailing political conditions drew his attention to an element of this earlier thought and caused him to emphasise it. Thus his view of the political thought or the philosophy in general of his predecessors must have been to some extent determined by the political circumstances in which he was writing. Indeed it might be necessary to see several contemporary problems as leading to one conclusion. There is no need, therefore, to discount any of them.[58]

Clearly pre-eminent among external influences must be the impact of Alexander who had irreparably altered the political situation at both an international and on domestic levels, only to confuse it still further by his premature death. There was no longer a barbarian threat to Greece from the other side of the Aegean; the balance of power which the Greeks had known for generations had been overturned. Instead Alexander's successors struggled with one another to secure their own territory; mainland Greece became the centre of attention only in so far as it was important to their strategy. Athens was redundant as an independent political force and for much of the time before 229 was garrisoned. It is hard to imagine that changes of this degree would not leave their mark on political thought.

Alexander has often been introduced into the discussion of Zeno's political thought. The relationship does not have to be understood as literally as Tarn, that Alexander formulated an idea of the brotherhood of mankind and Zeno adopted it. Yet, Baldry would appear to go to the other extreme claiming that Alexander's conquests had little relevance to Zeno's thought, and indeed little relevance to the idea of unity, because Alexander's legacy was not unity, but disunity which lasted until the second century BC.[59] Perhaps this is exactly the point of its influence on Zeno; Alexander, albeit for a short while, had shown that almost all the known world could be combined, that barbarian and Greek could be subjects in one empire, but the key point is that he failed and this led to the subsequent disorder. Zeno and his contemporaries suffered from this failure, yet the possibility of unity could be seen. It is significant that Zeno does not talk of unity as existing; it has become an ideal because it is so necessary and has been glimpsed, but gone. For Zeno unity can only exist if all men are wise;

[58] For discussion of some aspects of the relationship between philosophy and political changes in Athens, see Chapter 4.

[59] Tarn 1948: 2.448. For a refutation of Tarn's thesis, Badian 1958: 425-44. Baldry 1965: 153, 129.

for the good alone are true citizens, friends, kindred and free, while the bad or fools are enemies, slaves and aliens to each other, even parents to children, brothers to brothers, relations to relations (D.L. 7.32-3). This reflects not so much a belief in the unity of mankind as in the necessity of wisdom or good. An Alexander may unite the world, but unity not based on moral goodness is bound to fail and bring about the situation that existed in Zeno's day. For him the barrier to such unity was not differences between race or *polis* but sheer stupidity and moral badness.

It was argued earlier that the size of this ideal society was limited only by the number of people that there were, on the hypothesis that all were wise. This is a considerable shift from Plato's *Republic*, limited as it was to a single *polis*, and not the same as the Cynic thesis that wise men, scattered though they were, had a common bond in their wisdom. It seems plausible to see the scale of Alexander's conquests as a contributory factor; the limits of his empire may not have been fully comprehended, but men must have realised that it was enormous, probably envisaging it as larger than it was. Thus it no longer seemed totally absurd to go beyond the bounds of the *polis*. It may be objected to this that great empires were nothing new. Since the fifth century the Greeks had believed the Persian empire to be of inordinate size, so there was no reason why Alexander's empire should have any more influence than the Persian. However, the Greeks had merely observed the Persian empire from a distance, relieved that they were not part of it. Besides, it was a barbarian empire. But now whether they wished to acknowledge it or not, they had become part of Alexander's empire and subsequently subordinate to one or other of his Successors. Moreover Greeks had fought for it and emigrated there, living in Greek cities throughout Asia.

The cities of the early Hellenistic period also suffered seriously from internal instability. For instance, Athens between 323 and 261 had undergone numerous changes of government. Such instability was widespread throughout Greece, due partly to the determination of various Successors to have a government favourable to themselves, whether tyranny, oligarchy or democracy, and in part to the discontented within the population of the city. These two factors could work either together or independently. The former was merely a symptom of external problems and Zeno's approach to such disunity has been outlined above. The nature of the latter, however, needs to be considered more fully before Zeno's reaction to it is examined. Social polarisation had been increasing throughout the fourth century only to be exacerbated by the conquests of Alexander; for the vast quantities of money that these put into circulation caused prices to rise, possibly by as much as 50 per cent by 300 BC, while the wages remained the same or declined.[60] This, combined with other social problems such as the

[60] Tarn 1923: 108-27, based on evidence from Delos, folowed by Fuks 1974: 57-8. De

increasing number of landless, led to social conflict within the Greek cities; this was characterised by demands for the 'redistribution of land' and 'abolition of debts'. The constant occurrence of these phrases indicates the nature of the problem. This social conflict has been described as 'one of the great historical processes of Hellenistic Greece'.[61]

A major early example of this social conflict which must have alarmed the propertied class throughout Greece took place in Argos in 370. Here more than 1200 of the rich were condemned and clubbed to death; their property was confiscated (Diod. 15.57.3-58). Isocrates said that the poor delighted more in this execution of the rich than a man delights in slaying an enemy in battle (Isoc. *Philip* 51-2). From then on there is a succession of outbreaks of class conflict, stemming from the widening gulf between rich and poor. Many tyrannies emerged because of it, such as Clearchus in Heracleia Pontica (364-352), Chairon in Pellene (336-335), Agathocles in Syracuse (317-316), Apollodorus in Cassandreia (280-276). Euphron, tyrant of Sicyon (368-365), was buried in the market place as a popular hero and founder of the city, much to the disgust of Xenophon (*Hel.* 7.3.12). Other outbreaks occurred at Corinth in about 365, Mytilene in mid-fourth century and probably Ceos and Naxos in 280. Yet these are only cases where the circumstances caused these feelings of discontent to explode. There must have been many more places where the tension between rich and poor was apparent but where it did not quite reach the point of revolutionary conflict.

This tension is seen in the extensive evidence for the concern and fear on the part of the propertied classes. Isocrates is constantly warning of the dangers to Greece from the poor, who, he says, would rather rob the rich of their possessions than find treasure (Isoc. *Archid.* 67). Aeneas Tacticus (14.1), similarly, fears that in a time of siege a city cannot trust the mass of its citizens and should use various influences, such as the cancellation of interest or even part or all of the principal, in order to secure their loyalty. Attention, he recommends, should also be paid to those who lack the necessities of life. The fears of the rich of revolution from below were not only expressed in this form, but they were also enshrined in legal documents and treaties. As early as 353 the judicial oath of the court of Heliaea in Athens included a clause in which the juror had to swear that he would not allow private debts to be cancelled, nor land nor houses belonging to the citizens of Athens to be redistributed (Dem. 24. 149). The League of Corinth had a clause providing that any attempt to confiscate property, divide land, cancel debts or liberate slaves with a view to revolution would be prevented

---

Ste Croix 1981: 186-7 accepts Tarn's view that the condition of the masses deteriorated significantly, but expresses doubts about his figures.

[61] Fuks 1966: 441.

by the League (Ps. Dem. 17.15). This seems also to have appeared in the Hellenic League established by Antigonus I and Demetrius I in 302 (SVA 446 line 53). These all imply that whether class conflict took place or not the threat of it was always there.

Against this background Zeno's *Politeia* is set. It has already been seen that he was concerned with the problem of internal stability. Since much of this problem was caused by class struggle, the poor against the rich, Zeno envisaged a classless society. Certainly there was nothing new in the perception that much internal conflict was the result of class divisions; both Plato and Aristotle had been aware of this (cf. Plato *Rep.* 8.551d, Arist. *Pol.* 1296b34-97a7). In these earlier writers there was a distinct unwillingness, or possibly inability, to envisage a society without class divisions of some sort. They saw society as a hierarchy and wished to preserve its stability. Thus Plato proposed the somewhat dubious move of detaching political power from economic activity. This did not solve the social problems that led to the violence, it only placed them outside the realm of politics, at the same time ensuring that the class in power was virtually hereditary. Aristotle thought that the stability of the *polis* and the class structure could be preserved if there were more people of moderate wealth to balance the extremes of very rich and very poor. Zeno too was seeking to ensure stability, but this stability was for a society radically different from the contemporary one. Aristotle and even Plato may have been more realistic, but Zeno was acknowledging the complaints of the discontented. He was examining the nature of a society that would render these complaints invalid rather than simply suppressing them. The two main demands of the discontented were abolition of debts and redistribution of land. Zeno proposed that there would be no money and no private property; for everything would be the common possession of all. He was tackling the problem of two classes being, as Plato had put it, at war with one another, on the one hand by eliminating what he saw as the cause of it, money and property, and on the other by abandoning the class society in which these causes had effect. It is of course possible that he did not see the relationship as directly as this, but that is not to say that it did not influence him in some way. Yet there is evidence to suggest that he might have sympathised with the condition of the poor; for his contemporary Timon wrote that he collected around him a crowd of *penestai*, the most beggarly and empty of the townspeople (D.L. 7.16). This is doubtless abuse implying that his followers went about in rags and were no better than serfs, but the reference to *penestai* suggests contempt also for their background, although we do not know the context in which Timon wrote it.

An objection might be made to this that Zeno would have considered internal instability to be caused not by social and economic difficulties, but by the fact that most men were bad and foolish, hence his solution that all men should be good and wise. While it might be true that there would be no problems in a world of good men, this does not answer or explain anything. Zeno has to expound how he imagines such men should live and take into account the character of the contemporary world, seeking to avoid the deficiencies of it. It is quite consistent, therefore, to acknowledge the social and economic problems as a cause of instability but see that they are there only because men are bad. Accordingly he would consider the wise as living in a society without these problems and show how this was so, for instance by the role of Eros and the characteristics of the wise men. This requires that he emphasises certain aspects of the wise men, for example that all wise men are friends.

Thus when he characterised the wise man as citizen, friend and free in the *Politeia* (D.L. 7.33), he does so because all these qualities are relevant to the ideal society. The Cynics, too, held that *eleutheria* (freedom) was important and Diogenes said he valued it above everything else (D.L. 6.71). Yet from the context it is clear that Diogenes considered this to be freedom from the restrictions imposed by convention. In Stoicism *eleutheria* is given different and greater emphasis. It is noticeable that the Stoics constantly referred to the wise man as free (SVF 1.218, 222, 3.355, 544), but the Cynics did not, although they implied it by calling the fools slaves in contrast to the wise who were men (D.L. 6.33, 43). For Zeno it is an integral part of his doctrines and needed emphasis. It is a more positive concept than the Cynic one, vital to the ideal society. It is not merely that the wise man is free to act morally, because he lives in accordance with nature and his reason; this need not entail a relationship with other wise men, yet a passage referring to the *Politeia* makes it clear that it is connected with relationships between the wise. For Athenaeus notes that Eros was the god of *eleutheria* and *philia* (friendship) and provider of *homonoia*;[62] Eros, *philia* and *homonoia* all involve relationships and cannot be practised in isolation, therefore presumably *eleutheria* must be seen in terms of these relationships. I would suggest that no relationship in the ideal society is conducted on the basis of superiority, but is between equals. This is how one would expect it to be among men who are equally wise.

It is possible that what prompted Zeno to highlight *eleutheria* in his treatment of the ideal society was its emergence as a major political issue at the close of the fourth century. For Antigonus I had in 315 proclaimed himself the champion of Greek freedom, promising to give back autonomy to the Greek states. Ptolemy I of Egypt, realising the propaganda value of this, quickly made his bid, but it was Antigonus

---

[62] See n. 23 above.

who was taken seriously by the Greeks (Diod. 19.61-2). His claims were consistent with his actions in the early years, especially after Demetrius, his son, had 'liberated' Athens in 307, but their credibility must have deteriorated with time. The siege of Rhodes, in particular, showed his lack of sincerity.[63] Moreover, although there may have been no garrison, Demetrius' scandalous behaviour in Athens in 304/3 could scarcely have helped. Athens may then have been free, but in fear of Demetrius it passed a motion to the effect that whatever Demetrius commanded was to be regarded as holy and just (Plut. *Demet*. 24). By 294 Demetrius had installed a garrison in the Museion. Thus, as freedom becomes the ostensible subject of political and diplomatic struggle, so it takes on a more significant role in philosophical debate. Zeno may have been responding to, or at least influenced by, this contemporary political atmosphere when he wrote that the ideal society and its citizens were free. For they alone were free and their relationships were conducted on the basis of equality; anything else was just a charade. Bad men in society as it was were slaves, so little could be said for their promises of freedom. Freedom is only freedom if it is correctly used and this requires wise men.

It has already been argued that the Stoic view of *eleutheria* was different from that of the Cynics. Indeed it had never been treated as a central philosophical issue and philosophical ideal before. The propaganda value of the freedom of the Greeks as a slogan had been recognised before by the Spartans in the Peloponnesian War (e.g. Thuc. 1.124, 4.85.1), but then Athens, the centre of philosophy, had been the oppressor, now it was the sufferer. Previously philosophers had not emphasised *eleutheria* as an ideal. Clearly freedom would be preferable to slavery and superior to it (e.g Arist. *Protrept*. B25). Nevertheless, essentially *eleutheria* is considered as desirable only for the upper classes, but not for the lower. For the latter slavery (*douleia*) is appropriate, a point made bluntly by the Old Oligarch.[64] Consequently Plato condemns the *eleutheria* which is present in tyranny or in democratic Athens as mere licence to do what one wants (Plato *Rep*. 562bc, *Gorgias* 492c). For it is *eleutheria* in the hands of the wrong people. For Aristotle *eleutheria* is a characteristic of democracy, something which should be limited by law (Arist. *Pol*. 1310a24-38). It is significant that Aristotle writes of the *eleutheros*, the free man, in terms applicable to an upper-class gentleman and totally unsuitable for a vulgar artisan: it is the mark of the *eleutheros* that he does not do work appropriate to a hired labourer nor does he live for the benefit of another.[65]

The Stoic emphasis on the freedom of the wise man may have

---

[63] Simpson 1958: 409.
[64] Ps. Xen. *Ath. Pol*. 1.8-9; for Aristotle's and Plato's views, see Chapter 2.5
[65] Arist. *Rhet*. 1.1367a28-32; De Ste Croix 1981: 116ff.

contributed to the view that Stoicism was a philosophy concentrating on the individual. But this is not strictly true. It is argued that Stoicism responded to the failure of the *polis* by producing a very inward-looking philosophy.[66] Yet, when the ideal society is examined, it is clear that each wise man is actively involved in it, not merely an inhabitant, but part of a unity. He is described as citizen, *politês*, which implies his active participation (D.L. 7.33). It has been explained earlier how the wise man is by nature made for society. In the ideal society the wise man is far from individualistic, rather he is in his natural environment to which he would have a far stronger sense of belonging than to the ordinary, conventional *polis*. It is not a case of abandoning the *polis* for the individual but for something greater, of which the wise man is more truly a part and into which he integrates himself. At the same time, however, the attitude of the wise man to present society may well give the appearance of a highly individual-orientated philosophy, but this is no different from Plato's wise man when he is living in an imperfect society (Plato *Rep.* 496de).

This is not to suggest that disillusion with the *polis* is irrelevant. As the *polis* diminished in importance and became submerged in a world of enormous kingdoms, it was no longer self-evident that political thought should be limited to the *polis*. Aristotle himself may have been becoming aware of this towards the end of his life.[67] Perhaps people who no longer felt the former affinity with the *polis* needed to feel that they belonged to something and Stoicism offered a suitable alternative. At the same time the tradition of political thought of which Stoicism was part had developed within the *polis* system. So even when going beyond the *polis* it would be likely to continue to apply the ways of thinking which would be more appropriate to the *polis* environment in which they originated.

Another aspect of the political situation that may have influenced Zeno is the rule of Demetrius of Phalerum as virtual tyrant of Athens from 317 to 307. Demetrius was a pupil of Theophrastus and an associate of Nicanor, the son-in-law of Aristotle. After he had lost power he eventually went off to work as a philosopher in Alexandria. Thus it would not be surprising to find evidence of his Peripatetic education in his legislation. Cicero certainly felt that Demetrius had introduced philosophy into government (Cic. *De Leg.* 3.14, cf. 2.66). Most modern commentators agree that he did put elements of Peripatetic political theory into practice.[68] For instance by setting the

---

[66] E.g. Tarn 1952: 327, Zeller 1923: 283-4, Davidson 1907: 127-8.

[67] Weil 1960: 367-415.

[68] Bayer 1942: 21-93, Ferguson 1911: 38-49, Vatai 1984: 118-20. Gehrke 1978: 149-93 argues that the politician must be separated from the philosopher. As a politician Demetrius was pragmatic. It is certainly misconceived to imagine that in Demetrius' period of supremacy there should be a detailed match between political practice and political theory. Nevertheless, the approach to political action could still be consistent

property qualification for franchise at 1000 drachmae he limited citizenship, but still gave it to the majority of the people in the interests of stability. At the same time it is probable that the magistracies were only held by the upper sections of the citizens.

Although this is generally acknowledged, some dispute that moral reform entered his programme.[69] It is argued that his sumptuary laws had economic motives, but this does not necessarily invalidate the claim that they were also influenced by philosophy. Often it is the case that the choice of a particular economic policy is conditioned just as much by ideology as its likely effectiveness. Otherwise one would be compelled to claim that this policy was the only one he could possibly have chosen or that he chose it at random. The Samian historian, Duris, active in the early third century, wrote that Demetrius made laws for everybody else and arranged their lives, but led a lawless life himself (FGH 76 F10). Duris may not be a very reliable authority, but, while his attack on Demetrius' character may be doubted, the contrast really only has any point if he did try to improve morality. To promote morality by legislation would be consistent with an Aristotelian programme. For Aristotle had argued that the majority of men would not be influenced by argument but only by fear of punishment.[70] This attempt to impose political and moral order from above is the complete opposite of Zeno who held that, if there was to be a stable society in which all people behave morally, men must want to be moral, thus they must be wise. Hence it is possible that Zeno's work was a reaction to Demetrius. This animosity to Demetrius on a political level may be reflected in the absence of any explicit evidence to associate Zeno with the Peripatetic school in spite of being linked with the names of most other philosophers.

Zeno evidently began the *Politeia* by asserting that it was relevant to contemporary Greek society (Philod. 12.1-12). In what way was such an impossibly idealistic society relevant? It was relevant because it provided an ideal against which contemporary society could be matched to show how far it fell short of that ideal. It was not an ideal selected at random, but one which had developed out of the contemporary situation and thus closely linked with it. By writing it Zeno was condemning the way the world then was. It described not

---

with the basic principles of Peripatetic political thought. For the present argument whether Demetrius was influenced by Peripatetic thought is not as important as the fact that he was perceived to have been. This is apparent for instance in the reaction against the philosophy schools that followed his expulsion. Sophocles passed a law banning philosophical schools that did not have the support of the *dêmos*. What remains of Demochares' defence of this law demonstrates the political nature of this law; he cites examples of students of philosophy who became tyrants. D.L. 5.38, Athen. 13.610f, 11.508f-9a.

[69] Cf. Ferguson 1911: 41.

[70] Arist. *NE* 10.1179b4-20, 1179b31-80a5; Burnyeat 1980: 69-92, esp. 74-82.

only the ideal society of the wise, but the wise man's attitude to present society, an attitude which would be implicit throughout the book.[71]

The first head of the Stoic school expounded an ideal society of indefinite size and filled it with wise men; this was a direct, although rather impracticable, response to contemporary problems. To seek a solution by calling in the assistance of wise men may seem a somewhat facile one that need have no relevance to his particular time. For it might be said that anyone could solve the world's problems by making all the inhabitants wise. Yet this would be to neglect the context in which these ideas developed. Zeno's thought represented a solution to these problems in relation to the ideas of his predecessors and, as such, it was inextricably entwined with his own time. It was not a simple matter of everybody being wise, which would explain little, but of the relationship between the wise themselves and their whole environment. He was concerned to reach conclusions about the nature of such a society and hence produced a *Politeia* that was radically different from contemporary society. It is the Stoic analysis of contemporary society which will be the subject of the next chapter.

[71] Murray 1966: 369.

2

Slavery and Society

1. Introduction

In this chapter I intend to examine the role of the concepts of *douleia* (slavery) and *eleutheria* (freedom) and their relation to *homonoia* (unity/harmony) in the political philosophy of Zeno and Chrysippus. It will be argued that the early Stoics were not merely influenced by contemporary society, but they also attempted to analyse it. Hence they had their own view both of an ideal world and of the present. Indeed their approach to the ideal world was greatly conditioned by their approach to the present. They considered contemporary society to be a hierarchic structure, which came about largely because of the moral badness of its members. The relationships of subordination that exist in such a society were described by them as slavery; this slavery embodies the hostility and lack of harmony which are features of bad men and as such is completely incompatible with *homonoia*. This is a marked contrast to Plato and Aristotle, for whom slavery was an integral part of a harmonious ideal. This Stoic theory of slavery was originally formulated by Zeno and had a place in his *Politeia*, although it was perhaps at that stage somewhat confused; it is probable that Chrysippus clarified and systemised it.

This theory has to be reconstructed from scattered evidence, but that is not an argument against this interpretation. The distribution and quantity of evidence on a particular subject reflects not the interest of the early Stoa, but that of later writers and presumably their readers. For instance the fragments which we do possess of Zeno's *Politeia* survive mainly for their shock value, a suitable subject for polemic. On the subject of freedom and slavery there is a sufficient degree of detail and consistency in the evidence to make it reasonable to believe that it is the remains of a theory.

Central to a discussion of the concept of *douleia* in the early Stoa must be a series of types of *douleia* recorded by Diogenes Laertius (D.L. 7.121-2, SVF 3.355) in his summary of Stoic doctrine:

> The wise man alone is free, the morally bad are slaves. For freedom (*eleutheria*) is the power of independent action (*autopragia*), whereas slavery (*douleia*) is the absence of independent action. There is a second

form of slavery that consists in subordination (*hupotaxis*) and a third
which consists in both possession (*ktêsis*) and subordination. The
opposite of this is mastery (*despoteia*); this too is bad.

Here there is a fairly systematic presentation of several forms of
douleia, although the original clarity has been doubtless somewhat
obscured in the process of summarising, perhaps several times over,
but it will be shown that they represent elements of a consistent point
of view. This passage has not been given the attention that it deserves.
Indeed, when slavery in Stoic thought is discussed, it generally centres
on the first form, that is the moral slavery of the bad, and the third
form, slavery as property, in other words chattel slavery. I can find no
discussion of the second form, that of subordination (*hupotaxis*) alone.[1]
Yet, since the early Stoics did draw up this list of different types of
slavery and did give consideration to the first and third, it would be
curious if they ignored the second; it is to this second type of slavery
that this chapter will be chiefly devoted. It might be suggested that
this was just an incidental remark, but it will be shown below that
such suggestion must be rejected.

Before looking at the notion of slavery as subordination alone, it will
be necessary to examine briefly the Stoic position on the first and third
forms, in order to see the framework into which the second should be
fitted.

2. Moral freedom and moral slavery

At the beginning of the quotation *eleutheria* is described as the power
of independent action, while slavery is its opposite, the lack of this
power. The passage makes it clear that the wise man is free in this
sense and the bad man a slave; this is confirmed, for instance, by
Origen SVF 3.544, where it is said that every wise man is free, because
he derives the power of independent action from divine law. It is
generally accepted that this first statement is talking of the moral
freedom of the good and the moral slavery of the bad.[2] In the writings
that we can be reasonably certain represent the views of the early Stoa
we have no clear continuous account of what it means to be free in this
sense although we are frequently told that only the good man is free
(e.g. SVF 3.593, 3.618, 3.597).

The key notion in moral freedom is that of independence and only
the morally good man can attain this. For he is restrained by one thing
alone, the divine law, but paradoxically this is no restraint at all; it is
the essence of his freedom; for this is what is natural for man, in
agreement with which men should live. The wise man has a fully

[1] Griffin 1976: 459 refers to it in passing as political slavery.
[2] E.g. Pohlenz 1966: 137, Griffin 1976: 459.

developed reason (*logos*) which is in harmony with the *logos* of the universe, that is divine law. All men have reason, but only in the good man is it strong and uncorrupted; as a result he will both be able to live in agreement with nature and choose to do so. For since he has the knowledge of how he should live he cannot choose not to live like this. Moreover, because he will always do what is in agreement with nature he can never be compelled to do what he does not want to do (Stobaeus SVF 3.567). This is put explicitly by Zeno, who said that it is easier to force a bladder filled with air under the water than to force a wise man to do something he does not want to do; for the soul which is strengthened by right reason (*orthos logos*) is invincible (Philo SVF 1.218). Thus the wise man will be free and independent. All that matters to him is the moral good and this is his standard of evaluation. He will not be swayed in his judgments or actions by anything else, because none of these can be more important than what is morally good. This is how he should live; it is the way nature meant him to live. Clearly the individual is restricted in his freedom by the very fact that he is human, but within this sphere the wise man, because he lives as nature intends he should, is attaining the freedom his own nature can allow. This is closely linked to the notion that virtue is sufficient for happiness (SVF 1.187, D.L. 7.127). Both emphasise the independence of the wise man from things external to him and the moral freedom of the wise man in Stoic thought is dependent on the self-sufficiency of virtue.

In contrast to the wise man, the fool or bad man is denying his nature. Instead of acting with a view to the moral good, which would be to fulfil his nature, he often acts against it. His *logos* is weak and corrupt, so his criterion for action is not the moral good, but various things that are morally indifferent, that are not in the slightest commensurate with the good. If he is going to value things that have no moral value and are external to him, it is inevitable that he will lack the independence which the wise man has. For the wise man has no need of things external to him, although he may of course use them. It may be thought that the fool is free to deny his nature, but he is not making a free choice; rather he acts against his nature through ignorance; for he is ignorant of the good and how he should live. So not only does the fool have no choice whether to live according to nature or not, but once in this condition he is dependent upon indifferents and by mistakenly placing value upon them imposes even more restrictions on his life. Chrysippus makes this point clearly in a discussion of weakness in the soul: 'One man draws back through fear, another grew faint and gave in when a reward or penalty was brought, another when faced with one of the many similar things. All these types of situation overcome and enslave us (*douloutai hêmas*), so that by surrendering to them, we betray friends and cities and give ourselves up to many shameful acts after our earlier impetus has subsided.'[3] The wise man would have his life restricted by none of these, only by nature, which is the right way to live.

This is briefly the Stoic view of freedom and slavery in the first sense and for simplicity they will be referred to as moral freedom and moral slavery. Thus it should be viewed in the context of their whole ethical theory, but it should also be linked to their views on the last two types of slavery. In later writers, influenced by the Stoa, such as Seneca, Dio Chrysostom and Philo in the Roman imperial period, much emphasis is placed on this moral slavery to the complete neglect of the other two types. They hold that, since the freedom of the wise is the only type that has any moral significance, it is the only one that matters, so there is little point in examining other types. In their accounts there is a total disinterest in any political or social problems.[4] They were essentially sermons, encouraging men to be satisfied with their position in society. Nevertheless one should be wary of letting the large amount of material available on the later Stoa make us minimise the extent to which the early Stoics did analyse contemporary society. The emphasis need not have been the same nor should we necessarily attribute to them ideas identical to those in the later Stoa.

3. Chattel slavery

The third type is slavery in the orthodox sense, chattel slavery, described as consisting of both subordination and possession (*hupotaxis* and *ktêsis*). Prior to the Stoa there had been two opposing views on this, one put forward by Aristotle that some people were natural slaves and that slavery was in their interests (Arist. *Pol.* 1255a1ff), the other that slavery was contrary to nature, an artificial distinction between men based on force (Arist. *Pol.* 1253b20ff). The Stoics followed the second line, making no significant change, but they did put it in the context of their own theoretical framework. We have no statement that slavery is contrary to nature which is definitely attributable to the early Stoics, but various pieces of evidence make it clear that this was their view. Certainly their psychology would have prohibited them from offering an argument in favour of the natural slave in the manner of Aristotle. It has been argued convincingly that Philo SVF 3.352 is derived from Chrysippus:[5] 'For no man is a slave by nature, *ek phuseôs doulos*.' Support for this can be gained from the inclusion of ownership in the definition of slavery, because property in Stoic thought is a matter of convention, as is apparent from its absence

---

[3] Chrysippus, quoted by Galen, *HP* 4.6.7-8, SVF 3.473 p. 123, lines 28-33, cf. Philo *Quod omnis probus liber est* 2.

[4] Milani 1972: 221. For instance Dio Chrys. *Or.* 14 and 15, Philo *Quod omnis probus*.

[5] Griffin 1976: 459.

in Zeno's *Politeia*. Indeed a later Stoic, Panaetius, who certainly had no objection to private property, was prepared to concede that it was contrary to nature (Cic. *De Off.* 1.21). If property is contrary to nature, then slavery which involves possession must also be contrary to nature.

Chrysippus' views on slavery lie behind a passage of Cicero's *De Finibus* (3.67); Chrysippus is reported as saying that man can use animals for his own purposes without injustice, but between the individual and the human race there is what could be described as a code of law. This suggests that for one man to use another for the benefit of the user would be unjust. According to the Stoics this is exactly what the *despotes*, the master, does:[6] 'The master shows his concern for the slave, but for his own benefit (*dia heauton*), as the Stoics say.' This conception of *despoteia* (mastership) as rule which is exercised for the benefit of the master is already apparent in Aristotle, but far from considering this unjust Aristotle approves of the institution of slavery; indeed he considers the natural slave to be virtually no different from an animal.[7] From the passage of Diogenes quoted above we learn that *despoteia* is bad; this is consistent with the argument that to use another man for one's own benefit is unjust. It is not clear whether *despoteia* in the context of this passage is meant to be the antithesis of chattel slavery alone or both the second and third types of slavery. Whichever it is, the consequences of a bad and unjust act can hardly be described as according to nature. As will be seen later, the Stoics' use of *despoteia* is not limited to this third category of slavery, chattel slavery. In the light of this condemnation of *despoteia* as unjust, it is interesting to note that Zeno is said to have possessed no slaves (Seneca *ad Helv.* 12.4, SVF 1.15).

Status in society is morally indifferent (cf. on high and low birth at D.L. 7.106) so as a result being a slave is morally indifferent, although, as it is contrary to nature, it is something to be rejected; at the same time its rejection should not be allowed to override what is morally good. But what is often not realised is that it is not possible to go from this to the conclusion that to treat someone as a slave is morally indifferent. To use a man in this way is unjust, perhaps because one is deliberately bringing about a situation which is contrary to nature. Moreover what is unjust is bad (D.L. 7.93). One could draw an analogy with pain; for pain is morally indifferent (Stob. *Ecl.* 2.58.2-4, SVF 3.70), but to inflict pain on another for one's own pleasure would be

[6] Damascius (ed. Westerink 1977), pp. 42-3, part of a commentary on Plato *Phaedo* 62c-3c where the gods are described as *despotai*. Westerink emends the punctuation which appears in SVF 2.1118. A similar conception of *despotês* appears also in Dio Chrys. 1.22.

[7] Benefit of another: Arist. *Pol.* 1333a3-6, *Protrep.* (Düring) B25. Approval: Arist. *Pol.* 1253b23-55a2, 1277a33-b7; similarity between natural slave and animal: *Pol.* 1254b23-6.

unjust and morally bad. In this one can see part of the difference between the early and the later Stoa in their attitude to slavery. For the later Stoa were concerned not with the justice of keeping slaves, but with treating them well (e.g. Seneca *Ep.* 47).[8] Indeed when the notion of justice is introduced, slavery is generally seen not as the injustice of men but of fortune (e.g. Seneca *Cons. Marc.* 20.1) which would obviously be out of men's control. Yet for the early Stoa, regardless of how well slaves were treated, it would still be unjust to use them as slaves.

A further distinction between the early and the later Stoa would be as follows. The latter could assent to both these propositions: first, that you can still be virtuous even if you are a slave and secondly, that it is not important whether you are a slave or free so long as you are virtuous. Although the early Stoa would assent to the first, it is not clear whether they would do so to the second; if 'important' meant 'morally important' they would agree, but if it just meant 'important at all' they could not, because as a human being it is preferable not to be a slave; this is never the natural human condition. The wise man, if given a choice between virtue and virtue plus preferred indifferents, would have to choose the latter.[9]

4. A Stoic theory of slavery

The Stoics produced a classification of different types of slavery according to certain basic features: lack of independence, subordination and ownership. This systematic approach suggests that they were proposing some form of theory of slavery, although slavery in the orthodox sense would only be an element of such a theory. This is supported by the notion of slavery as *hupotaxis* which is an unusual conception of individual slavery, not found in this form in earlier writing. So its introduction is relevant because it implies not just reiteration of other people's ideas but fresh thought and adds to the importance of the passage as a whole.

In order to investigate slavery as subordination it is useful to begin with this word, *hupotaxis*. The noun is rare,[10] but the verbal form *hupotattô* is more common. It is a term which can cover numerous relationships. When referring to living entities, it involves inferiority in status, for example, to a general, to a state such as Rome or to God.[11]

---

[8] A point which can also be seen in the Stoic justification of empire discussed in Chapter 8 below.

[9] Alex. Aphrod. SVF 3.192, Cic. *De Fin.* 4.30, SVF 3.61, Kidd 1971: 159-60.

[10] Liddell and Scott give D.H. *AR* 1.5, Philodemus *Vol. Rhet.* (Sudhaus) 2.207. In a different sense Apollonius Dyscolus, the second-century AD Alexandrian grammarian, uses *hupotaxis* as a grammatical term, e.g. *Pron.* 116.5, *Adv.* 125.6, 180.8, *Coni.* 213.6, ref. to pages of *Grammatici Graeci* II.i, ed. Uhlig and Schneider.

[11] Rome: D.H. *AR* 1.5; General: Polyb. 3.138, Onosander 1.17; God: Epict. 1.12.7, Arius

It does not imply merely inferiority in status; it can also be a relationship which entails being subject to instruction from the superior.[12] This situation can either be imposed or voluntary.[13] The word implies hierarchy as, for instance, in its use in the Stoic classification of virtues into primary ones (*prôtai aretai*) and subordinate ones (*hupotetagmenai aretai*).[14] One would suggest that it should be subordination to something of a similar basic type; thus one virtue can be subject to another, one living entity to another (which includes God). The term is purely descriptive; unlike *douleia* it lacks a pejorative sense, hence its suitability for classification. *Hupotattô* and its cognates are rare in the Classical period, at least in literary Greek. They are not to be found in Herodotus, Thucydides, Xenophon or Plato, but they do occur very occasionally in New Comedy.[15] It is only in the Hellenistic period that their use becomes more frequent.[16]

That the Stoa should choose to use a term that was previously uncommon, particularly in philosophical language, indicates that they were trying to give serious consideration to slavery. They may have been deliberately using a word that was free from connotations and thus one which would be better suited for analysis. Its early Stoic associations are still visible in Epictetus who often uses the term and here again it lacks evaluative content.[17] This creation of a new vocabulary for the purpose of discussing slavery is also apparent in the choice of the term to describe independent action, *autopragia*. It is a word rarely, if ever, used before the Stoics.[18]

Is there a relationship between the three types of slavery? There is one obvious difference between the first and the others. Moral slavery can exist in isolation, but slavery in the second and third sense must necessarily involve relationships between people. Nevertheless, the basic definition of slavery which is giv⌐n, the absence of independent action, is relevant to all three types. That chattel slavery does entail this should require no discussion. The importance of moral slavery for

---

Didymus SVF 2.528, *Ep. Jac.* 4.7.

[12] Philodemus *Vol. Rhet.* (Sudhaus) 2.207.

[13] D.H. *AR* 1.5, Posidonius EK Frag. 60.

[14] Stob. *Ecl.* 2.60.9-18, 63.25, SVF 3.264, 280, D.L. 7.92, SVF 3.265, cf. also its use for classification by Polybius 3.36.7, 18.15.4.

[15] '*hupotetagmenos*' occurs in Arist. F.392 from Harpocration, but it is unlikely that it appeared in the original text; Poll. who is also quoted under the fragment did not use it. Comedy: Antiphanes F.268.2 (Kock vol. 2, p. 123), Phrynichus F.59.2 (Kock vol. 1, p. 385), but Kock would emend the latter to eliminate it.

[16] Welles 1934: 372-3 and Letter 53, E.4, Polybius 3.13.8, 36.7, 18.15.4. On Polybius 10.36.4, 36.7, 24.13.2, see Chapter 8. It occurs over fifty times in Diodorus. The phrase, *hoi hup'autous tassomenoi* and variations is found in an inscription of the 160s BC, Triantofyllos, *Arch. Delt.* 28 (1973 (1978)), Chron., Plate. 418, lines 17, 25-6, 31, 34-5. On its date, Derow 1984: 234.

[17] Epict. 1.4.18-19, 3.24.65, 3.24.71, 4.4.1. Epictetus does use it of subordination of one thing to something of a different type, e.g. man to law, 4.3.12.

[18] The only earlier occurrence I can find is the spurious Plato *Def.* 411e.

an understanding of the other two types will be examined later in this chapter.

There is clearly a relationship between the second and third types. For the third is a subset of the second; both involve subordination, but chattel slavery also involves possession of the subordinate person. That these two are meant to be related is further supported by a fragment of Chrysippus (Athen. 6.267b, SVF 3.353). *Doulos* and *oiketês* are both terms that can be used to describe chattel slaves, but in his *On Homonoia* Chrysippus pointed out that there is a difference between them: a freedman is still a *doulos* (even though he has been freed), but a man who is someone's property is both a *doulos* and an *oiketês*. This would appear to correspond to the distinction between *doulos* as a subordinate and *doulos* as both subordinate and property. For the distinguishing element of property is introduced and emphasised, while subordination which would be common to both is not. This also indicates that the classification of types of *douleia* was not merely written down and ignored, but that it was seriously considered and used when discussing slavery. Similarly another passage derived from Chrysippus conforms to this framework. For Seneca noted that Chrysippus described a chattel slave as *perpetuus mercenarius*, permanent hired labourer (Seneca *De Ben.* 3.22, SVF 3.351).[19] Although this is in Latin, it does contain the essential features of the description of chattel slavery found in D.L. 7.122, quoted above. *Mercenarius* clearly corresponds to the notion of subordination, although it is more limited than *hupotaxis*. It is qualified by *perpetuus*, which transforms the *mercenarius* into a slave. *Perpetuus*, by bestowing permanence in status on the *mercenarius*, supplies the other feature of the description of the chattel slave, that of being property. The neatness with which these two passages fit with D.L. 7.121-2 gives reason to believe that this classification is the remains of a theory of slavery. Since these two are from Chrysippus, it must have been formulated by him or one of his predecessors. The classification itself may be due to Chrysippus; for he had a reputation for clarifying and systemising Stoic thought.[20]

So what did the Stoics have in mind when they spoke of slavery in the second sense, slavery as *hupotaxis*? One might suggest on the basis of the *perpetuus mercenarius* example that the subordination, if it does

[19] I am grateful to Julia Annas for drawing my attention to the similarity between this passage of Seneca and Cic. *De Off*. 1.41 where it is advised that slaves be treated like *mercenarii*; she has suggested that Chrysippus had argued that slaves should be treated as if they were parties to a contract. But the stress on contractual/legal obligations in Cic. *De Off*. 1.21-41 seems alien to the early Stoa and more appropriate to Rome. It will be argued in Chapter 7.3 that such obligations only became the subject of debate in the second-century Stoa. It may have been that Chrysippus' original argument was reinterpreted, so that analysis was replaced with prescription.

[20] D.L. 7.179; Sandbach 1975: 15, 19 and Long 1974: 113.

correspond to *mercenarius*, entails being subordinate in the sense of being a hired labourer. But this need not be the only type of subordination that Chrysippus has in mind; to derive its content from the definition of the chattel slave alone would inevitably impose unnecessary limits. The other example, the reference to Chrysippus' *On Homonoia*, does not indicate clearly what kind of subordination might be involved. The freedman would not necessarily be a hired labourer, so one could be justified in seeing the subordination as embracing more than merely working for another. Since the example of the freedman in particular is used, it may be saying something about his position in society, a subordination that results either from being at one of the lowest levels or from the restrictions that accompany exclusion from the citizen body. Metics would be in a similar position and it is interesting that Heracleides Criticus in about the third century BC describes the condition of foreigners in Athens as *douleia*.[21]

The early Stoics did think that non-citizens should be taken into account and not simply ignored. They conceived a city as being the sum of all its inhabitants and not merely its citizens. Whereas for Aristotle the city is 'a mass of citizens', for the Stoa it is 'a mass of people living in the same place and governed by law'.[22] When Zeno says that a city should be distinguished by the virtues of its inhabitants (Stobaeus SVF 1.266), it is significant that he does not refer simply to the virtues of citizens alone. Stoic interest in the non-citizen may be due, in part, to the fact that none of the first three heads of the Stoa were Athenian citizens (although Chrysippus eventually became one). This interest is apparent also in a passage by Arius Didymus quoted by Eusebius (SVF 2.528). Here the Stoics are said to have compared the world (*kosmos*) to a city; the former consisted of gods and men, the latter of citizens and inhabitants (i.e non-citizens). In the world the gods have leadership (*hêgemonia*) and men are subordinate (*hupotetagmenoi*). The nature of the relationship between citizens and non-citizens is not explained, but it is clear from the analogy that non-citizens are subordinate to citizens. Although *hupotaxis* is a neutral term and so does not necessarily entail *douleia*, such a characterisation of the citizen/non-citizen relationship is obviously possible.

It can now be seen that the early Stoics, in particular Chrysippus, argued that certain forms of *hupotaxis* were slavery. These included, but were not limited to, chattel slavery; other relationships within society also came into this category. Ownership provides a criterion for

---

[21] Heracleides Criticus (ed. Pfister 1951), F.1.2, Pfister emends *douleias* to *boulimias*, discussed Pfister 1951: 113-15. But *douleias* seems to make adequate sense without emendation, Ferguson 1911: 465.

[22] Arist. *Pol.* 1274b41, Dio Chrys. SVF 3.329, cf. also Clement, Stob. *Ecl.* 2.103.17-23, SVF 3.327-8.

making the distinction between the second and third types of slavery, but the relationships are essentially the same. In both cases a subordinate person is used for the benefit of the *despotês*. Another feature of slavery was seen to be restrictions on independent action – such a restriction can be seen clearly in the case of the non-citizen, whose power of action is limited by laws over which he has no control and who may need a *prostatês* to represent him.

Just as *douleia* is not limited to chattel slavery, so *despoteia*, mastership, is not limited to slave-ownership. Rather it is a characteristic of the bad man, who is such that he does despotic things, *despotika* (Stob. *Ecl.* 2.104.3-6, SVF 3.677); in other words he would use another person to serve his own interests. An indication of what the bad man does is found in the following description óf the good man (Stob. *Ecl.* 2.99 SVF 3.567): 'The good man is neither compelled by anyone nor does he compel anyone (*anankazein*), he neither obstructs nor does he obstruct (*kôluein*), he is neither forced by anyone nor does he force anyone (*biazein*), he neither masters nor is he mastered (*despozein*) ... The opposite is true of the bad man.' All the verbs used here could describe *douleia* and *despoteia*; as the passage says, none of them could describe the good man. *Douleia* and *despoteia* are clearly the products of bad men.

Up to now this discussion of slavery as *hupotaxis* has concentrated on Chrysippus, but it is probable that Zeno in his *Politeia* had also used the notion of slavery as subordination and that Chrysippus was attempting to clarify it. So it would be useful to look again at the *Politeia* to understand further the concept of *douleia* and the use to which it was put. Zeno's role in its origin may have been discussed by Chrysippus in his book, *On Zeno's Proper Use of Terminology*, which is mentioned by Diogenes just after the three types of slavery (D.L. 7.122). On the other hand, the juxtaposition of the two passages in Diogenes may mean nothing, given Diogenes' rather haphazard method of working, although both do concern *eleutheria*. Yet that may be the reason why he placed them together.

Zeno began his *Politeia* with a condemnation of contemporary society.[23] Indeed much of the *Politeia*, in so far as it can be reconstructed, has its starting points in the deficiencies of the present. We are told that at the beginning he said that what he wrote was relevant to his own time and place (Philod. 12.1-12). Although to a certain extent his proposals for an ideal society would reflect his attitude to the present, one can assume at least a brief treatment of contemporary society at the beginning. What this condemnation consisted of is far from certain; the remains are very limited and the only fragment that can definitely be ascribed to such a prologue is the

[23] Baldry 1959: 11, Chroust 1965: 182.

remark that he condemned the standard educational curriculum, *enkuklios paideia*, as useless (D.L. 7.32). Diogenes proceeds to say that for Zeno the bad were all foes, enemies, slaves and aliens to each other, *echthroi, polemioi, douloi, allotrioi allêlôn*. This theme would also have come in this early section on contemporary society, partly because of the passage's close proximity to the remark on education and partly because the fools were an issue of the contemporary world, indeed the students of such an education. Thus for reasons of both context and content it is highly likely that Zeno discussed the fool as enemy and slave in his brief critique of contemporary society.

This society is full of fools in contrast to the wise men of the ideal society, but central to the problem of determining Zeno's views on the present society is the way the foolish or bad are described. It is the description of all the fools as *douloi* that is particularly interesting here. While it is true that they would have been in a state of moral slavery, it is not obvious that this is the meaning of the passage. If it is, it stands oddly in the context; for the rest of the statement is about relationships between fools, that they are hostile to each other, even children to parents, brothers to brothers, relatives to relatives. This is a very strong emphasis on relationships, so to place *douloi* in the middle as meaning 'moral slaves' would be very peculiar, totally out of keeping with the context. It might be argued that Cassius the Sceptic, Diogenes' source, had culled the various epithets from several chapters of Zeno's *Politeia* and joined them together. Even so it is curious, especially as *douloi* is placed in the middle of *echthroi, polemioi* and *allotrioi* as if it is natural that these four should be related. A more suitable explanation would be that '*douloi*' here does not refer to moral slavery at all, but rather slavery as subordination, which makes far more sense in the context. Thus fools are enemies to one another and slaves also of one another, although one would suggest that this slavery or subordination is not a reciprocal relationship, as hatred would be, but that a man would be a slave of another who might in turn be a slave of someone else. This would, therefore, be a view of the structure of society as a hierarchy of slavery.

Diogenes Laertius also tells us that the wise by contrast are friends, kindred and *eleutheroi* (D.L. 7.33), which suggests that *eleutheria* too should be seen in terms of relationships (D.L. 7.33, cf. Athen. 13.561c SVF 1.263; Chapter 1.5 above). If *eleutheria* here referred to moral freedom alone, it would have nothing directly to do with relationships between men, deriving as it does from the wise man's virtue which can exist independently of anyone else. This leads to the conclusion that among the wise in the ideal society of the *Politeia* there is no slavery in any of these three senses. Contemporary society, on the other hand, is made up of unequal relationships in which men use those subordinate to them to serve their own interests. This is the normal condition among the bad, but it has no natural foundation. The surviving evidence does not tell us explicitly how this hierarchy of slavery comes about; certainly it is because men are bad, but this does not have much explanatory force. It is possible to make a rough sketch of its origins which is compatible with the evidence.

All bad men are moral slaves, as has been said, and this entails a mistaken sense of values; for they do not know what is good. As a result morality will have no special significance in the agent's list of priorities. He will seek merely to obtain those ends which he incorrectly values most highly, regardless of the injustice that their attainment might entail. If he is to place indifferents above virtue, although they are in fact incommensurate with each other, then he will ignore any obligation he might have to treat other people justly. Thus he will force others into subordination to serve his own particular aims and those in subordination would do likewise if they had the opportunity or capability. Moreover, those who are subordinate may well be prepared, although not necessarily happily, to put themselves in this position in order to satisfy their own desires. Several centuries later the Stoic, Epictetus, puts forward a similar thesis: every bad man is a slave to someone and this is due to his ignorance of what is good. But Epictetus concentrates on the slave who values the wrong things and therefore subordinates himself to another.[24] The early Stoa was concerned with both the slave and the master and emphasised the despotic nature of the bad man.

This sketch receives support from a passage in Stobaeus (*Ecl.* 2.108.20-3, SVF 3.630): 'Among the bad, who are untrustworthy and fickle and have hostile views, there is no friendship (*philia*), but there are certain other unions and bonds which are brought about by external compulsion (*anankai*) and opinions (*doxai*).' Slavery as subordination is one of the key relationships in contemporary society, so one would expect it to be included in the 'other unions and bonds', the relationships that exist among bad men. These relationships are held together by *anankai* and *doxai*. The use of *anankai* carries implications of slavery, but the word may also be referring to the needs of a bad man which force him into a certain sort of relationship.[25] What is particularly important is the role of *doxai* in these relationships. Whereas only the good man possesses *epistêmê*, knowledge, only the bad man possesses *doxa*, opinion or belief (Sext. Emp. SVF 2.90). The good man's knowledge will include knowledge of the good, which the bad man lacks. The person who has only *doxa* will be 'out of touch with reality' and so in error.[26] In the passage from Stobaeus *doxa* refers to

[24] Epict. 4.1, 3.24.71, 1.4.18-19, 4.4.1.
[25] *Anankê* is closely connected to *douleia*; it can be used both to describe the state of slavery and the torture of slaves, Thomson 1938: 2.345.
[26] Watson 1966: 53.

the bad man's mistaken sense of values, his failure to know what is good. It is *doxai* along with *anankai* which are important determinants of the nature of these relationships. This would be consistent with the sketch of the origins of *douleia* as subordination put forward above.

So the surviving evidence for Zeno and Chrysippus produces the following picture. In the ideal society all the wise are free in all three senses; in contemporary society all the bad will by definition be moral slaves, but this slavery will not be confined to the realm of morals. For as a result of a mistaken sense of values, their moral slavery will infect the political sphere, producing this hierarchy of subordination which will embrace the whole society. This slavery is a result of the moral badness of men, but one could also argue that the continuing badness of men is to a certain extent the result of their social structure. The Stoics held that the environment is important in the moral development of the individual.[27] Thus a child brought up in such an environment is likely to absorb its values and emulate the behaviour of the people there. The badness of men and the problems such as slavery that co-exist with it are therefore self-perpetuating.

This hierarchy of slavery was considered to be one of the most striking features of contemporary society. At the very lowest level there could be the chattel slaves, followed by the freedmen and hired labourers; the gaps in our evidence leave the details of the rest open to conjecture. Athenian society does furnish various social divisions itself, such as *thetes, zeugitae* and *pentacosiomedimnoi*, which show that the classification of social groups was not alien to it. Perhaps it was simply the subordination of the poor by the rich who in turn were subordinate to men external to the city, such as in Macedon. It could have been made more complex by the introduction of a distinction between those within the citizen body and those without, as the example of the freedman might indicate. The position of the men at the top is unclear. It is possible that Zeno had not made the distinction between moral slavery and subordination as clear as Chrysippus did. If so, the problem of the men at the top, who would be few and may be as far away as Macedon, may never have been dealt with in depth. For if they were not slaves as subordinate, they would always be slaves in the moral sense. Any such vagueness is all the more problematic for us when compounded with the state of the evidence.

Although the theory may be clear-cut in some ways, a problem presents itself. For the wise are not only inhabitants of the ideal, they also occur in society as it is, albeit as rarely as the phoenix (Alex. Aphrod. SVF 3.658). What was their status in this society? Clearly they would be morally free; the evidence also suggests that they would be free in the other two senses. For it has already been said that the

[27] See Chapter 1, n. 40.

wise man cannot be compelled to do anything he does not want to do (cf. Stob. *Ecl*. 2.99 SVF 1.216, Philo SVF 1.218). Yet *hupotaxis* in the contemporary world would entail being subordinate to a bad man and so subject to his instructions; but the wise man could not possibly do everything that was asked of him, only what he did not consider to be wrong. Thus he would not let the bad man's values usurp his own. Since the wise man could not and would not be obedient in every respect, it is hard to see him as subordinate. One might object that a fool could just as easily disobey; but it would always be possible to compel him to obey, because the fool does not see the moral good as being the only thing of any real worth. One could ensure that a subordinate did wrong by a financial inducement, for instance (cf. Galen SVF 3.473, see above, §3). The wise man would never be faced with such a dilemma. So one would not expect the good man to be a *doulos* in either of the other two senses, that is subordination and both subordination and possession together, because both involve *hupotaxis* to a bad man. So Zeno could claim that a man who goes to a tyrant will not become a *doulos* if he goes there as a free man (Plut. *Mor*. 33d, SVF 1.219). This would be the case that showed the wise man's freedom from slavery at its most explicit, because the tyrant is commonly the example of the very worst kind of man, who thus is most likely to give commands which the wise man could not carry out. Moreover, since the wise man will neither *despozein* nor *despozesthai* (Stob. SVF 1.216), he could not be a slave in the third sense recorded in D.L. 7.122. Plutarch can write that the wise man is uncaptured when sold into slavery by his enemies (Plut. *Mor*. 1057e). This might seem curious, but the Stoics were not denying that he could be chattel. For this third type of slavery had two elements, first that the slave should be the property of somebody, secondly that he should be subordinate to that person. The one is regardless of character since anyone can be property, while the latter is the operative part of the definition. For as a result of his virtue the wise man cannot be subordinate to a bad man and thus is rendered immune to slavery, although in a rather technical sense since he could still be the property of someone. In society as it is, then, the individual wise man's moral freedom prevents him from being a slave in the second and third senses (as in D.L. 7.122).

Nevertheless not all types of ruling were to be rejected. It is *douleia* and the relationships that existed between bad men to which Stoics objected. Although the wise man cannot be a *despotês*, there are forms of rule such as *archê* and *hêgemonia* which were approved by the Stoa and were appropriate to the wise man.[28] It is reasonable to believe that the wise man, when in a position to rule, would act in the interests of

[28] The wise man can be *basileus, archôn, stratêgos, hêgemôn*, SVF 3.615, 617-19; there is a best *archê, hêgemonia, politeia*, Origen SVF 3.368; the law is *archôn, hêgemonia, basileus, prostatês*, Marcianus SVF 3.314.

his subjects. Proclus in his commentary on Plato's *Timaeus* discusses why Plato describes the soul as *despotis* and *archousa*. It is because the *despotês* looks after its own interests, while the *archôn* looks after those of its subjects; the soul looks out for its own good but also for the needs of the body. This way of interpreting Plato has been held to represent a Stoic distinction.[29] Certainly it is compatible with what has been said. For the Stoics, however, the term *archein* is limited only to the wise. They alone will *archein* and *archesthai*, rule and be ruled, but neither is true of the bad; for the bad will disobey, whereas the wise will obey (Stob. *Ecl.* 2.102, SVF 3.615). So *archê* entails obedience; a wise man will appreciate that a wise *archôn* is issuing morally good commands, but these will be ignored by the bad man for whom virtuous action is of no importance. But for the wise ruler to force a bad man to obey would itself be morally wrong; for he cannot compel anyone. All the wise man can do is to recommend to the bad what is morally correct. In this he would be analogous to god and the law, neither of which can force men to do what is morally good. The wise man, the gods and the law are all described as *hêgemones*.[30] This rather vague term may have been used for the relationship between the wise and the fool, representing leadership without implying any compunction to obey. There is no indication that the Stoics believed that the wise should force their will on the rest; such behaviour was left to the bad (e.g. Stob. *Ecl.* 2.104.3-6, SVF 3.677). Such ideas are reflected by Zeno in the remark which he is alleged to have made to Crates, that a philosopher should be taken by persuasion, not by compulsion (D.L. 7.24, SVF 1.278). Chrysippus did allow that a good man could knowingly make false statements in order to promote a certain course of action, for instance a general encouraging his troops by claiming that reinforcements are coming.[31]

A similar outlook is apparent in another group of philosophers who were reacting against Plato at about this time, the Epicureans.[32] For them, too, the wise man is a *hêgemôn* and such *hêgemonia* involves the rejection of that element of compulsion which is apparent in Plato. Epicurus, who was held to be the *hêgemôn* and wise man, said that

[29] Proclus on *Timaeus* 34c, Diehl, 2.118,14-17, Westerink 1977: 42-3 on Damascius, cf. Dio Chrys. 2.70: Gods are *despotai* and *archontes*, most important for God is himself, then his subjects (*hoi hup'autôi tetagmenoi*); Dio Chrys. 36.32: God as *despotês* and *hêgemôn*. But God as *despotês* is not compatible with the early Stoa, given their hostility to *despoteia*. For God as *hêgemôn*, cf. Arius Didymus SVF 2.528. Nevertheless, it is clear that the wise man would not be a *despotês*. The distinction which appears in Proclus is hinted at in Arist. *Pol.* 1333a3-6.

[30] Wise men: Proclus SVF 3.618, cf. Philo SVF 3.620; gods: Arius Didymus SVF 2.528; law: Marcianus SVF 3.314.

[31] Plut. *St. Rep.* 1057a, SVF 3.177, Stob. *Ecl.* 2.111.10-17, SVF 3.554; Long 1971: 99-101.

[32] On the Epicurean reaction against Plato, Rist 1972: 1-2, Farrington 1967: 76, De Witt 1954: 10-11.

human nature should not be coerced but persuaded (*Vatican Sayings* 21, cf. Zeno in D.L. 7.24, SVF 1.278).[33]

It has been proposed above that this theory of slavery as subordination was developed by Zeno and hence prior to Chrysippus. This is further strengthened by a passage of Philemon, the comic poet, which presents the following picture of a hierarchy of slavery in the mouth of a slave:[34] 'One man has control over me, law has control over these and you and thousands of others, there is a tyrant over the rest and over tyrants fear. Some are the slaves (*douloi*) of kings, the king is a slave of the gods, the god a slave of necessity (*anankê*). If you think about it, everything is inferior to all those other things that are stronger. It is necessary that all these are slaves to them.' This reflects the currency of such ideas of slavery and subordination. Since Philemon died in the 260s, it sets them firmly in the period before Chrysippus became established. What is expressed in this verse, however, is not identical to Stoic thought as outlined above, although it is akin to it. The passage contains a mixture of different types of slavery as one might expect from a comic poet who would take a selection of ideas and mould them into one. Thus there is not a pure hierarchy of one type of slavery. The tyrant is slave to fear but this is not subordination, rather it is moral slavery; many are subject to the laws, something which is not relevant to the early Stoic account. Philemon does not use the word *doulos* at all points, but it is the presence of the ideas rather than the vocabulary that is of interest. His presentation of this hierarchy of slaves is far more one of acceptance than the Stoics' presentation. The latter viewed society as a hierarchy, but it could not be said that they thought this was how it should be; the present fell far short of their ideal, as Zeno attempted to show in his *Politeia*.

5. Slavery, freedom and *homonoia*

The Stoic analysis of contemporary society is not limited merely to characterising it as a hierarchy of slavery. It is necessary now to consider other features of this analysis which are concomitant with this idea of slavery. For slavery is linked to hostility and disharmony, while freedom is linked to friendship and harmony. This may seem unsurprising but in the previous century Plato and Aristotle had seen slavery as an integral part of a harmonious ideal. In the *Politeia, douleia* is found associated with *echthra* (hostility), while *eleutheria* is associated with *philia* (D.L. 7.32-3). *Eleutheria* is also found closely connected with both *philia* and *homonoia* (Athen. 13.561c, SVF 1.263).

[33] De Witt 1954: 93-5, cf. Rist 1972: 9-10, Farrington 1967: 125-6.
[34] Philemon Frag. 31, Kock vol. 2, p. 486.

Stob. *Ecl.* 2.108, SVF 3.630 also makes it evident that relationships between bad men, which would include slavery, are linked with hostility and lack of *homonoia*. Moreover, as we have seen, Chrysippus wrote a work, *On Homonoia*, in which he discussed types of slavery (Athen. 6.267b, SVF 3.353). Sometimes *homonoia* is virtually identified with *philia*, and *dichonoia* (disharmony) with *echthra*, but although the one cannot exist without the other, *homonoia* is logically prior to *philia* (Stob. *Ecl.* 2.105.12-15, SVF 3.661, cf. *Ecl.* 2.94.1-6, 108.15-25, SVF 3.625, 630). So an examination of the concepts, *philia* and *homonoia*, and their opposites, *echthra* and *dichonoia*, should help to illuminate further our account of *douleia* and *eleutheria*.

Homonoia was a feature of Zeno's ideal society. It was a relationship between individual wise men which represented a concord and stability which did not exist in the present world. The Stoics held *homonoia* to be a type of knowledge; it is defined as 'knowledge of common goods, *epistêmê koinôn agathôn*' (Stobaeus SVF 3.625, cf. Clement SVF 3.292, Stobaeus SVF 3.630). The wise man has this knowledge and will act in accordance with it. Any action he performs will benefit all wise men (Stobaeus SVF 3.625, 626, Plut. *Comm. Not.* 1068f, SVF 3.627). This was a claim that was mocked in antiquity, for instance by Plutarch, but in a typically extreme fashion it was emphasising a serious and important point: among the wise there could be no conflict of interests. For what is considered good by one wise man is considered good by all. In such a situation in which there is complete agreement about what is good, *philia* is possible. Indeed, whereas *homonoia* is the knowledge of common goods, *philia* is the practical application of this knowledge. Friendship is said to be a sharing of those things which relate to life; for we treat friends as we treat ourselves (D.L. 7.124, SVF 3.631, cf. Stob. *Ecl.* 2.74.3-5, SVF 3.112). Since friendship is based on the consensus about common goods which exists among all wise men, it is plausible to claim, as the Stoics did, that friendship exists even between men who had never met one another (Cic. *De Nat. Deo.* 1.121, SVF 3.635). It is clear, therefore, that among the wise all are treated as equal, a marked contrast to relationships among the bad for whom self-interest is paramount. It is hardly surprising that among the bad or foolish there is no such thing as friendship (Stobaeus SVF 3.625, 626, 630, D.L. 7.124, SVF 3.631).

Instead of *homonoia* it is *dichonoia* which is characteristic of the bad (Stob. *Ecl.* 2.106.12-20, SVF 3.661). This is another term that is unknown before the Stoics and was probably coined by them.[35] Whereas *homonoia* is the knowledge of common goods, *dichonoia* is its opposite; it is marked by the lack of such knowledge and the lack of

---

[35] For other occurrences in Stoic writing cf. Philodemus SVF 3. Diog. 83, 85, Epictetus 3.3.18. *Dichonoia* appears in the spurious Platonic dialogue, *Alc.* I, 126b-7d.

sharing. Rather than having knowledge the bad men will have only opinion about what things they imagine to be good, as has been said above. Epictetus, a much later Stoic, reflects the ideas of the early Stoa when he describes *dichonoia* as a judgment about things which although not objects of moral choice are believed to be good or bad.[36] Consequently the interests of bad men, or what they perceive to be their interests, will conflict. Thus *dichonoia* is related to *echthra* in the same way as *homonoia* is related to *philia* (Stobaeus SVF 3.661).

Dichonoia* and *echthra* are conceptually distinct, but in practice they are aspects of the same thing, the relationship between bad men in contemporary society. The most significant such relationship is *douleia* as subordination, and this embodies both *dichonoia* and *echthra*. *Douleia* is an instance of *dichonoia* in so far as it is derived from and sustained by bad men's mistaken sense of values, their opinion (*doxa*) about the good. Rather than implying a multitude of different opinions, *dichonoia* implies disagreement between only two parties, a sense which the word is especially likely to have had in the early stages of its use. This sense is particularly appropriate to the dualism of the slave/master relationship. *Douleia* is an instance of *echthra* in so far as it involves a conflict of interests, whereas the interests of friends are the same; a man treats his friends as he would himself. In a similar way *eleutheria* reflects both *homonoia* and *philia*. Moreover, these two groupings are mutually exclusive; the early Stoics would think it ridiculous to suggest, for instance, that *homonoia* and *douleia* were compatible.[37]

It is clear that contemporary society was viewed as a centre of mutual antagonism, an antagonism that was made all the more concrete by being embodied in and derived from a network of subordinating relationships. The ideal society, on the other hand, is characterised by *homonoia* and the absence of slavery in any form. The originality and political implications of these ideas can best be appreciated if they are considered in relation to earlier Greek thought. For the relationship between slavery and *homonoia* put forward by early Stoics is completely at odds with Plato and Aristotle. Plato held that the statesman, the king and the slave-owner performed analogous

---

[36] Epict. 3.3.18-19: *dogma peri tôn aproairetôn hôs ontôn agathôn kai kakôn*. The terminology is not that of the early Stoa but the idea is; for Epictetus' use of *proairesis*, see Inwood 1985: 240-2.

[37] Athen. 13.561c, SVF 1.263, might be expected to add something useful to this discussion of the relationship between *douleia, echthra, dichonoia* and their opposites, but the reading of the text is disputed. Schweighäuser prints: *ton Erôta theon philias kai eleutherias, eti de kai homonoias paraskeuastikon*. Kaibel's reading in which *eleutheria* and *homonoia* are transposed is the more attractive, especially given the affinity between *homonoia* and *philia*. It is consistent with the argument above that *philia* and *homonoia* are both aspects of *eleutheria*. But the only conclusion that can safely be drawn is that Zeno believed the three to be intimately related.

functions (Plato *Politicus* 258e-59d). He took the institution of slavery and used it as a metaphor for ruler/ruled relationships which he considered to be good. The ruling element in the soul, reason, is identified with the master and the desires with the slaves (e.g Plato *Laws* 5.726, *Rep.* 444b7), similarly in the case of the rule of the soul over the body (Plato *Phaedo* 79e-80a, *Tim.* 34c, 44d). In the just city of the *Republic* the lowest class submit as slaves to the ruling class of philosophers (Plato *Rep.* 9.590cd). Aristotle adopts a similar approach, but makes rather more distinctions. He rejects Plato's comparison between the king and the slave-owner (Arist. *Pol.* 1252a1-23). Thus he can argue that the rule of the rational part of the soul over the irrational is monarchic and constitutional while at the same time follow Plato in maintaining that the rule of the soul over the body is despotic. Moreover, some men are suited by nature to be slaves and so needed instruction from above (Arist. *Pol.* 1253b23-55b15).

So in Plato and to a certain extent Aristotle slavery is a feature of the ideal. It is slavery in the interests of the slave, but in order to promote the interests of the slave it may be necessary to resort to compulsion and force, something which the Stoic wise man would refrain from doing. In the just city the lower class is enslaved by having to obey the reason of their betters (Plato *Rep.* 9.590cd). This is not to suggest that either Plato or Aristotle approved of slavery in all its forms, but they did approve of the basic principle. When they object to slavery it is because the wrong element is master. The tyrant enslaves the best men in the state (Plato *Rep.* 9.577c-e); in the unjust soul the desires enslave reason (Plato *Rep.* 4.442ab). In the ideal soul or state the best element should enslave the worst.

Gregory Vlastos has argued that for these philosophers the slave/master relationship represented not something undesirable and disruptive but a fundamental principle of the universe by which order was maintained. Plato thought that in the fields of slavery, the state, man and the world there was a superior element which had *logos* and which should control and instruct the inferior; reason must impose order on irrational desire.[38] In his ideal city Plato considered that *homonoia* resulted when all these elements were kept in their proper place (Plato *Rep.* 4.432a). Whereas the Stoics were showing that slavery and *homonoia* were incompatible, Plato devoted himself to proving their compatibility. In the just city of Plato there is harmony, stability and slavery, both metaphorical and real.[39] But for the Stoics it was self-contradictory to suggest that *despoteia* could be good or just. The master acts in the interests of his subjects only in so far as it benefits himself and in the process deprives them of independence of

[38] Vlastos 1941.
[39] On real slavery, Vlastos 1968: 291-5.

action. So the Stoics are rejecting the validity of the slave metaphor as it appears in Plato and Aristotle. They instead contend that such a metaphor is only appropriate to the corrupt society of the present where bad men use each other for their own advantage. For slavery in any form is anathema to the ideal society. Its absence is consistent with their psychology and ideal of a classless society in the same way as its presence in Plato is consistent with his just soul and just city (on this, see Chapter 1.4).

The close association which Zeno draws between freedom and *homonoia* is not common and a rare case of it is found in speech of Lysias, dating from the early fourth century BC. Here the speaker is praising the Athenians of old and says that they established democracy because they believed that the freedom of all was the greatest *homonoia* (*Or.* 2.18). It is interesting to note that this point is made in connection with democracy; for Plato, according to Vlastos, was led to his position by attacking Ionian philosophers with their democratic sympathies.[40] Now Zeno in what is a refutation of Plato is putting forward a view which is akin to these democratic sentiments of Lysias, giving an indication of where his own political sympathies lay.

Freedom is found in association with *homonoia* elsewhere, but the nature of the relationship is generally not the same. William C. West has argued that initially domestic *homonoia* was thought to be desirable because it gave the city strength to fight for freedom against an external threat (cf. Ps. Dem. 26.11); later this idea was extended to the international arena, where *homonoia* between the Hellenes was a necessary prelude to fending off threats from either Macedon or Persia.[41] Nevertheless, the relationship that Zeno posits between these two concepts is of a different nature, because for him *homonoia* is not a method of preserving threatened freedom but rather freedom and *homonoia* naturally co-exist. In the one case it is the freedom of the whole city, in the other it is of the individual within that city or society.

As will be seen in Chapter 8, Stoics in the second and first centuries BC rejected this conception of slavery and reverted to a more Aristotelian view. No longer was slavery incompatible with *homonoia*; instead it was by means of slavery that *homonoia* was imposed on subordinates. Part of the reason for this rejection may have been uneasiness with its democratic connotations, particularly when removed from democratic Athens to the far less liberal and more hierarchical Rome. Not only was Roman society very hierarchical, but Rome itself was an imperial power, ruling over numerous subordinate peoples. The later Stoic view of slavery was to play its part in justifying this rule. But the early Stoic conception did not disappear entirely.

---

[40] Vlastos 1941: 303-4.
[41] West 1977. For reservations about this argument, see Chapter 4.4.

Epictetus in the late first/early second century AD provides a vivid description of society as a hierarchy of slaves (Epict. 4.1, esp. 33-40). His emphasis, however, is on the slave to the neglect of the master. No doubt the upper-class audiences to whom this was addressed were pleased to learn that their position at the top of the hierarchy was due to the moral weakness of their subordinates, even if it was uncomfortable to be told that they were the slaves of the emperor (Epict. 4.1.41-50).

By saying that everyone was really a slave in some way the early Stoics were no doubt intending to shock. Yet by applying it to relationships more generally than before they weakened the distinction between the slave and the non-slave. Consequently later writers, such as Seneca and Epictetus, could say that it did not matter whether one was a slave or not because in fact everyone was a slave. This is unlikely to have been their intention of the early Stoics. For they did make an effort to distinguish different types of slavery. Moreover, initially there would have been no point applying the term to other relationships unless it had already been demonstrated that chattel slavery was bad and unjust and in what way this was so. Nevertheless, it does indicate that their interest in chattel slavery itself was limited.

In conclusion we should be wary of accepting the claims of those who say that the early Stoics paid no attention to contemporary society or its conditions. It is true that they may have examined it on a very theoretical level, but our evidence suggests that they developed a very critical analysis of their society.[42] Furthermore, the next chapter will show that as well as analysing contemporary society the Stoics also considered the question of active participation in it. Their successors gradually warped and discarded their analysis, but initially the Stoics subjected various types of slavery and freedom to careful examination in both a moral and a political context and justified Zenodotus' description (D.L. 7.30) of the school as the mother of unfearing freedom.

---

[42] Their theory of slavery may lie behind the *Suda*'s third definition of *douleia* as one that results from a *politeia*.

3

Political Participation

1. Political life

Plato's good man would abstain from political involvement in the corrupt society of the world as it is, but the Stoics were more flexible on this point. They held that the wise man would engage in political life not only in the ideal but also in contemporary society.[1] This chapter will seek to examine the nature of this involvement and its limits. In the early Hellenistic period the subject of political activity attracted much attention. Discussion of it was not limited to the Stoics. More controversial was Epicurus' advice, 'Live unknown'; he argued that most people should abstain from political life, because the competitiveness of such a life could jeopardise their happiness.[2]

Much of our knowledge of Stoic thought on this subject derives from what Chrysippus is reported to have said. For he examined the question of the wise man's political participation in some depth and considered the object of it to be the restraint of *kakia* (vice, badness) and the promotion of *aretê* (virtue, excellence) (D.L. 7.121, SVF 3.697). In addition to his writings on government which would have considered this subject, he also wrote four books *On Lives*, which discussed various ways of life open to the wise man.[3] The passages that give evidence for these books tend to concentrate not so much on ways of living, as ways of earning a living. According to Diogenes Laertius, who in this passage is clearly using authorities that were critical of Chrysippus, in the second book of *On Lives* he wrote that the wise man would get money from kings, friends and wisdom (*sophia*) (D.L. 7.188, SVF 3.685). Plutarch says that Chrysippus advocated three sources of income for the wise man, from kings, friends and lecturing (*sophisteia*) (Plut. *St. Rep.* 1043e, SVF 3.693); elsewhere Plutarch notes that the wise man will live with kings for profit and give lectures for money

---

[1] Plato *Rep.* 9.592ab, D.L. 7.121, Stob. *Ecl.* 2.94.7-20, SVF 3.611.

[2] His advice, *lathe biôsas*, is found in Plut. *Mor.* 1128a-30e, which is devoted to attacking it. Also note D.L. 10.119, Epicurus *Vatican Sayings* 58. On Epicurus and political participation, Aalders 1975: 39-42, Rist 1972: 128-9, De Witt 1954: 185-7.

[3] Writings on government: e.g. Plut. *St. Rep.* 1033b, SVF 1.27, 1044b, SVF 3.706. *On Lives (Peri Biôn)*: Plut. *St. Rep.* 1043a, SVF 3.703.

(Plut. *St. Rep.* 1047f, SVF 3.693). None of these passages provides strong grounds for believing that this work dealt with the wise man in political life, although there is an emphasis on the wise man's association with kings. But in the first book, presumably introductory, Chrysippus evidently argued that the wise man would participate in politics if nothing prevented him (D.L. 7.121, SVF 3.697), which would suggest that this was an issue relevant to *On Lives*. This is confirmed by a passage in Stobaeus, which, although not directly attributed to Chrysippus, parallels the passages from Diogenes and Plutarch mentioned above, but without having the polemical slant (Stob. *Ecl.* 2.109.10-110.8, SVF 3.686). As a result, it is more informative and sets them in a context.

According to the passage in Stobaeus the Stoics held that there were three preferred ways of life (*bioi*), 'the kingly, the political and thirdly the scholarly'; corresponding to these there were three preferred ways of making a living (*chrêmatismoi*), from kingship, from a *politeia* (government by citizens) and from lecturing. This is very similar to the categories noticed in Diogenes and Plutarch, but Stobaeus has as his second category income from a *politeia* instead of friends. Initially this appears to have little connection with the claim that the wise man would obtain money from friends. The passage in Stobaeus expands on this second category by saying that the wise man would 'make a living from the *politeia* and from those friends who were in prominent positions'. This would suggest that in the interests of polemic the context was abandoned in the accounts of Diogenes and Plutarch and the impression was left that the wise man would be a parasite on his friends. The first two ways of life clearly relate to public activity, while the last, education, if not an overtly public action, can at least be seen in terms of the restraint of *kakia* and promotion of *aretê*, perhaps sometimes being subsumed under the other two (cf. Stob. *Ecl.* 2.94, SVF 3.611).

If the wise man was to take part in political activity he could do so in an official capacity or by exerting his influence. In the case of kingship he would either be the king, which was improbable, or he would advise a king (Stob. *Ecl.* 2.111.3-9, SVF 3.690). Unfortunately most of the evidence for what the Stoics and Chrysippus in particular said about the wise man's relations with kings comes from Plutarch who is preoccupied with the wise man and his income. He gives little information on how he will assist the king. Nevertheless certain conclusions about his involvement with monarchy can be reached. The wise man would live with the king and be constantly in his company; for he would even go on campaign with him (Plut. *St. Rep.* 1043bc, SVF 3.691). So the advice that he gave would be of a type that could be required at any time. Two examples are given of kings who may be assisted, Idanthyrsos the

Scythian and Leucon of Pontus.[4] So Chrysippus did not limit his support of such activity to an area close to Athens, but perhaps suggested that there was no limit. None of this can be understood as advocacy of kingship; both the kings cited are from people traditionally ruled by kings. While the wise man would presumably seek to ensure that the king's actions were morally right and that he ruled justly, there is no direct evidence for what this would be. We can perhaps learn indirectly from what is said about the wise man's actions in a *politeia*. Stobaeus provides a slightly more detailed treatment of this, which may be a sign that Chrysippus gave more attention to this than to kingship and to think otherwise is to be misled by Plutarch's selectiveness and preoccupations.

In a constitutional government (*politeia*) the wise man, as in a monarchy, may hold office or he may only seek to influence, in this case, friends who are prominent in the state (Stob. *Ecl.* 2.109.14-20, SVF 3.686). Zeno's and Cleanthes' friendship with Chremonides could be construed as being of this nature (D.L. 7.17). The wise man in a *politeia* would make laws, educate men and would even suffer and die for it (Stob. *Ecl.* 2.94.11-17, SVF 3.611, for death cf. also D.L. 7.130). He would see it as his duty to marry and have children (Stob. SVF 3.611, 686). He would not, however, do those things which were bad, which are listed in Stobaeus as demagogy, sophistry and producing harmful literature. Thus the wise man is clearly expected to be actively involved in the life of the city and at a more practical level than simply being some sort of moral arbiter. He will seek to have an influence beyond what might normally be defined as moral. Indeed Chrysippus wrote that the wise man would speak in public and participate in government as if he considered wealth, reputation and health to be goods (Plut. *St. Rep.* 1034b, SVF 3.698). Such a statement is not a denial of Stoic values or an acknowledgment of the failure of Stoic thought in practical matters; it is consistent with Stoic theory which holds that certain things such as those mentioned are preferred (D.L. 7.106-7) and, if one was speaking loosely, might be described as 'goods' (Plut. *St. Rep.* 1048a, SVF 3.137). The corollary of this would be that these things which were to be rejected such as poverty (D.L. 7.106) would be treated as 'bad'. To be 'good' or 'bad' in this sense would be to be *kata phusin* or *para phusin* respectively. Thus one would expect the wise man in politics to take account of this and, since poverty is to be treated as something to be rejected and contrary to nature,[5] he would seek at least to alleviate it. Otherwise he would be failing in his task. The activities of Sphaerus and Blossius, which will be examined in Chapters 6 and 7, might be seen as examples of this.

---

[4] Plut. *St. Rep.* 1043bc, 1043e, *Comm. Not.* 1061d, Strabo SVF 3.691-2.
[5] D.L. 7.106, SVF 3.127, Cic. *De Fin.* 3.51, SVF 3.129, Sextus SVF 3.122.

Throughout the evidence for Stoic thought on political participation there is a proviso: the wise man will only take part if there is no obstacle,[6] a statement ascribed to both Zeno and Chrysippus. We are given little assistance as to what would constitute an obstacle. From Stobaeus we can gather that although the wise man would be prepared to risk danger on behalf of his country, he would not do so if he was not likely to benefit it (Stob. SVF 3.611, 690). This is consistent with the Stoic view that failure should be accepted and if one knew in advance that one would fail in some action one would not do it.[7] Yet political participation is not a single action, which may be likely to fail owing to a particular set of circumstances, existing at that moment, rather it is a series of actions that would be performed over a period of time. This abstention would have to be due to some long-term reason, a general condition of the state. This leads one to ask what condition this might be.

A couple of passages indicate that the morality of the state had a bearing on the wise man's decision to participate or not. For he would prefer to be active in a state that was 'making progress (*prokopê*) towards the ideal society' (Stob. *Ecl*. 2.94.8-11, SVF 3.611).[8] In the case of monarchy it is the nature of the king that is relevant; the wise man would 'live with a king who demonstrated a good disposition and a readiness to learn' (Stob. *Ecl*. 2.111.3-5, SVF 3.690). The phrase 'making progress' is a Stoic technical term used to describe those men who were bad, but were making an advance and is here transferred to states. Unlike the good/bad distinction there was a certain vagueness about who or what it delineated. It would not, however, be correct to assume that he would only consider a state that was making progress as worthy of his assistance. He preferred such states, but he was not limited to them. Chrysippus, quoted by Plutarch, specifically wrote that the wise man would not be concerned only with those kings who were making progress (*St. Rep.* 1043d, SVF 3.691). So it could be concluded that it would be an obstacle to participation if a state was irredeemably bad. If the wise man felt that his participation was likely to improve a state, he would be justified in taking part in its affairs. Merely because a state was bad would not provide sufficient cause for abstention. For only the ideal state could possibly be good; thus, if badness itself was the criterion for the decision, the wise man would just have to abstain from all states and wait for the miraculous appearance of his ideal. But all the evidence that has been considered

---

[6] Sen. *De Otio* 3.2, D.L. 7.121, Stob. *Ecl*. 2.111.3-9, SVF 3.690.

[7] E.g. Chrysippus in Epict. 2.6.9, SVF 3.191.

[8] *Teleia politeia* as an ideal or perfect society is analogous to the use of *teleios* to describe the wise man, a man with all the virtues (Plut. *St. Rep*. 1046ef, SVF 3.299), the *katorthôma*, a truly moral action (Stob. *Ecl*. 2.85.18-20, SVF 3.494) or the soul of the wise man (D.L. 7.128, SVF 1.569). In all these cases it refers to something that is perfect and morally good.

shows that the early Stoa thought that the wise man should participate in existing states in spite of their badness or even because of it.

This explanation of what would be considered an obstacle to participation gains some confirmation from Seneca's *De Otio* in which he advocates *otium*, retirement from public life. Here he suggests three reasons for non-participation; first when the state is too corrupt to be helped, secondly if he has too little influence or power and the state will not accept him, finally if his health is too poor (3.2-4). Only the first requires a decision on the part of the wise man, the latter two are out of his control. Seneca's belief that one of these will invariably be the case does not seem to be true of the early Stoa. At the beginning of the extant text he acknowledges that what he is arguing is contrary to the generally held view of the Stoic attitude to political participation (1.4ff). This helps to explain why his advocacy of *otium* is based not so much on what the Stoics explicitly said about *otium* as on conclusions drawn from Stoic first principles.[9] Seneca's interpretation of the views of the early Stoics on this matter must be treated warily, but the idea that some states are irredeemably corrupt seems valid for the early Stoa. Such a circumstance might arise from the disposition of the ruler, for instance, if he is a tyrant.

There is no doubt, therefore, that the early Stoics advocated political participation as an appropriate activity for the wise man, but it is necessary to distinguish two types of political activity. The first is the acceptance of a particular regime or system of government and consequent participation within it. The second is the rejection of the existing political institutions or practices and thus an attempt to change them. It is sometimes held that, although the Stoa may have encouraged participation if the regime was acceptable, it could not justify revolutionary activity of the latter type because of its metaphysics. Such a view has been explicitly attributed to the early Stoa by one writer: 'The Stoic considers the form of government under which he lives to be determined by natural law and therefore to be both rational and unalterable'.[10] Yet there are no grounds for this assumption, which prevents change of any sort in any sphere of life or indeed any action, since action entails alteration. The naturally ordained rightness of any situation can only apply to the present, not the future, and there is no reason why the form of government should be more sacrosanct than anything else, especially given the state of constitutional flux in the time of the early Stoa.

Chrysippus had described all existing laws and constitutions as mistaken (*hêmartêsthai*), a view which lies behind Stoic criticisms of

[9] Griffin 1976: 331, 328-34 on Sen. *De Otio*.
[10] Devine 1970: 329, cf. Kagan 1965: 241-2. It is suggested more cautiously by Brunt 1975: 17.

Solon, Cleisthenes and Lycurgus.[11] He had compiled a collection of differing burial customs of peoples, described by Cicero as *nationum varii errores*, the various errors of nations (Cic. *Tusc. Disp.* 1.108, SVF 3.322). It would seem reasonable that the Stoic should seek to correct at least the more extreme of these *errores*, just as he should put a man who has lost his way back on the right road.[12] It may be suggested that because the Stoics accepted existing societies they inevitably became conformist and conservative.[13] This, however, would be too simple. It was not absolute acceptance; they accepted it only in so far as they could be politically involved in it and this entailed change and improvement.

It may seem as though a Stoic would have little incentive to be interested in political reform or improving people's external circumstances. A person has the potential to be virtuous and happy whatever his external circumstances, whether he is rich or poor, slave or free. For happiness (*eudaimonia*) is solely a consequence of virtue and virtue is not dependent on external conditions.[14] Therefore there is no need to improve them.

Nevertheless the early Stoics did not hold a person's environment to be unimportant. If they had, Chrysippus' claim that the wise man in politics should be concerned with the restraint of *kakia* and the promotion of *aretê* would be meaningless, as would the belief that some societies were preferable to others. A person would not *need* a good environment to be virtuous, but he could be influenced favourably by one.[15] It would be partly with this object that the wise man would be concerned with law-making and education. As has been argued in the last chapter, the Stoics were particularly interested in social relations. The slave/master relationship which is characteristic of contemporary society not only stems from the moral badness of people, but also helps to perpetuate it. An environment which limited it would therefore be preferable. In this sense it is the values that underlie the environment that are important, affecting all levels of society, rather than the particular circumstances of any one individual.

The Stoic stress on virtue should not be taken to imply a disregard of other people's circumstances. For virtue is not to be understood only with reference to the virtuous person, but also involves the relations of that person with the rest of society. The wise man in politics will act virtuously and the object of virtuous action is not necessarily to make other people virtuous and therefore happy. If someone were drowning,

[11] Chrysippus' remark: SVF 3.324. Stoic criticisms: Plut. *St. Rep.* 1033f, Cic. *Acad. Pr.* 2.136, SVF 3.599.

[12] Lactantius SVF 3.629, Cic. *De Off.* 1.51-2.

[13] Aalders 1975: 84.

[14] See Chapter 1.2, cf. also Irwin 1986.

[15] See Chapter 1, n. 40.

a virtuous man would try to save them, but whether or not he succeeds is morally indifferent; it will not make the drowning person any more virtuous or happy to be saved, but that is not a reason to let them drown. It is in accordance with nature, *kata phusin*, and preferable that they live and the wise man should try to bring this about.[16] Concern with political reform or improvement would be similar to this in so far as the existing situation was contrary to nature, *para phusin*. The extent to which the Stoa would advocate change would depend in part on the degree of criticism of contemporary society. In the early Stoa, as has been seen, it was intense.

The Stoic ideas on political participation were a response to their dissatisfaction with the existing state of affairs, as outlined in the first two chapters. Yet this was not the only possible response. The Epicureans experienced a similar dissatisfaction, but their solution was to opt out; this has echoes of the Cynic viewpoint from which the Epicureans were at pains to dissociate themselves.[17] Although this was a rejection of contemporary society, it was not replacing society with the individual. Rather, Epicurus was proposing the stability of a community of friends as an alternative to the hazards of contemporary political life.[18]

2. Constitutional preference

Did the advocacy of political participation combine with a preference for a particular form of constitution? It has been suggested that it was not the system of government that was important but the worth of the individual state, and this depended on how far the statute law was in accordance with the common law of reason.[19] This may be true, but it is too strict. It could be that the system of government also affected their judgment about the worth of a state. It should not exclude the possibility that they had a preference, although not an absolute one, for a particular type of government, perhaps depending in part on circumstances. The early Stoics are unlikely to have completely ignored questions about the relative merits of different types of constitution, a subject that had figured so prominently in the writings of Plato and especially Aristotle. The fact that over a period of several hundred years they acquiesced in various forms of government should not be used to determine the ideas of the early Stoa. Moreover, their apparent indifference to constitutions need not be as extreme as the fragments suggest, because we are relying for evidence on what fairly late authorities thought interesting at a time when such distinctions

---

[16] For the example Rist 1969: 220-1.
[17] Cf. D.L. 10.8, 119. On Epicurean hostility to Cynicism, Aalders 1975: 53-4.
[18] Rist 1972: 127-39 on Epicureanism and friendship.
[19] Pohlenz 1970: 139.

were largely irrelevant.

Plato and less markedly Aristotle had been noted for their animosity to democracy. The early Stoics were in many ways reacting against these predecessors. Zeno had directed his *Politeia* against Plato; Persaeus wrote seven books attacking Plato's *Laws* (D.L. 7.36); Chrysippus' *On Justice* was aimed at Plato with particular reference, as might be expected, to his *Republic* and probably at Aristotle too (Plut. *St. Rep.* 1040a-41a). Furthermore Zeno and Chrysippus' analysis of slavery is in direct opposition to Plato and Aristotle. Refutation of the arguments of Plato and Aristotle need not in itself imply that the early Stoics had democratic sympathies, but the nature of this opposition argues strongly for this claim.

A recurrent theme in Plato's philosophy is that there is a better element which should rule and a worse one which should be ruled. Often, as has been said in the last chapter, this is expressed in terms of the slave/master relationship. In the state, philosophers should rule the rest, in the soul reason should rule the desires, in man the soul should rule the body. The maintenance and justification of this ruler/ruled distinction was an essential feature of the anti-democratic argument. It is this particular aspect of Plato's thought which is rejected by the early Stoa. The ideal state contains only the wise. The soul is a unity; it has parts, but they do not conflict. There is no harsh division between soul and body. For the soul in the form of *pneuma* (breath) permeates the whole body; body and soul are material and their combination is described as total blending, that is to say both occupy the same space. So intimate is the relationship that what affects the body affects the soul also and *vice versa*.[20] Thus the ruler/ruled distinction which is apparent in Plato's thought is rejected in favour of a more unitary conception of the world. It was a distinction which would not meet with the approval of the proponents of democracy. These, as Aristotle pointed out, advocated that there should be no rulers or, if this was impossible, men should rule and be ruled in turn (Arist. *Pol.* 1317a40-b17). This all suggests that Stoic thought had a democratic bias. Such a bias would be consistent with their condemnation of subordination in contemporary society and their stress on the importance of freedom, both of which have democratic connotations.

Other aspects of Stoic thought reveal a similar tendency towards democracy. A contrast with Aristotle is useful here. Aristotle held that without virtue one could not be a citizen. Whether a man could attain such virtue was dependent on his occupation. Artisans could not become citizens because their work was degrading and they worked for

[20] Nemesius SVF 1.518, Galen SVF 2.885, Hierocles *Found. of Ethics*, col. 3.56-4.53, Themistius SVF 1.45.

the benefit of another; nor could agricultural workers, because they did not have the leisure to become virtuous (Arist. *Pol.* 1328b33-29a2, 1337b4-15). For a Stoic, on the other hand, anyone can be virtuous, regardless of their position in society, even a slave (e.g. Lactantius SVF 3.253). In contrast to Aristotle this has strong democratic overtones. For Aristotle, social position dictates whether or not one can be virtuous and, therefore, whether one can be a citizen. Moreover, those with leisure are likely to be well-born and wealthy.

So it is hardly surprising to find that Aristotle often clearly associates good birth and virtue. Good birth is related not only to the virtue of a person's forefathers but also to their economic status. In the *Politics* good birth is defined as 'ancient wealth and virtue (*archaios ploutos kai aretê*)'.[21] A noble ancestry will not guarantee virtue, but it gives a person a better chance of being virtuous. This association of virtue and the upper or propertied class is fairly common; it is apparent in the moral terms in which they are described, for instance *kaloi kagathoi, aristoi, beltistoi*.[22] The Stoic separation of virtue from birth and class prepares the ground for a democratic position.[23] For Chrysippus it is irrelevant whether one's parents are well-born or not.

In contrast to Aristotle wealth-orientated virtues play a very insignificant role in Stoic accounts of the virtues. For Aristotle both *eleutheriotês* (liberality) and *megaloprepia* (magnificence) cover the use of wealth alone and *megaloprepia* involves expenditure on such a large scale that a poor man would be completely incapable of being virtuous in this respect (Arist. *NE* 2.1107b8-21, 4.1119b22-23a33). These virtues hardly receive a mention in the Stoa, and when they do, *eleutheriotês* is not limited to wealth (Andronicus SVF 3.273) and *megaloprepia* seems to have nothing to do with money at all (Andronicus SVF 3.270).

Thus the whole tenor of Stoic thought inclined towards democracy. It was produced at a time when democracy in Athens was far from secure and was for periods non-existent. In such circumstances the democratic tendency of Stoic thought had a particular relevance. Their support for democracy in Athens will be examined further in the next chapter. On the other hand, the pronounced aristocratic bias of Plato

[21] Arist. *Pol.* 1283a34-7 (with Newman's commentary), 1294a21, 1301b3, cf. *Rhet.* 2.15.1390b22ff. In the extant passages of Aristotle's *Peri Eugeneias* wealth seems to be less significant, Chroust 1973: 23-4, 293-5, but Arnheim 1977: 181 differs on this. In Plato *Theat.* 174e the view is reported that a man is noble, *gennaios*, if his family has been wealthy for seven generations.

[22] For discussion of such terms and a fuller list, see De Ste Croix 1975: 10-11, cf. also Denniston on Euripides *Electra* l. 253.

[23] Sen. *De Ben.* 3.28, SVF 3.349, Ps. Plut. SVF 3.350. Chrysippus is not the first to put forward such ideas, cf. Eurip. *Electra* ll. 367-72 (contrast ll. 38-9), *Dictys* frag. 336, Antiphon frag. 44B (DK). Chrysippus apparently cited Euripides in support of his case. Guthrie 1969: 152-5.

reflects his hostility to a democracy which in the mid-fourth century must have seemed fairly deep-rooted.

Some scholars have argued that the early Stoa favoured a mixed constitution,[24] others that they favoured kingship. Both suggestions should be rejected. According to Diogenes Laertius the Stoics held that the best constitution was a mixture of democracy, kingship and aristocracy (D.L. 7.131, SVF 3.700). But he omits to say which Stoics believed this. To attribute it to the early Stoics is implausible because such a constitution would institutionalise divisions within a society which they clearly rejected. Panaetius, a Stoic in the second century BC, is believed to have advocated such a constitution. It would be more appropriate for his conception of the divided soul and interest in Peripatetic thought.[25]

Tarn has argued convincingly that Kaerst was mistaken in his belief that the early Stoics were monarchists; in fact they disliked monarchy.[26] There is little evidence for any monarchic sentiment on the part of the early Stoa and none at all for Zeno.[27] That their names should in some degree be linked with kings is scarcely surprising in a world in which kings were becoming increasingly prominent and so reveals nothing of their attitude to monarchy. Persaeus, Cleanthes and Sphaerus all wrote works *On Kingship*, but nothing is known of their contents (D.L. 7.36, 175, 178). The Stoics certainly had the concept of the ideal king and only the wise man was such a person. This claim effectively condemned all contemporary kings and explains Sphaerus' alleged denial of Ptolemy's kingship. When charged with this he is recorded as replying ambiguously 'being such a man as he is, Ptolemy is indeed a king'.[28] What the Stoics present is not the idealisation of the king, but the idealisation of the wise man. In Hellenistic kingship treatises the virtues which the king should traditionally have include *epieikeia*, equitable consideration, and *praotês*, gentleness,[29] but this also could not be true of the early Stoic conception of the good king. For although the wise man who has kingly qualities will have *praotês* (Stob. *Ecl.* 2.115.10-12, SVF 3.632, Plut. SVF 3.255), he will not be *epieikês* (Stob. *Ecl.* 2.96.4-9, SVF 3.640, D.L. 7.123, SVF 3.641). For in spite of being unaccountable he cannot be above the law, yet the exercise of *epieikeia* requires making an exception to the law. This limitation condemns not only contemporary kings, but also the idealisation of them. In the Hellenistic context it would have been difficult to avoid the question of how a king should behave, but to

[24] For instance, Kargl 1913: 63, Sizoo 1926: 230.
[25] See Chapter 8 and the Conclusion below.
[26] Tarn 1948: 2.424-6, Kaerst 1926/27: 2.306ff, cf. also the *aufgeklärten absolutismus* of Wilamowitz 1881: 218.
[27] Murray 1970, Aalders 1975: 88-91.
[28] D.L. 7.177, interpreted as hostile by Hobein, RE Sphairos col. 1688f.
[29] Murray 1965: 168, 176-7.

propose that the wise man will be the only true king is not to show a preference for monarchy; it merely asserts that the wise man will have the qualities appropriate to a true king, whether he is in practice a king or not (Stob. *Ecl*. 2.102.13-15, SVF 3.615).

Much of this discussion on participation in politics has concerned the wise man. Stoic philosophers, however, never claimed to be wise men themselves. Chrysippus did not consider himself, his associates or his teachers to be wise (Plut. *St. Rep*. 1048e, SVF 3.668, cf. Sext. Emp. SVF 3.657, Plut. *Comm. Not*. 1076bc). Although the philosopher need not be identified with the wise man, it is reasonable to assume that the philosopher would seek to emulate the wise man as far as he was able, in this field as in others. Since the Stoics did advocate participation in politics, it is now necessary to find out if there is any evidence to suggest that they went beyond theorising and actually did take part in political life. First the role of the Stoa in Athenian political life will be examined and then Chapters 5 and 6 will consider the relationship between Stoic ideas on the just distribution of property and the Spartan revolution of the 220s.

4

Third-Century Athenian Politics

1. Introduction

In the third century Athens was a politically insignificant state in a world dominated by powerful kings with extensive territories, such as the Antigonids in Macedon and the Ptolemies in Egypt. For much of the time Athens was subject to the Antigonids, although there were occasions on which it sought to assert its independence, often with the help of Ptolemaic Egypt. It tended to be the supporters of democracy in Athens who favoured independence from Macedon. I wish to argue that the Stoics were among those who supported an independent and democratic Athens and that their behaviour can be seen as directed to this end.

In the early part of the third century when Athens was in the possession of the Antigonids Zeno had associated with Antigonus Gonatas. Later, when it became clear that Macedon was determined to keep its garrison in the Piraeus, he moved into the sphere of the radical democrats, such as Chremonides and Demochares, the nephew of Demosthenes. From then on, if the Stoics were associated with any foreign power, it was Egypt, not Macedon. Zeno's ideas were adapted for the propaganda of the war against Macedon in the sixties, known as the Chremonidean War. Subsequently when Athens had lost and was firmly back in Macedonian control, there is a lull in any known political activity on the part of the Stoa, as in our knowledge of the anti-Macedonian element in Athens. In the 230s, however, the Stoa is found to be linked with the re-emergence of those opposed to Macedon and was among the supporters of the liberation of the city in 229.

Plutarch criticised the early Stoics for their lack of participation in politics. Zeno, Cleanthes and Chrysippus were happy to write numerous books on government, ruling and being ruled and similar subjects, but none of them were prepared to do anything themselves (Plut. *St. Rep.* 1033bc). It is, however, clear that Plutarch was thinking of political action in a limited sense, that of official acts, such as going on an embassy, being a general or contributing to an *epidosis* (public benefaction). Even this is not strictly true; Zeno, for instance, did contribute to the repair of the public baths (D.L. 7.12). Nevertheless it will be seen that although they did little in an official capacity, the Stoics were involved in the politics of their time.

As advocates of political participation they could be expected to hold views on current political problems. It has already been argued that their work reflected an awareness of the contemporary situation. Yet, many scholars give the impression of a school that was comfortable with theory but confused and inconsistent on matters of practical politics. It may have been a particularly confused period, but even so one would expect some degree of consistency in approach. There is an apparent conflict between the revolutionary nature of the *Politeia* and their association and alleged support of Antigonus Gonatas, between an ideal of equality and a supposed advocacy of monarchism, between their links with Antigonus and those with the Ptolemies.

Any inconsistency between the *Politeia* and Zeno's association with Antigonus would be diminished if the *Politeia* could be dated as early as possible. W.W. Tarn, for instance, emphasises both its earliness and impracticability, the former suggesting that it may have represented discarded views by the time that Zeno came to know Antigonus, the latter that it had little bearing on Zeno's views of the actual world anyway.[1] It might also be said that as an ideal state for the wise alone it need be of no importance to the present or to fools.[2] H. and M. Simon adopt a different approach to reconciling these problems. They argue that Zeno was a supporter of the Antigonids as early as Demetrius Poliorcetes' first approach to Athens in 307. Zeno's ideas supported the lower classes and were in sympathy with Demetrius who was relying on those hostile to the ruling class. With the consolidation of the Antigonids in Macedon the Stoics remained aligned to the new power. Thus from revolutionary beginnings they became the exponents of Macedonian power and later of kingship. The possibility is even put forward that Zeno's radical views were not so much sincere as dictated by his support for Demetrius.[3] All these arguments rely on the early dating of the *Politeia*, a dating which has already been questioned. Even if it was an early work, similar ideas were held in the Stoa as late as Chrysippus. Moreover, although the *Politeia* may be an ideal, it still embodied a view of the world antipathetic to one such as Antigonus.

Further apparently inexplicable changes in the political direction of the Stoic school occurred later in the third century. For W.S. Ferguson the Stoa changed from being 'the Macedonian court philosophy' under Zeno to being 'the creed of uncompromising republicanism' under Chrysippus, a radical change. For the Simons too there is a change of direction, the Stoics at some point in the scholarchy of Cleanthes abandon their supposed strong allegiance to Macedon for Egypt,

[1] Tarn 1913: 230.
[2] De Lacy 1958: 60-3.
[3] Simon 1956: 7, 15, 26f.

although they provide no adequate explanation for this. Tarn also notes this about-turn, dating it to shortly after the Chremonidean War. He attributes it to Cleanthes' personal inclinations, now that the main link, Zeno, was dead. All these scholars agree that the Stoa leaned towards Egypt in the last half of the century, but none of them offer a satisfactory explanation for what would appear to be a very important change.[4]

Nevertheless it is possible to see the approach of the early Stoics in general as being consistent throughout if one can ascertain and understand the premises on which it was based. To do this it is necessary to look at their political writings. Some of these were examined in earlier chapters where it was argued that the views of Chrysippus and Zeno on the ideal society were greatly influenced by their analysis of the contemporary situation. Fundamental to this was their view that the prevalence of certain forms of subordination which they described as slavery was incompatible with *homonoia* (unity) and unjust. It was suggested that they saw this subordination within Athens and that Athens itself could be seen as subordinate to Macedon. We might, therefore, expect them at least to sympathise with those elements which desired an independent Athens and to be averse to any power which wished to make Athens subordinate to itself, in other words to enslave Athens. It was also argued that many of their ideas had democratic connotations. This would strengthen the likelihood that they would sympathise with those seeking to secure an independent Athens; for these were generally associated with democracy.

The objection could be brought that the Stoic ideas contained an elitist division between wise men and fools and that Athens could not be considered to be a city full of wise men.[5] If such an objection were really valid it would render impotent the entire Stoic ethical system which concentrated on the wise man. Yet the bad man could make progress and could seek to emulate the wise man. Similarly the fact that a state could make progress towards the ideal society makes it clear that the ideal had relevance to the present. The *Politeia* may have been a philosophical enquiry rather than a practical proposal, but Zeno himself had emphasised that it was of importance to the present world.[6]

In the following discussion it will be shown that this desire for a democratic and independent Athens represents the consistent viewpoint of the third-century Stoa, manifesting itself in various ways. That this was their attitude has hitherto been obscured by the

---

[4] Ferguson 1911: 232, 261; Simon 1956: 26f; Tarn 1913: 331.

[5] Cf. De Lacy 1958: 60-3.

[6] Stob. *Ecl.* 2.94.7-20, SVF 3.611, for *teleia politeia* in this passage see Chapter 3 n. 7. Relevance: Philod. *Peri St*. 12.1-11, cf. Sandbach 1975: 24.

over-emphasis placed on the relationship between the Stoic school and Macedon and the tendency to see any kind of connection with kings as being evidence for monarchist theory; yet it is a period in which all the major powers were monarchies. Moreover, it is a mistake to try to find complete duplication of their political ideals in practice. For this results in two undesirable extremes; the one is to argue that any political activity by the Stoics was an attempt to set up their ideal society, for instance Sphaerus in Sparta, the other is to point out that they never did and never could, so this ideal society and the ideas associated with it had no political validity. It has already been said that Chrysippus accepted that the wise man would have to cope with imperfect states. Furthermore, it will be suggested that the Stoics could participate in two ways, on the one hand in direct political activity, on the other as proponents of the ideology of a democratic and independent Athens.

It is not unusual to see the relationship of the philosophical schools with external powers as reflecting the political persuasion of those schools. The Peripatetics were generally inclined to Macedon, which traditionally supported oligarchies in Greece. Thus Demetrius of Phaleron, the Peripatetic tyrant of Athens from 317 to 307, had the support of Cassander, while the hostility of the democrats to the oligarchic Peripatetics was manifested in the prosecution of Theophrastus (D.L. 5.37) and in 307 in the law banning all philosophical schools in Athens that did not have the consent of the *dêmos*.[7] Such a law presupposes that some philosophical schools could meet with the approval of the *dêmos*. This affinity with Macedon was only upset by the confusion in Macedon that followed the death of Cassander in 297. Once there was stability in Macedon and the approval of the new Antigonid rulers was clear, it was not long before normal relations resumed. After the Chremonidean War, with a pro-Macedonian government installed in Athens, Lycon, the head of the Lyceum, associated with Antigonus and donated money to the Athenian *epidosis* of 243,[8] while Hieronymus of Rhodes conducted an annual festival in honour of Halcyoneus, the dead son of Antigonus (D.L. 4.41-2, 5.68). The reconciliation between Macedon and the Peripatetics is evidenced in Antigonus' appointment of the grandson of Demetrius of Phalerum to the *thesmothetai* (Athen. 4.167f) a position which may have been particularly important at this time.[9] As a result of this Macedon-oligarchs connection it would be expected that the democrats and those philosophers with democratic sympathies would turn to a power that was prepared to assist them, in this case Egypt.

[7] Pollux 9.42, D.L. 5.28, Athen. 13.610f.
[8] D.L. 5.65, IG II^2 791, line 71; Habicht 1982: 26ff; Walbank in Hammond and Walbank 1988: 310 argues that the threat was not an Achaean invasion.
[9] On the importance of the *thesmothetae*, Habicht 1982: 18-19.

They did not have to believe that Egypt was in favour of democracy in principle, only that in these circumstances it would be.

2. Zeno and Antigonus Gonatas

Before proceeding to examine the part played by the Stoa in third-century Athenian politics it is necessary to clear up any misconceptions there may be about the relationship between Zeno and Antigonus Gonatas. The anecdotal nature of some of the evidence on this subject and indeed on Stoic political activity in general means that it has to be treated with caution.

The dominant view for many years has been that there was a very close relationship between Zeno and Antigonus. Ferguson says that when Athens was in Antigonus' possession, he was 'a constant auditor of Zeno, his friend and teacher' and even goes so far as to see the Macedon policy of installing tyrants in Greece as Antigonus' conception of the Stoic wise men. For Wilamowitz too Zeno is the friend and teacher of Antigonus; Stoicism is ideologically suited to support monarchy and is intrinsically antipathetic to democracy. Tarn does not go quite so far as these, but places great emphasis on the constant friendship of Zeno with Antigonus, while noting that at the same time he avoided being labelled as a pro-Macedonian. Such views underlie the arguments of many other scholars.[10] All these scholars tend to overstress the connection between Zeno and Antigonus, although there are dissenters who would not do so.[11] This view perhaps reflects the over-enthusiasm of earlier scholars for seeing philosophers behind powerful men as opposed to the gradual dissemination and consequent acceptance of philosophical and political ideas.

Christian Habicht has recently re-examined the history of Athens in the third century BC and concluded that the city remained independent of Macedon from 287 until the end of the Chremonidean War, although the presence of the Macedonian garrison in the Piraeus was a constant irritation.[12] This casts doubts on the prevailing view of the Zeno-Antigonus relationship. For this view assumed that Antigonus had frequent and unhindered access to Athens and hence to Zeno's lectures until the outbreak of the Chremonidean War in the sixties,[13] but it now appears that he did not enter the city again after the Antigonids lost Athens in 287. Thus, although there are extant several passages which describe meetings between the two men, these meetings must have fallen in the only years when Antigonus could

[10] Ferguson 1911: 168f, 175f; Wilamowitz 1881: 217f, 231; Tarn 1913: 34f; cf. also Grilli 1963: 287-301; Sartori 1963: 117-51.
[11] Reesor 1951: 14.
[12] Habicht 1979, esp. 68-75.
[13] E.g. Ferguson 1911: 168; Tarn 1913: 34.

have been in Athens, that is 294-87, the period of Macedonian occupation,[14] although for some of this time he was preoccupied with the revolt of Thebes (Plut. *Demet.* 40). Diogenes Laertius (D.L. 7.6) tells us that Antigonus attended Zeno's lectures whenever he was in Athens, which fits well with his movements because he was not in Athens for the whole of this period. The other passages refer to two anecdotes about various drinking parties in which both men were involved (Aelian SVF 1.289, Athen. 13.603d, SVF 1.23, D.L. 7.13). All these must be placed before the Athenian revolt of 287.

After this Zeno showed distinct reluctance to meet Antigonus again. Antigonus wanted Zeno at his court, just as he wanted many other literary men and philosophers there, such as Menedemos of Eretria and Bion of Borysthenes. Although Zeno was invited several times, he consistently refused, until in about 276 he sent his pupils Persaeus and Philonides (D.L. 7.6-9). It is said that he refused because he was too old, but the only grounds for this view are two letters quoted by Diogenes which are generally agreed to be forgeries.[15] Moreover, if he died at 72 years old,[16] then he was in his late fifties in 276 when he would scarcely have been decrepit. Indeed we are told that he was in good health until his death, although there is one mention of illness (D.L. 7.28, 162). Such refusals then call into question the assumption of close friendship.

If Zeno and Antigonus were only acquainted for so short a period of time, why should there be a disproportionate number of anecdotes about them to the point that Epictetus in the second century AD takes for granted their association (*Diss.* 2.13.14-15)? The answer lies in Zeno's pupil Persaeus. Not only did Persaeus become part of the Macedonian court but he also wrote a book on the subject of drinking parties (*sumposia*), which I will argue is the source of much of the material on the relationship between Zeno and Antigonus. This work offered advice, particularly on drinking parties, and provided anecdotal examples from things familiar to Persaeus, such as a Macedonian dinner for an Arcadian embassy. Zeno was clearly central to the book; it was said to have been compiled in part from the memoirs of Zeno and Stilpo and one of the few certain passages describes how Zeno invariably declined invitations to dinner.[17] Thus, given Zeno's

---

[14] Habicht 1979: 72.

[15] Forgeries: Wilamowitz 1881: 110, Tarn 1913: 230, Pohlenz 1970: 2.14, Murray 1970: 230, Dorandi 1982: 110-11. Genuine: Grilli 1963: 287-301.

[16] Diogenes Laertius accepts a tradition that Zeno died at the age of 98, but he also records that Zeno's pupil, Persaeus, gave his age at death as 72 and even cites the work in which this claim was made (D.L. 7.28). So the age of 72 years comes complete with writer and book; also it is a writer who should have been in a position to know. Cf. Beloch 1927: 561f, Rohde 1878: 622f, Pearson 1891: 2.

[17] Athen. 4.162bc, 13.607a-e, D.L. 7.1, SVF 1.451-3. Persaeus' book goes under several titles, primarily *Hupomnêmata Sumpotika, Sumpotikoi dialogoi*, all of which refer to the

importance to a work that is for a large part made up of anecdotes about drinking parties, it is very probable that other stories that involve Zeno in such parties originate from it, particularly if they involve Macedon in any way. There are a disproportionate number of such stories about Zeno, too large to be a coincidence, especially for an ascetic who was reluctant to attend such functions at all. For instance, Zeno knees a guest at a drinking party (D.L. 7.17); he criticises a glutton (D.L. 7.19, Athen. 8.345c); although he is austere, he relaxes when drinking just as the bitter lupin becomes sweet when steeped in water (SVF 1.285 appearing in Athenaeus, Galen, Eustathius and Diogenes). Persaeus introduces into Zeno's house a flute girl who had been bought at a drinking party (Athen. 13.607e, D.L. 7.13). On another occasion Zeno snatches back a fish that a glutton has taken (Athen. 5.186d), a story which is also told of Bion of Borysthenes, suggesting that it was current in the Macedonian court.[18] People, Zeno remarked, should not remember the way things are said but instead concentrate on the substance of what is said, just as they should not be bothered about how the food is cooked or dressed (D.L. 7.22).

Clearly the large number of these stories would be of little importance if they were only found in Athenaeus, who was after all writing on the subject of such parties, but they are, as can be seen, found in other sources. Anyone who was writing on Zeno would look to Persaeus for material – hence the proliferation of drinking and dining stories about Zeno. So anecdotes about drinking parties which involve both Zeno and Antigonus will also stem from Persaeus. In fact although few anecdotes refer to actual meetings between them, two of the anecdotes are linked to drinking parties. In one Antigonus takes Zeno off to a drinking party, in another he turns up from one (D.L. 7.13, Athen. 13.603c, Aelian SVF 1.289).

The *Life of Zeno* by Antigonus of Carystos is now lost, but it contained at least three drinking stories about Zeno, including one of those about Antigonus Gonatas mentioned above (Athen. 8.345c, 13.603c, 607e). All of these also occur in Diogenes Laertius 7.12-24, which Wilamowitz argued was derived from Antigonus.[19] In this section of Diogenes there are six references to Zeno and *sumposia* and one other to food alone. This concentration would tend to add further support to Wilamowitz's original thesis and suggest that these drinking stories all come from the same original source, Persaeus' book on the subject; for otherwise it is curious that Antigonus should find so many stories like these about a man renowned for his ascetic and frugal way of life (cf. D.L. 7.27). This section, D.L. 7.12-24, contains several anecdotes about Zeno and Antigonus Gonatas and it is highly

same work, Deichgräber RE Persaeus 929-30.
[18] Athen 8.344a; on Bion's relationship with Antigonus, Tarn 1913: 233-9.
[19] Wilamowitz 1881: 112ff.

likely that all of them, regardless of whether they take place at drinking parties, stem from Antigonus of Carystus' use of Persaeus. One paragraph does emphasise the closeness of Antigonus Gonatas and Zeno more than any other, D.L. 7.14-15. Here Antigonus Gonatas describes Zeno's death as the loss of an audience (*theatron*), a strange thing to say about a man he has not seen for over twenty years. It suggests a background more appropriate to a philosopher than a king. It recalls the statement of Epicurus: 'We are sufficient audience for each other', *satis eum magnum alter alteri theatrum sumus.*[20] Doubtless the philosopher was Persaeus.

So if Persaeus is the source of many of these anecdotes about Zeno and Antigonus, how reliable is he? Anecdotes of this type are notoriously unreliable as historical evidence, and Persaeus is hardly an impartial source. It is in his interest to emphasise a friendship between Zeno and Antigonus and hence his own position with the king. He would want to put Zeno in a favourable light and thus himself. For it was through Zeno that Persaeus had been introduced to Antigonus and consequently any dubious action on the part of Zeno would arouse Antigonus' suspicions of Persaeus' loyalty. This would necessitate dissociating Zeno from those elements hostile to Antigonus in imagination if not in fact. There is an anecdote in which Zeno is at yet another *sumposium* where ambassadors from Ptolemy want to know his views and he refuses.[21] In D.L. 7.14-15, mentioned in the last paragraph, after Demochares, the Athenian democrat and nephew of Demosthenes, tells Zeno that he could obtain whatever he wanted from Antigonus, Zeno is said never to have spoken to Demochares again. This is a rebuff of silence similar to that given to Ptolemy's ambassadors. The immediate beneficiary in both cases would have been Persaeus, whose position in court might be adversely affected if it were known in Macedon that Zeno was involved with such people. If he could not deny that Zeno had met these people, he could at least claim that it was only to reject them. Demochares obviously did not expect such a snub, if indeed he got it. So such material, derived from Persaeus, cannot be relied on where it concerns Antigonus Gonatas. For he would be bound to stress the connection, hence producing that disproportionate emphasis that seemed so odd earlier on, given the short time that it was actually possible for Zeno and Antigonus to have known one another.

It might, however, be contended that Persaeus' continued presence in Macedon reflects the affinity of the Stoa as a whole with Antigonus.

---

[20] Tarn 1913: 310.

[21] D.L. 7.24. There is a different version, Stobaeus SVF 1.284, in which it is Antigonus' ambassadors who get rebuffed, but D.L. 7.24 is more likely to be the original. If the argument that Persaeus is the source of all these stories is right, he is unlikely to have amused Antigonus by such a story.

Yet, he was not considered by the ancients as true to his Stoic beliefs. He chose the court life, not the life of a philosopher (SVF 1.441). There is also the story of his dismay after hearing of the loss of his estate; 'in an instant Zeno vanished, Cleanthes vanished'. As he must have discovered soon afterwards, he was the victim of a practical joke designed to test the sincerity of his Stoic beliefs (Themistius SVF 1.449).

A final piece of evidence that might be used to argue, if not Antigonus' friendship for Zeno, at least his respect, is the Athenian decree in honour of Zeno, passed after his death when Athens was under Macedonian rule.[22] This decree is quoted by Diogenes Laertius and is generally thought to be genuine, although some have suggested that it might be a forgery.[23] It honoured Zeno with a gold crown and burial at public expense in the Ceramicus. It is referred to four times by Diogenes (D.L. 7.6, 10, 15, 29), but only on one occasion is it mentioned that Antigonus was supposed to have been the instigator (D.L. 7.15). The proposer of the decree, Thraso (D.L. 7.10), served as an Athenian ambassador to Antigonus; Diogenes reports a story that Antigonus asked Thraso to ensure the burial of Zeno in the Ceramicus – no mention is made of the crown (D.L. 7.15). This story does not appear elsewhere. It is difficult to gather from the tone of the decree whether it was done grudgingly by the Athenians as Wilamowitz supposed or by a man overwhelmed by 'strong feeling' as Tarn believed.[24] Regardless of the emotional content of the decree, it is noticeably apolitical, which might be surprising if it were sponsored by Antigonus. One might expect some such reference given the nature of the government. Instead it is very cautious, concentrating solely on Zeno's virtue and his role as educator. It would be a mistake to consider all decrees passed under pro-Macedonian governments as being pro-Macedonian. Phaedrus, a moderate democrat involved in the liberation of 287, was honoured in the 250s.[25] It is interesting that Menon of Archarnae appears as one of the supervisors to carry out the terms of both these decrees.[26] Further problems are added by the probability that the decree as we now have it is actually a fusion of two decrees.[27] It is certainly unparalleled for a crown to be given posthumously and it is plausible to believe that the crown was voted him in his lifetime and that this was under a democratic regime.[28] So while it is not possible to reach any firm

[22] D.L. 7.10-12. The eponymous archon is Arrhenides who was archon the year after Macedon occupied Athens, Apollodorus FGH 244 F44.
[23] Susemihl 1891: 1.54 n. 186 suggested that it was a forgery. Habicht in a forthcoming article, 'Analecta Laertiana', accepts the decree as authentic; its formula and vocabulary are consistent with other third-century inscriptions.
[24] Wilamowitz 1881: 232, Tarn 1913: 309.
[25] IG II² 682; Habicht 1979: 58ff; Osborne 1979: 187ff.
[26] Shear 1978: 56, although based on an emendation by Droysen 1881: 296.
[27] Droysen 1881: 291, Tarn 1913: 309; Rhodes 1972: 277 notes signs of re-editing.
[28] Wilamowitz 1881: 343, Tarn 1913: 309.

conclusions about the political implications of this decree, it is likely that it does not reflect any pro-Macedonian or pro-Antigonus sympathies on the part of Zeno.

3. Zeno and Athenian politics

Thus it was in the early years of the third century before 287 that Zeno associated with Antigonus, who was not yet king. At this time there existed a volatile political situation in which it was hard to predict the eventual standpoints of the protagonists. The great Hellenistic kingdoms were still in the process of being established. It is against such a background of uncertainty that Zeno's position must be considered, although as with much of the history of this period it is impossible to obtain a full picture of his relations with Athens.

In 307, after overthrowing Demetrius of Phalerum, Demetrius Poliorcetes had reactivated an Athenian democracy of sorts, which he was bound to do, partly because he had to try to live up to his liberation propaganda, but also because the oligarchic elements were favourable to his Macedonian opponent Cassander. Later, when he re-occupied Athens in 294, Cassander was dead, so that, if he wanted a government that would support him, democracy was not the only choice. Indeed an oligarchy would be dependent on him in a way that democracy would not; he had already experienced rejection at the hands of the moderate democracy after the battle of Ipsus in 301 and democracy in Athens traditionally sought independence. A democracy that was subordinate and so did not have control over its own affairs would be a contradiction. For power would ultimately rest not in the hands of the *dêmos*, but in those of the occupying force. An oligarchy, on the other hand, would be more reliable. It has often been believed that from 294-287, the period of Demetrius' control of Athens, there was a moderate democracy, but recent research has shown that the government was in fact an oligarchy.[29] It may have retained certain democratic institutions, but it had the essential features of an oligarchy. The archons were not elected, but appointed by the king and their term of office was not always limited to a year. The democratic secretaries were replaced by oligarchic *anagrapheis*.[30] Moreover, he secured his control of the city by installing garrisons in the city itself on the Museion and in the Piraeus.

Rather than elections and the renewal of democracy Demetrius appointed to the magistracies those who were popular with the people.[31] These would be men such as Olympiodorus who held the

[29] Moderate democracy: Ferguson 1911: 136-7, Beloch 1927: 447. Oligarchy: Habicht 1979: 22-33.
[30] Plut. *Demetrius* 34, Habicht 1979: 27.
[31] Habicht 1979: 27f.

archonship in 294/3 and 293/2. Yet it may well be that Olympiodorus and those like him had had hopes that Demetrius would allow a complete restoration of democracy and had acquiesced in his government for this reason, only to be disillusioned. Olympiodorus had fought for Athens against Cassander, arranging an alliance with the Aetolians for this purpose in 306, probably being in contact with Demetrius from 307 to 301.[32] It is likely that he was a general in the reconstituted League of the Antigonids of 302/1.[33] As a result he was clearly sufficiently close to Demetrius in 294 to obtain a leading position in the new government, but by 287 he was so dissatisfied with the course of events that he was one of the main figures in the rising against the Macedonian overlords.

There were perhaps several reasons for this alienation. He may have resented the Macedonian garrisons from the beginning. The annexation of Boeotia led to conflict between Demetrius and Boeotia's allies, the Aetolians, with whom Olympiodorus had been close.[34] Moreover, with the acquisition of the Macedonian throne in 294 Demetrius would have appeared to the Athenians as taking on the role of Cassander. When in 292/1 Demetrius allowed the return of the oligarchic exiles who had originally fled from him in 307 (Plut. *Mor.* 850d on Deinarchus), it must have been clear that he had no intention of restoring democracy, but was adopting the policies and adherents of Cassander's Macedon. It is significant that Theophrastus was involved in the moves to bring about the return of these exiles (Plut. *Mor.* 850d), indicating that the Peripatetics and the Antigonids were already coming to terms. As Demetrius' policy changed, so did people's attitudes to him. Those who were once the enemies of Cassander and friends of the Antigonids, men such as the Boeotian leader, Pisis of Thespiae, were now the enemies of Demetrius.[35] In this way any hopes that Olympiodorus and his associates may have had were abandoned and the Macedonians were expelled from Athens, though not from the Piraeus. The Athenians, Phaedrus of Sphettos and Philippides of Cephale, were probably men of a similar disposition.[36]

The liberators of Athens received assistance from Egypt, as the decree in honour of Callias of Sphettos, the brother of Phaedrus,[37] makes clear, and for most of the century Egyptian help was to remain important to those who advocated a democratic and independent Athens. Since the Piraeus was still occupied by a Macedonian garrison,

[32] Ibid. 42f.
[33] Beloch 1925: 166, De Sanctis 1936: 146.
[34] Habicht 1979: 43.
[35] Ibid. Tarn 1913: 39.
[36] Habicht 1979: 58ff, Osborne 1979: 187ff, against Shear 1978: 10. On Philippides, Davies 1971: 541.
[37] Text of Callias decree in Shear 1978.

Egypt helped with the import of grain through other ports.[38] The Athenian concern with grain is attested by the owl-in-wheat-wreath motif of their bronze coins.[39] The loss of the Piraeus was a severe blow to the Athenians and the recovery of it became one of their main policy objectives (cf. IG II^2 657 lines 31-8). It was an obstacle to reaching any kind of understanding with Antigonus and was a major cause of the Chremonidean War as Athens attempted to reunite its state.[40]

Zeno was in Athens throughout this period, but there is little certain information on what he was doing or what he thought about the political situation. It may be said that as a native of Citium and not an Athenian citizen he had little reason to be concerned about it at all. Nevertheless as a man who advocated political participation it is unlikely that he was indifferent to it. It has already been argued that his political views grew out of the political problems or failings that he observed and that they inclined him in favour of a democratic and independent Athens. All we do know for certain is that Antigonus Gonatas attended his lectures when in Athens and that sometimes he met the Macedonian prince socially. It may be objected that there was no political significance at all in their association, that it was purely a pupil-teacher relationship, but could it really be divorced from politics, given the position of Antigonus in Athens? Some have argued that Zeno and his school were supporters of Demetrius and Antigonus from the time of Demetrius' initial occupation of Athens until sometime after the Chremonidean War, probably until the 230s.[41] While this seems to be going against the evidence, it is plausible to suggest that until some time in the government of 294-287 Zeno had hopes of them in the same way that Olympiodorus did. Like Olympiodorus and those others who were initially pro-Antigonid, only to become hostile when Antigonid policy changed, he became disillusioned. From Zeno to Chrysippus there is no evidence of significant change in their analysis of society and, as has been said, this analysis was inconsistent with Macedonian suzerainty. As this chapter proceeds, it will be seen that in the ensuing years there were signs of Zeno's alienation from the Antigonids and he was eventually to be involved with the anti-Macedonian movement associated with Chremonides. It is probable, then, that this split occurred during the time of Demetrius' occupation of Athens as it became apparent that the interests of Zeno were no longer in harmony with those of the Macedonian rulers. This coincided with the increasing connection between the oligarchic

[38] IG II^2 650 and addendum p. 662; Osborne 1979: 190, Habicht 1979: 48ff against Shear 1978: 20f.

[39] Kroll 1979: 145.

[40] Paus. 1.26.3. has been taken to show that the Macedonian garrison was expelled by Olympiodorus between 295 and 270, but Habicht 1979: 95-112 demonstrates that this passage should be understood to refer to an event before 295.

[41] Simon 1956: 7, 15, 26f.

Peripatetics and the Antigonids and the general disaffection of those who were formerly pro-Antigonid. For the circumstances demanded a reassessment of allegiances.

In the period following the liberation Zeno's initial ambivalence was reflected in his cautious approach to Antigonus. He refused repeated invitations to visit the Macedonian king's court (D.L. 7.6) which cannot be explained on grounds of age, because he was probably only in his fifties. Yet one might cite the visit of Persaeus some ten years later as evidence of a continuing friendship between the two men. This need not be significant; it has already been said that many Greek intellectuals visited Macedon. We do not have to assume a complete breakdown of relations, rather a gradual deterioration, which may on occasions even have improved, depending on circumstances. Zeno did support attempts to influence kings and this may well be such a case. Persaeus' visit occurred not long after Antigonus had taken up the Macedonian throne and there may have been hopes in Greece itself that relations could improve, particularly after the joint effort to repel the Celts. With the victory over the Celts at Lysimacheia in 277, Antigonus became even more threatening,[42] but this is to a certain extent historical hindsight and it may have taken the Athenians a while to realise this. Changes in the political situation often lead to fresh hopes, however irrational. Demochares himself, probably at this time,[43] had allegedly asked Zeno to use his influence on Antigonus, which indicates a desire for dialogue on the part of the extreme democrats (see below). There is an enigmatic statement in Aelian (*VH* 7.14) that Zeno negotiated with Antigonus on behalf of the Athenians, but about what did he negotiate? The main preoccupation of Athens was the Macedonian garrison in the Piraeus and the consequent lack of access to its harbours. It is possible that it was this question that was behind Persaeus' visit. It is interesting that he should be accompanied by Philonides of Thebes, another Stoic, about whom little else is known.[44] For at this time Boeotia had good relations with Antigonus but may still have had the Macedonian troops that were stationed there by Demetrius.[45] In which case both visiting Stoics came from cities with similar problems in their relations with Macedon, problems which may have some bearing on their visits. To go on an embassy would be consistent with Stoic thought; they included going on an embassy among appropriate acts (Stob. *Ecl.* 2.85-6 SVF 3.494). The two philosophers may have made representations, perhaps informal,

[42] Habicht 1979: 85.
[43] Cf. Ferguson 1911: 172.
[44] D.L. 7.9, which also notes that Epicurus, writing to his brother, Aristoboulos, mentioned that Persaeus and Philonides lived at Antigonus' court. Bion of Borysthenes apparently accused both these Stoics of attacking him, D.L. 4.47.
[45] Good relations: D.L. 2.141; garrisons: Gullath 1982: 198, 210.

on behalf of their cities. It was becoming increasingly common to use philosophers as ambassadors, regardless of whether they were citizens. In 322 Xenocrates of Chalcedon, the head of the Academy, went as ambassador to Antipater (D.L. 4.9); in 287 Crates, also of the Academy, went to Demetrius (Plut. *Demetrius* 46); while later in around 226 Prytanis of Carystus was sent to Antigonus Doson (Moretti no. 28). At some point Arcesilaus of Pitane in Aeolis visited Antigonus Gonatas on behalf of his native city (D.L. 4.39). Persaeus stayed on in Macedon and his reputation suffered in consequence (SVF 1.441) and Philonides appears to have lived there for a while (see n. 44). It is doubtful that he remained in Macedon long; if he had, one would expect to hear more of him, but instead he vanishes from the records. If there were such negotiations, they clearly failed and any hopes evaporated. After this relations deteriorated and attitudes hardened. Menedemus of Eretria, the friend of Antigonus, was expelled from Boeotia.[46]

Nevertheless, whatever the state of Athenian relationships with Macedon on Antigonus' accession to the throne, the Athenian attitude to him soon became more hostile in the late seventies. Its ties with Egypt were strengthened (cf. Callias decree of 270/69 and D.L. 7.24), it sent an embassy to meet Pyrrhus, the king of Epirus, at Megalopolis, but he died before anything positive could come of it (Justin 25.4.4) and generally there was an increasing radicalisation in Athenian politics (Hegesander *ap.* Athen. 6.250f). There must be a reason for such an intensification of anti-Macedonian activity. The disastrous failure to recapture the Piraeus in the eighties with the loss of 420 lives is inadequate as an explanation, because it was too far back. Possibly it was the recognition of the consequences of Antigonus' accession, but along with this there may have been some negotiations that failed, such as those that have been suggested above, and this left military action as the only hope. Of course it was also the case that the circumstances seemed right; there were sufficient allies to give the attempt some hope of success, as well as the assistance available from Ptolemy. It was this growing radicalisation and frustration on the part of Athens that eventually led to the Chremonidean War. Unfortunately our knowledge of this war is limited, although we can have a rough idea about its causes as has been indicated. It is likely that the initiative for the war came from Athens, not as some have assumed from Egypt which did not seem fully committed.[47]

There is evidence that leads to the conclusion that Zeno was involved with the anti-Macedonian politicians and that by the late seventies his alienation from Antigonus was complete. There are only two reports of

---

[46] D.L. 2.142, Gullath 1982: 210.

[47] Habicht 1979: 112 against Tarn 1913: 290ff, Sartori 1963: 117ff. Habicht's view is criticised by Fraser 1981: 242.

Zeno associating with Athenian politicians and curiously the men in both cases are fervent anti-Macedonians, Chremonides and Demochares. It might be contended that there is no significance in this; for he would have spoken with many politicians, the names of whom go unrecorded. This would, perhaps, be a legitimate objection if there was no evidence to corroborate an anti-Macedonian position on the part of Zeno. One of these anecdotes (D.L. 7.17) records a conversation between Chremonides, Zeno and Cleanthes. It has been objected by some that this does not mean that Chremonides was a Stoic,[48] but such a point is not relevant. It does mean that Chremonides was known to have associated with two of the leading Stoics of the day and listened to them. It will be argued later that Chremonides does appear to have been influenced by certain Stoic ideas. This association was probably not long before the Chremonidean War.[49]

In the other anecdote (D.L. 7.14) Demochares told Zeno that he had only to make a request of Antigonus and it would be granted. After hearing this, Zeno allegedly had nothing more to do with Demochares. It has been suggested above that this anecdote should not be taken at face value; for if it derives from Persaeus, then it is the only answer Zeno could have given, but whether he did respond in this way is doubtful. A common modern view is that Demochares was trying to seek some personal advantage from Antigonus.[50] If Habicht's reconstruction of the years 287 to the end of the Chremonidean War is correct, this cannot be a valid explanation. For Demochares did not return from exile until after the liberation and died in about 271 – thus the association between Demochares and Zeno must fall in the period of Athenian independence when Demochares could make no personal gain from Antigonus and to do so would be inconsistent with his position. If Demochares did make some form of request of Zeno, it must have been of a political nature, regarding Athenian relations with Antigonus, perhaps the Piraeus. It may well have been this that led to the dispatch of Persaeus to Antigonus, hence Persaeus' subsequent eagerness to play down any association between Zeno and Demochares. Even if he did not make a request, the anecdote would have been derived from the known association of Zeno and Demochares and carries in it the implication that the two men had enough in common for Demochares to have certain expectations of Zeno.

There is another request with similar implications, also discussed earlier (D.L. 7.24). For Zeno evidently met an embassy from Ptolemy. That this embassy should want to speak to him also suggests that they had made certain presumptions about his position. This would certainly be odd if he was as pro-Macedonian as some scholars

---

[48] Cf. Wilamowitz 1881: 224.
[49] Cf. Immerwahr 1942: 345.
[50] Tarn 1913: 94 n. 11, Ferguson 1911: 172.

suppose,[51] but not if he was known to favour a democratic and independent Athens and with it the recovery of the Piraeus. It is probable that the embassy came to Athens not long before the Chremonidean War and its business was connected with the ensuing struggle against Macedon.[52]

Symbolic of independence was the right of a city to mint its own coinage, and the loss of this right was a public humiliation.[53] Athens had apparently lost the right during its subjection from 294-287 and did not resume the minting of its own coins until after the expulsion of Demetrius.[54] It is within this context that Zeno's remark about Attic coinage should be viewed (D.L. 7.18), which has been ascribed to the period between the liberation and the end of the Chremonidean War.[55] Zeno draws a comparison between the Attic tetradrachms and the silver coins of Alexander, which is distinctly unfavourable to the latter. The Attic coins in spite of their crudeness by far outweighed the external attraction of the Macedonian ones. This criticism takes on an extra force in the light of the loss of minting rights from 294 to 287 and helps to confirm the conclusions already reached about Zeno's political position. For its implications would easily have been understood by his contemporaries.

4. The Chremonidean War

So Zeno had links with the anti-Macedonian elements in Athens, but did his involvement with them go beyond this? Can his ideas be seen to have influenced them? To argue that they did is not to propose that the Chremonidean War was some form of Stoic crusade, aiming at the introduction of an ideal society. It is mainly because he makes such an assumption that Franco Sartori argues that the aims of Chremonides, as expressed in the decree of Chremonides about the alliance between Athens and Sparta, were inconsistent with Stoic philosophy.[56] He suggests that, although Chremonides may have been influenced by Zeno, it was only at a very superficial level and consequently he did not understand the theory and failed to apply it properly. Sartori examines the decree, contrasting it with the Stoic ideal society, to show that it contains ideas a Stoic would reject. He concentrates on two particular aspects, its attitude to the *polis* and its attitude to the barbarians.

Sartori emphasises that the decree is concerned with the protection of the *polis* and its ancestral constitution (cf. lines 13-16), a policy he

[51] For instance, Simon 1956: 33.
[52] Tarn 1913: 294, Will 1979: 1.221.
[53] Ferguson 1911: 184.
[54] Kroll 1979: 144-5.
[55] Koehler 1884: 299-300, who also discusses Alexander's silver coins.
[56] IG II² 687, SIG 434-5, Sartori 1963, cf. also Wilamowitz 1881: 224.

considers outmoded and an anathema to a Stoic. For a Stoic would reject the *polis* in favour of the cosmopolis or at least a large national state. He implies that, if Zeno had a preference for either of the protagonists, it would be Antigonus; for it was Antigonus whose policy was nearest to achieving this. Wilamowitz has no doubt about this.[57] Although a Stoic ideal society would contain no *poleis* in the conventional Greek sense, the Stoics did not repudiate the *polis* totally. They recognised it as an integral part of Greek society as it was and advocated that the wise man should take part in political life, as has been made clear in the previous chapter. So emphasis on the *polis* in the decree is not in itself evidence for the lack of Stoic influence. Only if one makes the unjustified assumption that movements supported by the Stoics must have as their goal the ideal society, would it be legitimate to suggest that reference to *poleis* is out of place, and even this would not be certain. The decree is not meant as a philosophical document but a statement of alliance.

Sartori sees a second inconsistency in the reference to the glorious days of the Persian Wars in lines 9-13. The highlighting of the barbarian-Greek conflict would be inconsistent with the Stoic denial of ethnic and social differences and if it had any philosophical antecedents it would be Plato. The validity of this point has been disputed;[58] for the barbarians are not mentioned once in the decree and the Persian Wars are only alluded to, almost a self-conscious desire not to emphasise the opposition, which could even imply the contrary of what Sartori suggests. Nevertheless, even if barbarians were mentioned, it does not seem to have any bearing on the matter; it only represented a traditional way of designating a particular enemy. The Persian Wars did not cease to exist just because the Stoics decided that ethnic divisions were not important. These wars had been the time of the last significant alliance between Athens and Sparta, thus making it a natural subject for propaganda.

If, therefore, there is nothing in the Chremonidean decree which would preclude Stoic influence, is there any evidence to indicate that there was such an influence on the anti-Macedonians? Again with reference to the decree Sartori cites various expressions that, he says, are typical of Stoicism, *philia kai summachia koinê* (line 10), *koinê eleutheria* (line 19), *koinê homonoia* (line 32), *ta koinêi sumpheronta* (line 52), but he sees them as being in the tradition of Themistocles and Demosthenes.[59] While they certainly are linked to an older tradition, perhaps they indicate more than Sartori will allow.

Since his article was published in 1963, another inscription has been discovered which shows that *homonoia* and *eleutheria* were important

[57] Sartori 1963: 146. Wilamowitz 1881: 224.
[58] Heinen 1972: 124 n. 20.
[59] Sartori 1963: 149.

elements in the propaganda of the anti-Macedonian coalition in the Chremonidean War.[60] This is the decree of the League of the Greeks at Plataea in honour of the Athenian Glaucon, son of Eteocles. Glaucon was a leading anti-Macedonian politician and the brother of Chremonides. He is here honoured for, among other things, his contributions to the joint cult of Zeus Eleutherius and the Homonoia of the Hellenes. This is the earliest evidence for the existence of such a cult and, since Glaucon was in exile at the time of the decree, it was presumably set up prior to 261. The editors of the decree, Roland Étienne and Marcel Piérart, provide the most suitable dating for the establishment of this joint cult; that it was at the time of the Chremonidean War and symbolises the new alliance, although the cult of Zeus Eleutherius was probably established in the previous century. This would equate well with the emphasis on *homonoia* (lines 32, 35) and *eleutheria* (lines 14, 19) in the Chremonidean decree.

William C. West, however, prefers to date the establishment of the joint cult to the time of Philip II and Alexander and the re-building of Plataea, but his argument seems inadequate.[61] He considers it to be the result of the development of the association between *homonoia* and *eleutheria*, first in the domestic, then in the international sphere. But he tends to overstate the kinship of these two terms in the fourth century, particularly in the international sphere. For much of his evidence comes from material in which ideas similar to those expressed in these terms are linked but not the terms themselves. For instance, he assumes that *sôteria* is substitutable for *eleutheria*, but while in practice it may be describing the same event it is not expressing the same idea. His actual examples are few; given the quantity of literature available from the fourth century something more solid is required. While the joint cult is clearly that of Homonoia of the Hellenes, that is between Greek states, much of the evidence that West adduces for the interest of Alexander in *homonoia* in fact refers to the internal *homonoia* of the cities.[62] Finally it is odd that a leading anti-Macedonian should contribute so generously to a cult established by Macedonians, the enemies of Greek freedom. It would be more reasonable to adopt an existing cult of Zeus Eleutherius, even if established by Philip or Alexander, and by converting it into a joint cult to reclaim it for the Greeks.

These two inscriptions demonstrate that two of the key concepts in the propaganda of the Chremonidean War were *eleutheria* and *homonoia* and that they were closely linked. Consequently it is not surprising that there is reference to the enslavement of cities

[60] Published by Étienne and Piérart 1975.

[61] West 1977: 314ff. Étienne 1985: 259-63 defends his position and rejects West's arguments.

[62] West 1977: 317-18.

(Chremonidean decree, line 12). Indeed Macedon became cast in the role of enslaver of the Greeks; in 211 BC Chlaeneas, an Aetolian, said, according to Polybius, that the slavery (*douleia*) of the Greeks owed its origins to Macedon and it was as a result of the actions of Cassander, Antipater and Antigonus Gonatas that there was no Greek city that did not have a share in the name of slavery (Polyb. 9.28.1-3).

Eleutheria as propaganda slogan was not unusual. Since Polyperchon many of the successors in their attempts to win over the Greeks had made claims that they were seeking the freedom of the Greeks, but *homonoia* was never, as far as is known, mentioned in this context. This is scarcely surprising; the unity of the Greek world was not something they would have relished. Vacuous promises of freedom, on the other hand, were easy to offer; the freedom was dependent on the goodwill of the external power and it was up to that power to define this freedom.

Freedom, when it was combined with *homonoia*, as in the context of the decrees, is of a different order. In this case freedom is preserved or attained not by an external power (although Ptolemy was providing some sort of assistance in the Chremonidean War), but by the Greeks themselves, the beneficiaries of this freedom, acting in unity. It was not a novelty to suggest that a state with internal divisions or a group of states quarrelling among themselves were easy prey for another power, particularly a stronger one, often Persia (cf. Isoc. *Paneg.*). Various different words and phrases are used to convey this (cf. Lysias 33.6, Isoc. *Paneg.* 85), but the decrees of the Chremonidean War and the establishment of a joint cult represents something new. Once *homonoia* is transmuted into a divinity and one so closely associated with *eleutheria*, the relationship takes on a solidity and objectivity that it did not previously possess. Although ideas similar to those contained in these terms had been juxtaposed in the past, the terms themselves are not found to be regularly associated. So there is a lacuna between the ideas expressed in various forms and the emergence of a joint cult of Zeus Eleutherius and Homonoia of the Hellenes. One could say that they had evolved and we do not have the evidence to chart this evolution properly. It may be possible, however, to explain both the prominence given to the combination of *homonoia* and *eleutheria*, rather than some other combination such as *homonoia* and *sôteria*, and how they come to appear in the decree.[63]

It has often been suggested that Chremonides' love of liberty and hatred of tyranny were influenced in part by the Stoa, although this is

---

[63] As Pfister in RE Soteria 1222-31 shows, Soteria does become noticeable from the early third century onwards. There is a festival of Soteria in Priene for the liberation of the city from the tyranny of Hieron c. 297. Also at Delphi, after the invasion of the Celts under Brennan. When Aratus dies, a festival of Soteria is established with a priest of Zeus Soter to mark Aratus' liberation of Sicyon from tyranny, Plut. *Arat.* 53.

qualified by asserting that his position did not represent that of the school.[64] Their influence may have been stronger than this. For the Stoic school did lay very considerable emphasis, as has been pointed out in Chapter 2, on the interrelation of the concepts of *homonoia, eleutheria* and *douleia*. All of these find their way into the Chremonidean decree, while the former two, the ideals, are present as divinities in the inscription in honour of Glaucon. It is certainly not impossible that Chremonides as an associate of Zeno, perhaps even a pupil, should reflect the Stoic teachings in some way, especially as the object of the coalition was to ensure that Athens was not subordinate to Macedon in any way. Nor should one imagine that the theory should survive the translation into propaganda intact.

The Stoics, until at least the time of Chrysippus, held that society was made up of a series of subordinating relationships of such a type that they described them as *douleia*, which was inimical to *homonoia*. If there was to be any true *homonoia*, there had to be freedom. In the evidence we have (for discussion of this see Chapter 2), this was with reference to personal freedom and *homonoia* between individuals. But this was in the context of the ideal society and there is no reason why it could not be transferred to relations between cities. If a city was subordinate and therefore not free, how could any of its citizens be free? So an expanding Macedon would undermine both the freedom and *homonoia* of the Greek cities if they fell victim to it. Without a community of interests between the cities there could be no freedom even amongst themselves. It might be objected that these notions of *homonoia* and *eleutheria* are only valid in an ideal society, one which is full of wise men, whereas the present is populated with foolish and bad men. Nevertheless, some situations may be closer to the ideal than others (cf. Stob. *Ecl.* 2.94.7-11, SVF 3.611) and hence preferable. So one would not be talking of true freedom, but something that approximates to it. In this context a group of free states could strengthen their unity in the face of danger from a stronger power, such as Macedon, in order to preserve both their unity and their freedom. This may not be an exact duplication of Zeno's thought, and in the circumstances one should not expect it, but it does contain two important features. First there is the very close association between *homonoia* and *eleutheria*, particularly as exemplified in the joint cult, although the relationship is not quite the same. Secondly there is the hostility to any subordination and the injustice involved in this (cf. Chremonidean decree, line 33). So the Greek side was characterised by *homonoia*, freedom, friendship and justice (the latter implied), while the Macedonians were unjust and with a will to enslave. Thus it is presented in Stoic terms with no doubt about who is right.

[64] E.g. Will 1979: 1.223, Tarn 1913: 295.

It would be completely mistaken to see or try to see the Chremonidean decree as a Stoic manifesto. It is a decree about an alliance between Athens and Sparta and it is in those terms that it must be interpreted, but it does show Stoic influence, particularly in respect of the slogans, *eleutheria* and *homonoia*, which recur in the decree in honour of Glaucon. This is not to suggest that this was unconnected with the tradition of similar ideas in the fourth century, but rather that it was through the Stoa that Chremonides came to emphasise these terms in particular. Indeed it need not have been the case that these ideas should have been present at all in any precise form. In a sense this propaganda amalgamated the Stoic emphasis on these concepts with the tradition of the fourth century.

So Zeno, after his association with Antigonus in the early years of the century and his subsequent ambivalence, aligned himself with the anti-Macedonians in Athens. He supported their struggle for a democratic and independent Athens and his influence can be seen in their propaganda. His changing attitude to Antigonus and Macedon can be explained not by changes in his ideas, but by his response to an unstable political situation. The premises that underlay his own political position remained consistent. Clearly this view has to be to a certain extent hypothetical, but it seems the most plausible interpretation of the evidence available. Corroboration for this can be gained from the likelihood that the Stoa in Athens followed the same line for the remainder of the century.

Zeno himself died shortly after the war. Keeping up his interest in politics to the very end, he died on the way to the assembly (Lucian SVF 1.288). So he did not live long enough to see the consequences of the war's failure, the installation of new garrisons, the oligarchically-inclined government and the rule of Antigonus Gonatas.

5. Later Stoic activity

In the period after the fall of Athens there is a marked absence of any evidence for Stoic activity in the political field, whether it is in Athenian politics or by association with the Hellenistic kings. This is curious when it is contrasted with the degree of known activity in the case of the other schools and their members. Lycon the Peripatetic is said to have helped the Athenians a great deal by frequently giving them advice (D.L. 5.67) and this is most likely to have been while Athens was subject to Macedon; for he was one of the subscribers to the *epidosis* of 243.[65] The affinity between the Peripatetics and Macedon at this time has already been noted above. A further, slightly later, instance is assistance given by Prytanis of Carystus, a Peripatetic, to

[65] IG II² 791 line 71, Habicht 1982: 26ff.

Antigonus Doson in drawing up a code of laws for Megalopolis in the late twenties; he also attempted to negotiate with this king on behalf of Athens, probably in 226, doubtless because it was felt that the king would be favourable to him.[66]

It has been suggested that, as a result of the reaction of 307, philosophical schools were unwilling to be identified with a particular regime, hence Strato, head of the Peripatetic school, had contacts with Alexandria, and his successor, Lycon, had the patronage of Eumenes and Attalus of Pergamum as well as Antigonus Gonatas.[67] Nevertheless, while there may have been a certain degree of wariness among the schools in such matters, they would generally incline towards those with whom they had something in common. Yet the complete absence of such Stoic activity until Ptolemy's invitation to Cleanthes, probably in the 230s, seems to be taking wariness too far. Aside from this there are two possible explanations: first that there was such activity, but the evidence is now lost, an explanation that seems odd in the light of our information on other schools. The second possibility is that there was no significant activity. This seems to be the most probable, for one would expect them to keep a low profile in the years in which Macedonian authority was evident in Athens. Their absence from the political arena would be in accord with the lack of information about effective or futile opposition to Macedon in Athens after the Chremonidean War. It was a time of defeat and recuperation for the opposition whose leading figures had fled to Egypt, so a hiatus would not be surprising. Any knowledge of dissent in Athens can only be gathered indirectly; the incursions of the Achaean Aratus into Attica in the forties and early thirties suggest that the Achaeans believed that there were elements within Athens which were favourable to them. A similar conclusion can be drawn from the appearance of Chremonides with an Egyptian fleet in the Aegean in the same period.[68]

It is only with the resurgence of the movement for an independent Athens that the Stoa reappears in the political sphere. This revival was due to the increasing weakness of Macedon in Greece which had been taking place since Aratus' seizure of the Acrocorinth in 243. The Achaean League was expanding in the Peloponnese, undermining the Macedonian-backed tyrannies, the Aetolians were causing problems in central Greece, particularly in Thessaly, while Macedon itself faced a threat from invading Dardanians on its northern frontiers. As a result the Athenians, under the leadership of the brothers Eurycleides and Micion of Cephisia, had sufficient confidence in 229 on the death of Demetrius II, the Macedonian king, to buy their freedom by paying

[66] Law code: Polyb. 5.93; negotiations: Moretti no. 28, Dow/Edson 1937: 169.
[67] Momigliano 1977: 45; on reaction, §1 above and n. 7.
[68] Ferguson 1911: 197.

Diogenes, the commander in the Piraeus, 150 talents to leave (Plut. *Aratus* 34, IG II² 834 lines 10-14). The Athenians could only have taken this step if such a feeling had been becoming increasingly dominant in recent years.

It is not known what part, if any, Ptolemy III played in the liberation of 229. He is not recorded as making any financial contribution and it is possible that there would not have been time for him to do so anyway, although he would doubtless have been pleased by the outcome.[69] He is known to have been providing a subsidy, albeit a small one, for Aratus (Plut. *Aratus* 41). Athenian policy after the liberation was to pursue neutrality, unwilling to incur even greater displeasure from Antigonus Doson and be drawn into war. Thus they rebuff Aratus soon after the liberation in spite of his assistance and refuse to join the Achaean League. Polybius, admittedly prejudiced, wrote that they took no part in the affairs of Greece and gave honours to all kings, in particular to Ptolemy. The extent of Athenian relations with Ptolemy is unclear before the cult of Ptolemy was established, probably in 224/3,[70] although there is one inscription earlier from September 226, which honours Castor, an official of Ptolemy (IG II² 838).

There is sufficient accumulation of evidence to indicate that the Stoic position was in line with the one which I have argued that Zeno held. Approval of the newly liberated Athens can be seen in the actions of Aristocreon, the nephew of Chrysippus. He is honoured by the *dêmos* for his part in contributing to the *epidosis* for the strengthening of the Athenian harbour and also for making a loan, probably for paying off the Macedonian garrison (IG II² 786).[71] To emphasise the value of his assistance the Athenian *dêmos* also made him a *proxenos*. Aristocreon would have been familiar with the Stoic attitude to the political situation in Athens, because he had been educated there by Chrysippus (D.L. 7.185).

While philosophers with oligarchic leanings were associated with Macedon, the Stoics are found to be in contact with various anti-Macedonian states around the time of the liberation of Athens. For Sphaerus of Borysthenes, a Stoic close to both Cleanthes and Chrysippus, appears both in Alexandria and in Sparta, probably a second visit to the latter.[72] Sparta was a state which was traditionally

[69] Habicht 1982: 80 n. 7.

[70] Ibid. 105-12.

[71] Ibid. 81 n. 11 rightly rejects Ingholt's dating of the decree to 196 BC, Ingholt 1967-68: 165-73. Habicht points out the similarities between IG II² 786 and other Athenian decrees of the time on the same matter, such as IG II² 834 l. 14, IG II² 835 ll. 9-11.

[72] Sphaerus may have visited Sparta in the 230s, Plut. *Cleom.* 2.2, see Chapter 6. A visit to Sparta by a Stoic would have helped to off-set the unfavourable impression created by the renegade Stoic Persaeus as a Macedonian official in Corinth between 245

hostile to Macedon. The exact dating of Sphaerus' travels is uncertain,
but an approximate idea can be obtained. He is known to have helped
with the revolutionary reforms of Cleomenes, so he must have been in
Sparta in about 227 (Plut. *Cleom.* 11). Later he is found in the court of
Ptolemy IV Philopator, who became king in late 222 or early 221,[73] so
possibly he fled with Cleomenes after the Battle of Sellasia (D.L.
7.177). He had made an earlier visit to Alexandria during the lifetime
of Cleanthes (D.L. 7.185), which was probably to the court of Ptolemy
III Euergetes. This is more difficult to date; the invitation was
addressed to Cleanthes so it has to be before his death, which can be no
later than 230/29.[74] There are various reasons for believing that this
visit was made at some time in the thirties. Since Cleanthes was
unable to take up Ptolemy's invitation, it is possible that he felt that he
was too old, but this is not very strong grounds. Chrysippus too was
unwilling to go, so the invitation must have come after his arrival in
Athens and not immediately afterwards; for he would have had to have
been taught for some time before being considered a possible
candidate. His philosophical education in Athens is likely to have begun
in the mid to late 240s. According to D.L. 7.181 Chrysippus began
studying philosophy after the property which he had inherited from his
father had been confiscated to the king's treasury, an incident that
probably took place during the third Syrian War (246-241) when
Ptolemy occupied much of Cilicia.[75] This would gain support from a
papyrus that refers to the seizure of money in Soli, Chrysippus' home
town, in the early stages of the war.[76] This indicates a date in the
thirties for Ptolemy's invitation, a date which would also be more
suitable in the light of the lack of known relations between Athens and
Egypt earlier.

So, to sum up, at some stage in the 230s Ptolemy III Euergetes
invited Cleanthes to come to Alexandria or, if he was unable to do so, to
send another Stoic. Both Cleanthes and Chrysippus declined, but
Sphaerus accepted. He probably also visited Sparta in the thirties and
went there again in about 227 when he assisted Cleomenes in his

---

and 243, SVF 1.442-5. Some see Sphaerus as a sort of negotiator between Egypt and
Sparta in the 220s, Susemihl 1891: 73 n. 296; Zeller 1923: 3.1.39 n. 4; Jacoby FGH 585,
Comment.

[73] Samuel 1962: 106-8 puts the death of Ptolemy III between 18 Oct. and 31 Dec. 222.
Skeat 1937: 32 places the death of Ptolemy III and the accession of Ptolemy IV between
Choiak 21 (5 Feb. 221) and Tybi 2 (16 Feb. 221).

[74] Heinen 1972: 185, SVF 1.477.

[75] Ingholt 1967-68: 159f. In 197 Egypt lost various possessions in Cilicia, including
Soli, to Antiochus III, Hieron. FGH 260 F46. It is probable that these had been held by
Egypt since the Third Syrian War, Will 1979: 259, Bagnall 1976: 115. An inscription
attests Ptolemaic control of Soli in the late third century BC, Welles 1934, no. 30.

[76] Gurob papyrus, FGH 160. Holleaux 1942: 291-310, in particular 297 n. 2 where he
rejects his earlier view that the events referred to in the papyrus took place solely in
Syria.

reforms. Finally he went to the court of Ptolemy IV Philopator, probably with Cleomenes after the defeat at Sellasia. If he did accompany Cleomenes, he would have been in Egypt at the close of Ptolemy III Euergetes' reign.

It might be argued that there is no need to see any wider political overtones to Sphaerus' wanderings. Ptolemy III may simply have fancied having a Stoic in his court; but why a Stoic? Alexandria was certainly a great intellectual centre, but it attracted scarcely any philosophers.[77] Cleomenes may merely have needed some assistance and intellectual jusification for what he was doing in Sparta. Nevertheless, bearing in mind the overall political context and the international upheaval of the time, it is plausible to view the departure of Sphaerus from an Athens, subordinate to Macedon, to the court of Ptolemy as having political implications, especially as a member of a school that was not unaware of political realities. Indeed it is more than a coincidence that he should be both there and in Sparta at a time when Macedon was coming under increasing stress. Egypt had kept out of Athenian matters since the end of the Chremonidean War.[78] Now after the Third Syrian War had been brought to a conclusion in 241 and Macedon's grip on Greece was weakening, Egypt is found making approaches to the Stoa. This suggests that Ptolemy III was sounding out the situation, being aware of the Stoa's political position and their relationship to his own general, Chremonides. Given the Stoa's approach to politics up to this point, it is surely significant that a Stoic should be at the Egyptian court not long before Athens bought its freedom, especially when another Stoic is found contributing to this liberation.

Sphaerus' interest in Sparta would have been partly due to its internal politics, which included property reforms. These will be discussed in depth in Chapter 6 after an examination of Stoic views on property and justice in Chapter 5. But his interest in Sparta was also because Sparta had a tradition of anti-Macedonian activity, which dates back to long before it became embroiled in the struggle with Antigonus Doson.[79] While the exact details of Sphaerus' manoeuvres might elude us, it is apparent that he was actively involved in contemporary politics and his activities represent no divergence from the main Stoic position as it has been outlined so far. In the process he provoked abuse of himself and other Stoics in the verse of the

[77] The only philosophers of note are Demetrius of Phalerum, who was a political refugee (D.L. 5.78) and Strato, who was tutor to Ptolemy Philadelphos (D.L. 5.58). Fraser 1972: 1.480-85 considers there to be little significant philosophical activity in Alexandria in the third and second centuries BC.

[78] Habicht 1982: 105-6.

[79] Walbank 1957: 239, followed by Urban 1979: 131f, rejects Polybius' claim (2.45.1-5) that there was a Sparta-Aetolia-Macedon coalition early in Cleomenes' reign.

Megalopolitan oligarch and pro-Macedonian, Cercidas.[80]

There is no evidence for political activity on the part of Chrysippus, but at the same time there is nothing to suggest that he would have deviated from his associates in his stance. Certainly in his writings he supported and enlarged upon many of the views of Zeno, such as his analysis of society which has been discussed in Chapter 2. Thus he would be expected to reach similar conclusions about the political situation, but he may have had less interest in politics than some of his fellow Stoics. He wrote a vast number of books on logic, but there are few known titles of works on politics, although they do include a *Peri Politeias*. The list of his works given by Diogenes Laertius is incomplete (D.L. 7.189-202) and this could, therefore, produce a false impression. Indeed Plutarch tells us that he wrote a great many books on political matters (Plut. *St. Rep.* 1033b). His nephew, Aristocreon, did support the liberation of 229 and this may reflect Chrysippus' position. When Chrysippus was asked why he did not take part in politics, he is said to have replied that 'if anyone does bad political acts, it displeases the gods; if he does good ones, it displeases the citizens' (Stobaeus SVF 3.694). A context is lacking but the remark seems to reflect a despairing view of political life as it is practised by bad men.

The ancients clearly thought it significant that he dedicated none of his writings to kings (D.L. 7.185). Plutarch is scornful of his view that the wise man should advise a king and live with him (Plut. *St. Rep.* 1043b-e). What is important is that all references about this cite not contemporary kings, such as the Antigonids, the Seleucids, the Attalids or the Ptolemies, as good examples of kings to advise, but those distant in time and space. The kings referred to are Idanthyrsus, a king of the Scythians in the late sixth century, and Leuco, king of Bosporus, Theodosia and many Scythian tribes in the first half of the fourth century (SVF 3.690-2); incidentally, though perhaps not irrelevant, the latter was a friend of the Athenians. If he had cited contemporary kings, they would surely have been mentioned. This in combination with his refusal to dedicate any of his writings to kings indicates a hostility to these Hellenistic kings, such as the kings of Macedon. This would be consistent with his criticisms of hierarchy in society.

So Chrysippus' political outlook conformed to that of Zeno, whether or not he put it into practice. He was favoured by the renewed democracy, no doubt as the leading representative of a school which supported its existence. For he accepted their offer of Athenian citizenship (Plut. *St. Rep.* 1034a) and it is most likely that this was at the time of the liberated Athens. Between 261 and 229 there are only

---

[80] Powell 1925: 201ff, frag. 8 and 9; Dudley 1937: 82, 93; Walbank 1943: 11. The text is unfortunately very fragmented.

two, or possibly three, known decrees bestowing citizenship, one of which was to a *stratêgos* of Demetrius II, a very pronounced reduction compared to other years.[81] Chrysippus was buried in the Ceramicus and a statue of him was set up there (Paus. 1.29.15, D.L. 7.182), presumably not long after his death in about 206. More significant, perhaps, is the statue of him erected in the Ptolemaeum which was built in the late twenties. It is not known when this statue was erected there, but since the Ptolemaeum symbolised the close relationship between Athens and Ptolemy, the choice of this location for Chrysippus' statue may well have been connected with the policies that Chrysippus espoused. The festival of the Ptolemaia may have had a particular importance for Stoics in the second century BC.[82]

There were other links between the Stoics and Egypt, but it is not clear whether or not they have any bearing on the picture that has been outlined above, although they could result from partiality to Egypt. Zeno had one pupil from Alexandria, Posidonios, about whom nothing else is known (D.L. 7.38). Eratosthenes, who probably listened to both Zeno and Aristo (Strabo SVF 1.338), went to become librarian in Alexandria, probably in the 240s. Aristo is often seen as a heretical Stoic, but the divisions between Zeno and Aristo should not be overemphasised, because there was, as yet, no orthodoxy. None of the third-century scholarchs are known to have had pupils from Macedon, unless one accepts as true the story that Persaeus was sent to Zeno by Antigonus (D.L. 7.36).

So, in conclusion, although the third-century Stoics, as far as we know, did not participate in politics in any official capacity, they were actively involved in other ways and were fully aware of the political situation. Their political thought had developed out of their understanding of it and their behaviour was consistent with this understanding within the limits imposed by the real world – in contrast to their ideal society, which could develop unrestricted. As a result throughout the century they supported a democratic and independent Athens. Whether they had any impact on the course of events cannot really be known, but they did provide intellectual authority for the democratic movement in spite of Antigonus' attempts to have a monopoly over intellectuals. In the process they helped to shape the language in which the struggle against Macedon was seen.

These early Stoics were not politicians but philosophers in whose thought politics was only one element, albeit an important one. It was

---

[81] Habicht 1982: 25; IG II² 808, IG II² 707 and IG II² 570 are the only inscriptions recording the granting of citizenship which may fall within this period, on which Osborne 1982: 172-8. Osborne 1983: 89-90 proposes three other instances, although there is no direct epigraphical evidence for these – they probably fall in the 250s.

[82] On the statue: Paus. 1.17.2; on the Ptolemaeum: Habicht 1982: 112-17; cf. IG II² 1938 for possible Stoic interest in this.

in the role of philosopher that they sought to influence the leading figures of the day. It is not possible to determine with any certainty how far their influence extended, whether they had the support only of some of the prominent nationalists or of a larger proportion of the population. Zeno and his followers met in the Painted Stoa, a public place in a corner of the *agora*, so many had the opportunity to listen to him, though this is no argument that they did. The public nature of the place, however, suggests that they did want their ideas to reach a wider audience. Zeno could sometimes have quite a crowd around him but we are told that he would occasionally ask bystanders for money to make them keep their distance (D.L. 7.14, 16). Indicative of the popularity of the Stoa is an anecdote about Cleanthes (D.L. 7.173, SVF 1.603). When the poet Sositheus ridiculed Cleanthes in the theatre, he was driven off the stage by the audience who applauded Cleanthes.

5

Property and Justice

Within Stoic political thought there exists a tension between the ideal and the actual. How can the advocates of such a radical ideal society come to terms with the world as it is? While being harshly critical of it as their analysis shows, they at the same time advocated participation within the *polis*, within the very society that they condemned. A certain degree of compromise will be involved in this, even if they are concerned to produce change. The question of the nature and extent of their acceptance of contemporary society has been examined in some of its aspects in earlier chapters, but the problem seems particularly acute in the case of property. For in many cities property ownership was the criterion by which political rights were distributed and hence was constitutionally fundamental. In the ideal society there would be no property, but in the present world people, some at least, do possess it. The Stoics could either ignore it, which would be unrealistic if they wish to participate, or, given that there is property, they could ask what the best arrangement would be. They may nevertheless conclude that the only satisfactory arrangement is communal ownership. It is not clear how, if at all, this tension was resolved among the early Stoics, although it appears to be by distortion of the ideal by the time of Panaetius.

1. Property-holding

Since it is necessary to determine the Stoic position on property-holding in contemporary society, it would be appropriate to outline the possible positions they could have held. Their views could fall into three main classes. First, they could have proposed, in the light of their conception of the ideal society, that all property should be held communally. Alternatively they may have made allowance for the short-comings of contemporary society, but argued for reform, that is to say that property should be distributed among a larger number of people and/or that there should be a greater equality of holdings. These first two positions are not mutually exclusive. Thirdly, they could accept the *status quo* and justify the existing distribution of property.

None of these positions would be novel; discussion of all of them can be found in the second book of Aristotle's *Politics*. The examples which Aristotle cites, however, are such that communal ownership or equal distribution of property is limited to the governing part of the community. Yet Aristotle's criticisms of these theories are responses not only to the particular writer he is discussing but also to the whole issue of communal ownership and equal distribution of property, regardless of the proportion of the population it affects. He begins with criticism of common ownership as it is envisaged by Plato in his *Republic* (Arist. *Pol.* 1261b16ff), which would appear to have been limited to the governing class.[1] Later he complains that Plato has not made it clear whether farmers owned their own land or farmed it communally (1264a13ff). Using Plato as his starting point, he proceeds to a more general discussion of common ownership and its defects (1262b37ff). Further, Aristotle (1266a31ff) preserves the only extant account of the thought of Phaleas of Chalcedon, who is said to be the first to argue that social unrest would be reduced if there was an equal division of property. He also proposed that there should be equality of education (*isotês paideias*), though Aristotle professes to be ignorant of the nature and motive of this, but suggests that it is to ensure that everyone is trained to have the same appetites. It is significant however that this theory which could be taken to be democratic in tone demands that all skilled workers are public slaves and are not members of the citizen body. So Aristotle concludes that Phaleas must have had a small number of citizens in mind (1267b13-16). Perhaps Phaleas' conception of a city without conflict has been influenced by the *Homoioi* (Peers) of Sparta. Aristotle in his response to Phaleas does not remain within these limits, but discusses a wide range of problems which he associates with the equal distribution of property, not all of which would be relevant to Phaleas' city.

Although Aristotle is replying to the more conservative proponents of these positions, it is implicit in what he writes that there were others who did not seek to limit these ideas to such a small proportion of the community. Demands from the poorer classes for an equal division of property had a long history. As early as Solon there were unsuccessful attempts to obtain *isomoiria*, equal sharing.[2] Aristophanes in what appears to be a parody of Plato's *Republic* proposes a society where everything is common for all (Aristoph. *Eccl.* 583-729). 'Redistribution of land' became an increasingly popular political slogan in the fourth century and a particularly alarming one

---

[1] In the *Republic* communal ownership is limited to the guardians, *Rep.* 3.416c-17b. On the other hand, Plato *Laws* 5.739c appears to suggest that Plato also conceived of a society in which everything was common for all. But this is a very brief passage that seems to be referring to the ideal society of the *Republic*, so may only in fact be talking of the governing class, Stalley 1983: 92-3, England, *Commentary on Laws* 5.739c.

[2] Arist. *Ath. Pol.* 11.2, Plut. *Solon* 13.3, 16.1, Vlastos 1953: 352-5.

for those with property. In his discussion of the social upheaval in Syracuse in 356 Alexander Fuks has shown that the proposals for broad-based economic equality in the form of the redistribution of land were supported by theoretical justifications. Plutarch gives the justification for the reforms: 'Equality is the starting point of freedom whereas the poverty of the propertyless is the starting point of slavery' (*Dion* 37.5). This should be interpreted as meaning that freedom can only come from economic equality, while poverty leads to the 'economic and social servitude of one man to another'.[3] It is likely that Aristotle was aware of what happened in Syracuse; for Dion had close links with the Academy. Timonides of Leucas, a member of the Academy, took part in the expedition and sent a letter to Speusippus, giving an account of it (*Dion* 35). The roots of the anti-equality argument of Quintilian's 261st Declamation have been traced back to the time of Aristotle.[4] So equality in many forms was clearly a subject of discussion in the period prior to the emergence of the Stoa.

2. Property, the theatre and the Stoa

So what position did the Stoics hold? They certainly did not consider property to be natural. It is absent from the ideal society of Zeno's *Politeia* and in the *De Officiis* of Cicero, derived from the second-century Stoic Panaetius, it is still considered to be a matter of convention (*De Off.* 1.21). But it does not follow from this alone that they proposed that there should be no private property in contemporary society. In the same passage Cicero writes: 'Nothing is private by nature but rather by long occupation ... or by conquest ... or by law, by agreement or by allotment.' And he continues that this is how it should be. So it is quite possible to accept private property, while acknowledging that it is contrary to nature.

It has often been claimed that the early Stoa, at least from Chrysippus onwards, held the third of the positions listed above: whatever their views on property in the ideal society, in contemporary society they acquiesced and supported the *status quo*.[5] If they did adopt such a position, it would make the tension all the more extreme. This argument, however, rests on a passage of Cicero (*De Fin.* 3.67, SVF 3.371), some of which is, I believe, mistakenly attributed to Chrysippus:

> Just as the Stoics think that rights act as bonds between men, so they think that no rights exist between men and animals. For it was well said by Chrysippus that everything else was created for the sake of men and

[3] Fuks 1968: 218-23.
[4] Asheri 1971: 1.309-21.
[5] For instance, Africa 1961: 17, and more cautiously by Reesor 1951: 23, Aalders 1975: 84.

gods; and that men and gods were for community and society, so men could use animals for their own interests without committing an offence; and that since it is the nature of man that a form of civil right exists between himself and the human race, someone who upholds this will be just, someone who departs from this will be unjust. But in the same way as a theatre is common and yet it can rightly be said that the place which each man occupies is his own, so in the city or world, which is common, no right is infringed because what each person has is his own.

Sed quomodo hominum inter homines iuris esse vincula putant, sic homini nihil iuris esse cum bestiis. Praeclare enim Chrysippus cetera nata esse hominum causa et deorum, eos autem communitatis et societatis suae, ut bestiis homines uti ad utilitatem suam possint sine iniuria; quoniamque ea natura esset hominis ut ei cum genere humano quasi civile ius intercederet, qui id conservaret eum iustum qui migraret iniustum fore. Sed quemadmodum, theatrum cum commune sit, recte tamen dici potest eius eum locum quem quisque occuparit, sic in urbe mundove communi non adversatur ius quo minus suum quidque cuiusque sit.

The whole of this passage, including the theatre analogy at the end, is normally attributed to Chrysippus. If this attribution were correct, it would provide grounds for believing that Chrysippus sought to justify not only the possession of private property, but also existing property rights; for occupancy is seen as sufficient reason for continued possession. As it stands, Cicero's argument is hardly a compelling one.

While it is clear that the first part of this passage on the relationship between God, man and animals up to '*iniustum fore*' stems from Chrysippus, it is not at all obvious that the theatre analogy does. The only reason for believing this is because it follows a definite attribution to Chrysippus. The change from *oratio obliqua* to *oratio recta* might suggest that Cicero is no longer reporting Chrysippus' opinion, although there are instances of Cicero making this transition and yet continuing the quotation.[6] Nevertheless there are several other reasons for rejecting this attribution and holding that the theatre analogy, which justified private property, had its origins in the Roman Stoa and was intended as a counter-argument to Chrysippus' views on justice and property.

The analogy, as given by Cicero, would not be incompatible with the Greek theatre, although in a Greek context it would have more egalitarian overtones than in Rome. For the Roman theatre unlike the Greek was a class theatre.[7] In addition to Cicero the analogy also occurs in Seneca (*De Ben.* 7.12.3-6) and Epictetus (*Diss.* 2.4). It is the passage of Seneca which is relevant. For here the analogy between property and seats in the theatre appears in greater detail. Seneca is

[6] Madvig on Cic. *De Fin.* 1.130 gives examples.
[7] Bieber 1961: 189.

attempting to show that, although the wise have everything in common, it is nevertheless possible to bestow a gift on a wise man, because there are certain circumstances in which something can be common property yet at the same time it can belong to a particular individual. To make this clear he introduces the example of the theatre. Here a person might have a right to a seat among the *equites*, which, having occupied, he can give up to another member of the *equites* if he wishes to do so. The seats are the common property of all the *equites*, but a seat is also the property of the person occupying it, who will be bestowing a gift if he yields it. He adds that if the equestrian seats are full, he will not be able to exercise his right to occupy one, although he still possesses the right. Thus Seneca provides an interesting new dimension to the comparison with the theatre; for his example is clearly set in the Roman theatre and includes the question of class allocations. But why does Seneca introduce the *equites* into the argument? Class divisions in the theatre have no relevance to the argument as he presents it. Moreover it was not personally appropriate because he was not a member of the *equites* at the time.[8] It suggests that there was a fuller and earlier version of the argument possibly in the writings of Hecaton which Seneca is believed to have used.[9] Hecaton, a Stoic of the early first century, had an interest in property (cf. Cic. *De Off.* 3.63, 89) and the theatre analogy may be linked to his statement that the private fortunes of individuals are the wealth of the state, '*singulorum facultates et copiae divitiae sunt civitates*' (Cic. *De Off.* 3.63).

The *equites* had had a special allocation of seats since at least the late second century, possibly as early as 146, a right that was taken away at a later date, probably by Sulla.[10] It was restored to a wider range of *equites* by Roscius Otho in 67 BC, who gave them the first fourteen rows in the theatre behind the orchestra which was reserved for senators. So the analogy complete with a discussion of equestrian seating could have originated as early as the late second century BC, before the time of Cicero. It would not have been possible for a reader of the passage of the *De Finibus* to ignore the fact that allocations of seats according to class were an important feature of the theatre as they knew it. If the passages of Cicero and Seneca are considered together, it would indicate that they were both adopting an analogy that had been developed to justify both property rights and in some way the unequal distribution of property. It is not a valid objection to argue

---

[8] Griffin 1976: 455 n. 4.

[9] Ibid. 300, 358.

[10] Hill 1952: 160 suggests that it was the work of C. Gracchus, while Botsford 1909: 356f, 428f dates its origin from 146 BC. Badian 1972: 95 believes that the right was taken away by Sulla. Wiseman 1970: 80, however, argues that the *equites* had never possessed such a right before Roscius Otho, but this requires the rejection of Vel. Pat. 2.32.3, '*equitibus in theatro loca restituit*'.

that because Cicero does not refer to the division of seating by class, the original analogy did not contain it. For Cicero's version is so concise and abbreviated that we can obtain very little idea of how the original had been developed. Its very conciseness leads one to believe that Cicero was not the originator.

The proposition that occupancy justifies continued possession is a key feature of a series of Hecaton's arguments recorded by Cicero in the *De Officiis* 3.89-90. If a fool has grabbed a plank from a sinking ship in order to save himself, it would be unjust for a wise man to take it away from him; this is unjust, one assumes, because occupancy of the plank establishes possession. In a further case in which there are two wise men and one unoccupied plank, other criteria have to be used to decide who should have it. If a plank is occupied by one of the passengers, not even the owner of the ship is justified in seizing the plank; for the ship is said to belong to the passengers for the duration of the voyage because they have hired it. So this adds another element – the ship is seen as analogous to the theatre; it is the common property of the passengers.

These analogies to the theatre and the ship seek to show, as is apparent from Cicero in the *De Finibus*, that something can be both private property and in a sense common. Cicero put forward an earlier version of this argument about occupancy elsewhere in the *De Officiis*, an argument which almost certainly derives from Panaetius, the teacher of Hecaton.[11] Land, which is common by nature, becomes private property through occupancy. There are no analogies and the course of the argument shows that such analogies would be inappropriate. For no attempt is made to argue that something can be both common and private property. It is clear in this argument that it ceases to be common when it becomes private property (Cic. *De Off.* 1.21). Panaetius drew a clear distinction between what is private property and what is common: it is one of the tasks of justice to ensure that what is common is used for common purposes and what is private is used by the owner (Cic. *De Off.* 1.20, Panaetius F.105). So the theatre analogy that occurs in Cicero's *De Finibus* would appear to be a development from Panaetius' position, an attempt to make compatible the ideas of the early Stoa with those of the later.[12]

So far the theatre analogy has been discussed in isolation, but, if it is examined in its context, it gives little encouragement to the view that it is the work of Chrysippus. The part of the argument which is definitely attributable to Chrysippus is self-contained, but the link with property is not immediately obvious and so the reference to it

[11] Hecaton of Rhodes as a pupil of Panaetius, Cic. *De Off.* 3.63, Panaetius F.154.

[12] Although much of *De Finibus* 3 is held to represent fairly accurately the views of the early Stoa, chs. 62-8 are an exception, Reesor 1951: 38-40 suggests Posidonius as a source, cf. Schäfer 1934: 47.

appears to represent a digression. The early part discusses the relationship between men and that between men and animals. We are told that, while law governs relationships between men, it has no bearing on men's relationship with animals and hence man can use animals as he thinks fit. There are many references to these subjects, considering both the exclusion of animals from the sphere of justice (SVF 3.367-76) and the fact that animals and plants are created for the sake of man (SVF 2.1152-67), but it is only in Cicero that there is a defence of private property attached. The form of argument which is found in this passage of the *De Finibus* occurs several times in Cicero's works, although without reference to Chrysippus. In the *De Officiis*, a work heavily influenced by Panaetius, he refers to the produce of the earth being for the sake of men and common to all men, but he always adds the qualification that one should not imagine that this affects private property. So at *De Officiis* 1.51: 'All things which nature has produced for the common use of men should be kept as common, with the proviso that those things which are assigned by statutes and civil law should be held as laid down by those laws, while everything else should be considered as in the Greek proverb, everything is common among friends.' The emphasis on the statutes and civil law here adds further to the suspicions that this defence of private property had its origin in Rome with all its legal preoccupations. A similar view is expressed at *De Off.* 1.21. All three passages follow the same line of argument that everything may be common, but occupancy justifies private property.[13]

The curious jump which Cicero makes from Chrysippus' account of justice to a defence of property rights is only intelligible if that account did undermine property rights. Chrysippus had said that everything was for the sake of gods and men and talked of the community, *communitas*, that existed between gods and men. A similar view is preserved by Arius Didymus, who writes that there is a *koinônia* (community) between gods and men, because both share in reason (*logos*). Everything else, that is everything that does not possess reason, is for the sake of these (SVF 2.528, cf. SVF 3.367-76). It is clear from the response that this community of men and gods meant that those things which were outside the sphere of justice were not only for the sake of gods and men but also the common possessions of them. It is a recurring theme that all things are common but with the qualification that this does not affect private property. The link with justice is apparent too in Panaetius when he says that it is just that what is common is used for common purposes, but his conception of

---

[13] Ambrose, who modelled his *De Officiis Ministrorum* on Cicero's *De Officiis*, neatly comments on the inadequacies of this argument in a way that the early Stoics would doubtless have approved, Ambrose *De Off.* 1.132. Swift 1979 compares the two arguments.

what is common is much narrower than that of the early Stoa. Later Stoics, disagreeing with Chrysippus but not accepting Panaetius' solution, contended that it was possible for something to be both common and private, hence the theatre analogy.

The structure of the *De Finibus* precludes the possibility that the theatre analogy is Cicero's own. For book 3 gives an account of Stoic theory put into the mouth of Cato, a Roman adherent of the Stoa in the first century BC; Cicero's objections to it do not occur until the next book. Consequently any arguments against Chrysippus in book 3 must represent those of the Stoics themselves, attempting to counter Chrysippus' rejection of private property. It would certainly have been odd for Chrysippus himself to have put forward a thesis and then immediately have denied its implications. The early Stoics were notorious for single-mindedly pursuing the implications of their thought to the point of paradox. It is more understandable that later members of the school, embarrassed by the conclusions of their predecessors and writing in different circumstances, should react against them.

A similar fear that certain Stoic notions could undermine property rights is present in other passages. In the third book of the *De Officiis*, there is a debate between two Stoics of the second century BC, Antipater of Tarsus and Diogenes of Babylon. In this shock is expressed by Diogenes at the thought that the fellowship which exists between men (*societas inter homines natura coniuncta*) might deny private property (*De Off*. 3.53, words reminiscent of *De Fin*. 3.67). Seneca in the seventh book of the *De Beneficiis* devotes considerable space to proving that the thesis that everything belongs to the wise is not incompatible with private property (*De Ben*. 7.4-12). All these ideas (i.e. that everything is common by nature, that the wise possess all things, and those on the nature of justice and the bonds that link all men) are seen not as comfortable propositions but threatening ones. Instead of being vigorously espoused, they call for qualifications and defensiveness. All these passages see the rejection of property rights as implicit in these propositions, but they do not always make clear why this should be so. The ostensibly unprovoked determination to show that these propositions did not need to have undesirable consequences for property rights can only be explained if the early Stoics did indeed draw such conclusions. Otherwise it indicates paranoia on the part of the later Stoics. Thus the later Stoics were burdened with ideas which while agreeable in principle were distinctly distasteful in their consequences.

3. Christianity and Stoic arguments on property

It is with the emergence of Christianity as a significant factor that arguments which seek to question prevailing views about the legitimacy of wealth and property ownership again become current.

The concern of these arguments is usually not so much to alter radically the distribution of property, but rather to encourage the rich to give to the Church and engage in charitable activity.[14] Christian writers frequently denigrated pagan philosophers, arguing that their ideas were filched from the scriptures and that Moses had anticipated them in many areas (cf. Ambrose *De Off.* 1.133, Clem. Al. *Strom.* 1.25, PG 8.912-17). Nevertheless there was great ambivalence towards pagan philosophers and Christian intellectuals were prepared to borrow from them where necessary.

At this point it is useful to look at two Christian arguments in particular. There are several reasons for doing this. First, they show that such arguments about property as those which I have attributed to the early Stoa were put forward in the ancient world, even if at a later date. Secondly, although they were written well into the Christian era, they contain signs of Stoic influence. Consequently they can help to give a more complete picture of the arguments of the early Stoa.

One of these arguments is provided by John Chrysostom, Bishop of Constantinople at the end of the fourth century AD, a man whose denunciations of wealth and luxury did little to endear him to the rich. John was a pupil of the pagan rhetorician, Libanius, in Antioch and must have been well-trained in the classics, as is apparent from his pure Attic style, which has been compared to that of Demosthenes. He demonstrates a knowledge of classical authors, including philosophers, although he is not necessarily favourable to them. He could claim that the *Politeiai* of Zeno and Plato were inspired by evil spirits and demons.[15]

In his twelfth homily on 1 Timothy John creates a dispute with an imaginary rich man (PG 62.562-4). He argues that wealth, which includes such things as land, houses, slaves and money, is not a good; for if it were, then the possessor would be good and the more he acquired the better he would become. Yet, he says, there is an evident contradiction in this, because wealth is acquired by injustice. Against the objection that much wealth is inherited and therefore ownership does not involve injustice, John argues that it must originally have been acquired by injustice. For in the beginning God did not make one

[14] On Christian attitudes to property: De Ste Croix 1975, Grant 1978: 96-123.
[15] Baur 1959: 305-14. Wilamowitz 1912: 296 compares John's style to that of Demosthenes. The *Politeiai* of Zeno and Plato: *Hom. on Matt.* 1.4, PG 57.18-19. For John's knowledge of Stoicism: PG 48.670, Paul and the Stoics; PG 50.546, on Stoic incest; PG 60.270, on conflagration; PG 60.414, rebelling against Aristotle; PG 48.886, Zeno. Young 1983: 158 notes the 'subtle blend of Stoic and Christian motifs' in the letters to the rich deaconess Olympias. Coleman-Norton 1930: 305-17 demonstrates John's extensive knowledge of Greek philosophers. Sometimes John is hostile to pagan philosophers and classical education, but this should be seen in its context, cf. *Hom. in Eph.* 21.2, PG 62.152.

man rich and another poor. Instead he gave the same earth to all. 'Since the earth is common (*koinê*), how is it that you can have many acres of land and another man none at all?' Wealth which is acquired by chance, for instance by finding a gold seam, might seem immune from the charge of injustice, but to keep it for oneself is morally wrong. The Lord is common and so are his possessions; to attempt to enjoy alone what is common is therefore unjust. In the same way as the emperor's possessions, such as cities and market places, are common and shared equally (*pantes to ison metechomen*), so too are those of God. In support of this claim John introduces the fact that the sun, air, earth and water apply to all equally (*ek isês*) and that God made all men the same. Problems begin when people wish to possess things for themselves alone and use the words 'yours' and 'mine'. Where there is no property, there are no disputes and this situation is according to nature, *kata phusin*.

The second argument is put forward by an enigmatic writer called Epiphanes, about whom little is known, apart from some doubtful biographical details in Clement of Alexandria. He wrote a work, *On Justice*, passages of which are preserved by Clement.[16] Clement's hostility is mainly directed at Epiphanes' views on sex, in particular community of women; the distortion that this creates, however, is offset by the lengthy passages that Clement quotes. In these the chief subject is not women but justice and property. The way in which morally controversial ideas distort perceptions of the work as a whole recalls the similar treatment of Zeno's *Politeia*.

On Justice must have been written some two hundred years before John's homily, but the two works contain several common features. The argument is to show that property is not in accordance with God's design, i.e. it is contrary to nature, and that everything should be common. Like John he attacks the concepts of 'yours' and 'mine'. Justice is several times described as *koinônia met' isotêtos*, community with equality, and therefore everyone should share equally of God's creation. Some of the arguments used to justify this also appear in John. The light of the sun, which derives from God, is equal for all who can see. So God does not make distinctions between people, whether they are rich or poor, rulers or subjects, male or female, free or slave; Epiphanes goes so far as to include animals. God ensures that nobody can get twice as much light as his neighbour. Furthermore, within a species all are constituted the same. In addition to these arguments which feature with variations in John he also argues that equality is a integral feature of the universe; the heavens are a circle equidistant

[16] Clement *Strom.* 3.2. The question of Epiphanes' existence is discussed in Chadwick/Oulton 1954: 25-9, a volume that also contains a translation, but in the present discussion only the existence of the argument is relevant. Also Grant 1978: 105-7.

from the earth and, less plausibly, all stars shine equally brightly. Thus Epiphanes produces arguments from nature and the divine order to support arithmetic equality; all should be treated the same.[17] God, we are told, made every thing for man to be common property such as vines and corn, but men's laws were inconsistent with the community and equality established by divine law and put an end to it.

In spite of being present in Christian writers these two similar arguments owe much to the influence of ancient philosophers. It is significant and surprising that neither writer adduces evidence from the Scriptures to support his case.[18] The rejection of 'mine' and 'yours' appears as early as Plato (*Rep.* 5.462b-e, cf. *Laws* 5.739cd). The overall argument, however, with its stress on the natural and divine origins of equality and community of property, is not Platonic and has more in common with Stoic perceptions of the world. Indeed not only are the arguments similar in drift to those which I have attributed to the early Stoics, but they also show distinct Stoic traits. John's argument begins by asserting that wealth is not a good, recalling the Stoic thesis that wealth is indifferent and only the morally good is good. Stoic thought is also apparent in the claim that the absence of property is in accordance with nature, *kata phusin* (cf. Cic. *De Off.* 1.21). At one point John describes men as fellow slaves, *sundouloi*, a description that accords with Stoic views of mankind, at least in their present condition. Epiphanes proposes community of women, something concomitant with the abolition of property; his extreme version seems to be closer to Zeno than to the more restrained version of Plato. Further, he sees the produce of the earth as being for the sake of man, echoing Chrysippus, although he has an ambivalent attitude as regards animals, as he seems to lack the Stoic respect for rationality. His argument that the sun epitomises justice may be related to the importance of the sun in Stoic thought, in particular the thought of Cleanthes who made the sun the *hêgemonikon* (governing element) of the universe.[19] Both writers follow the Stoics in stressing how everything is naturally common and link this to justice. They differ from Cicero's presentation of Stoic arguments because they draw the conclusions which he rejected and which I have contended that the early Stoics also drew. It is not being suggested here that John Chrysostom and Epiphanes are simply putting forward Stoic arguments, but rather that the

---

[17] It is useful here to distinguish arithmetic equality from proportionate equality. The recipients will be a and b, the goods to be distributed will be c and d.

Distribution according to arithmetic equality: a=b, c=d.

Distribution according to proportionate equality: a:c=b:d, or a:b=c:d.

[18] In the case of Epiphanes it must be remembered that we do not possess a full text of this part, but it is true of the extant passages which include the argument discussed here.

[19] Arius Didymus, Ps. Censorinus, Aetius, Cicero SVF 1.499, D.L. 7.139. For the role of the sun in ancient, in particular Stoic, political thought, Bidez 1932.

arguments which they use have their origins in the early Stoa. Consequently they are affected by other influences and thus represent the integration of Christianity and Greek philosophy. Nevertheless, they do give some idea of how the Stoic argument was developed.

John's argument also gives a clue as to the original purpose of the theatre analogy. According to him God's creation is common in the same way as public property such as the *agora*, an argument which is intended to undermine accepted property rights. The theatre analogy in Cicero is very similar to this; the theatre is both a public property and common, but the interpretation of it is the opposite to that of John. Cicero's analogy can be most easily understood as providing a counter-example to an argument of the type put forward by John. Not all public property is common in the same way; the *agora* is not common in the same way as a theatre, because in the theatre people have possession of their seat for the duration of the performance. If the theatre analogy is meant to demonstrate an exception and thus act as a counter-example, then it no longer appears as weak an argument as it does at first sight. Its purpose is not so much to justify property ownership as to reject an attack on the *status quo* made by the early Stoa. The Stoic influence on John's argument has already been shown and is apparent in this analogy. Moreover, the description of public property as common can also be found in Panaetius.[20]

So the early Stoics and these Christian writers held that everything which was for the sake of man was common and argued that it was just that what was common should be for common use. The role of justice is important in both cases, but in the Christian writers this goes with a stress on equality. In the case of Epiphanes an examination of both God and nature shows that concern for arithmetic equality is a key feature of God's justice. It is necessary now to look further at the Stoic account of justice.

4. Justice and property

The Stoics emphasised the social nature of justice. Chrysippus had said that no man could be unjust in isolation and consequently he attacked Plato for concentrating on a single unjust man and his internal troubles (Plut. *St. Rep.* 1041bc, SVF 3.288-9). Indeed not only was the Stoic conception of justice social, but it transcended conventional social units. As Emile Bréhier has remarked, before the Stoics justice and right were inseparable from the social forms in which they were realised, afterwards they were independent.[21] For in Stoic thought a man was just because he was obedient to the law which

---

[20] Cic. *De Off.* 1.53; for Panaetius' interest in public property, see Cic. *De Off.* 2.60, Panaetius F.122, cf. D.L. 7.125, SVF 3.590..

[21] Bréhier 1951: 264.

existed by nature, right reason, which dictated what one should and
what one should not do (D.L. 7.128, SVF 3.308, Marcianus SVF 3.314).
This law could only be realised to a limited extent in the laws of any
city. Chrysippus even went so far as to condemn the laws of all cities as
off the mark, a comment that has similarities with Epiphanes'
condemnation of man-made laws (Eusebius SVF 3.324).

Our knowledge of Stoic thought on justice is limited, as so often, by
the nature of the sources. These, since they are summaries, tend to
repeat the same general statements and definitions without providing
details, often leaving statements that seem remarkable for their
blandness. Yet Chrysippus devoted a whole work to justice
(*dikaiosunê*), to which Plutarch gives much space, but Plutarch's
selectiveness obscures Chrysippus' thesis (esp. Plut. *St. Rep.*
1040a-42a); Zeno, Herillus, Cleanthes and Sphaerus all wrote on law
or legislation (D.L. 7.4, 166, 175, 178), books about which we know
little. As a result there are no clear statements of what justice would
demand in the sphere of social organisation, although the end-product
can be seen in their conception of an ideal society.

A limited reconstruction can be obtained from what remains of their
discussions of justice as a virtue. From Zeno onwards the central
feature of justice is seen as *aponemêsis* (Plut. SVF 1.200-1, Stobaeus
SVF 3.264). All forms of justice are reduced to this; justice is defined as
a disposition or form of knowledge which renders to each what is in
accordance with worth, *hexis aponemêtikê tou kat' axian hekastôi* and
epistemê aponemêtikê tês axias hekastôi (Stob. *Ecl.* 2.84.13-17, 59.9-10,
Andronicus SVF 3.266). Associated with justice are equality (*isotês*)
and fairmindedness (*eugnômosunê*) (D.L. 7.126, SVF 3.295). Justice is
said to have four subordinate virtues, piety (*eusebia*), kindness
(*chrêstotês*), justice in exchange (*eusunallaxia*) and *eukoinônêsia*. Of
interest in particular for political thought is *eukoinônêsia*, which is
defined as knowledge of equality in *koinônia* (Stob. *Ecl.* 60.22-4, 62.2-6,
SVF.264). So it is apparent that equality does have a role in their
account of justice.

A suitable approach might be to begin with the proposition, almost
certainly held by Chrysippus, that *oikeiôsis* is the starting point of
justice.[22] *Oikeiôsis* has two related senses for the Stoa. It is the affinity
between an animal and its constitution which begins at birth and
ensures its survival (D.L. 7.85-6, SVF 3.178). Because man has reason
this affinity with his own constitution develops into an affinity with
other human beings, so that he behaves justly to them.[23] This *oikeiôsis*

[22] Porphyry SVF 1.197 – Von Arnim lists this under Zeno, but its attribution to *hoi apo
Zênônos* could be taken to refer to those after Zeno. Chrysippus discussed the subject in
his *On Justice*, Plut. *St. Rep.* 1038bc, SVF 3.179, 2.724, cf. D.L. 7.85-6.
[23] For instance, Cic. *De Fin.* 3.62-8. This second form of *oikeiôsis* is not directly
attested for the early Stoa; it may be that *oikeiôsis* as the starting point of justice (see n.

to others is only truly present in the wise man who has fully developed reason. The problematic transition from egoism to altruism was never adequately resolved and became the subject of attacks from the sceptical Academy in the second century BC. The ideal situation is best presented by Hierocles, a Stoic philosopher of the second century AD.[24] A man is surrounded by concentric circles, the closest of these contains his relatives, further out are his fellow citizens and finally the whole human race. A good man should try to bring all these circles as close as possible. Ideally therefore there should be no difference between his attitude to himself and his attitude to everyone else. That the object of the second form of *oikeiôsis* is to treat all equally is apparent also in an anonymous commentary on Plato's *Theaetetus* from the second century AD, but which may reflect the arguments of Carneades in the second century BC. In the commentary it is argued that it is impossible to have equal affinity with everyone.[25] Hierocles' picture is in direct opposition to Aristotle's account of the obligations of justice and friendship to those close to and distant from one (Arist. *NE* 8.1159b25-60a8).

The account of *oikeiôsis* is concerned with how a person becomes just, how they make the transition from egoism to altruism, rather than with what justice entails or the principles on which justice is based. Nevertheless, it is important because it demonstrates the Stoic concern with the eradication of distinctions in matters of justice. It also draws attention to the opposition between Aristotle and the Stoics which will become more apparent below.

The drive towards equality which is evident in the account of *oikeiôsis* is also present in one of the subordinate virtues of justice, *eukoinônêsia*. This subdivision of justice is defined as the knowledge of equality in *koinônia*, in other words where there is community or sharing (Stob. *Ecl.* 2.62.3-4, SVF 3.264). This phrase, *epistêmê isotêtos en koinôniai*, bears a strong resemblance to Epiphanes' definition of justice as community with equality, *koinônia met' isotêtos*, which was noted in the last section. We have seen that there is a *koinônia* between gods and men, because they both share in reason, and that everything else is for the sake of these (Arius Didymus SVF 2.528, cf. SVF 3.367-76). Implicit in this is the idea that these things, the produce of the earth and heavens, are common to men and the gods.

---

22) is only personal *oikeiôsis*. But the fact that Chrysippus did talk of *oikeiôsis* not only to oneself but also to one's children (Plut. *St. Rep.* 1038b, SVF 3.179, 2.724) suggests that he did hold the second form as well. On this see Pembroke 1971: 122-3, 128-9.

[24] Hierocles, Fragment p. 61 lines 10-26, Arnim. Hierocles does not use the term *oikeiôsis*, but it is clear that this is what he means from a papyrus containing an argument which attacks this theory as *oikeiôsis*, see n. 25.

[25] *Anonymer Kommentar zu Platons Theaetet (Pap. 9782)*, ed. Diels und Schubert (Berlin 1905), *Berliner Klassikertexte*, Hefte II, col. 5.14-7.9. On Carneades, Pembroke 1971: 128-9.

This is brought out more clearly in the passage of Cicero's *De Finibus* which quotes Chrysippus. Here not only are such things understood to be the common property of the community of men and the gods, but this is related to justice, prompting the counter-argument of the theatre analogy. John Chrysostom goes a stage further and introduces equality: such things should be shared equally. While such passages demonstrate that everything should be common, they fail to show clearly why justice should lead to these conclusions, conclusions which the later Stoics and John Chrysostom in their different ways feel do little to justify private property.

Justice was defined by the early Stoa as rendering to each what is according to worth, *aponemêsis tou kat' axian*. Within the several subdivisions of justice equality is only used in the definition of *eukoinônêsia*. If this is applied to the community (*koinônia*) of men and gods, it would suggest that each person as a member of that community is regarded as equal in so far as they possess reason. For it is sharing in reason which makes them all part of this community, whereas anything that does not possess reason is outside the community and, therefore, also outside the sphere of justice (cf. Sext. Emp. SVF 3.370). Given this equality it would be just that everything else which is for the sake of those within the community should be common and shared equally. Nobody has more right to it than anyone else. This interpretation gains support from the arguments that Cicero puts forward in defence of private property, drawing on Stoic sources. On several occasions, as we have seen, he argues that occupancy justifies possession, an argument also put forward by John Chrysostom's imaginary interlocutor.[26] Since such an argument ignores the qualities of the occupant himself, it presupposes that the case for equality has already been made and concentrates instead on the fact of occupancy.

An objection might be raised against the above argument. For it is held by some scholars that the remains of the Stoic account of justice suggest that it was very similar to that of Aristotle. When such comparisons are made, it is Aristotle's account of particular justice in the *Nicomachean Ethics* that is meant, or more precisely his account of distributive justice. For Aristotle divided particular justice into two types, one of which was distributive justice, *to en dianomêi dikaion* (*NE* 5.1131a10-31b24). He argued that such things as money and honour should be distributed according to worth, *axia*. The criteria by which worth is determined might vary; for instance in democracy it is freedom, in an oligarchy wealth or noble birth and in an aristocracy excellence (*aretê*). Equality, *isotês*, is considered an integral feature of justice. Since people are not equal, however, the just distributor will

---

[26] The 'occupancy' argument was developed before Cicero, see above, §3.

not give equal amounts to each person, rather the ratio of a person's worth to the share awarded to him will be equal for all. Thus in an oligarchy a rich man will have a greater share of political rights than a poor man, but within the context of the oligarchy this is just, because wealth is the criterion by which worth is judged. Equality in this sense will be described as proportionate equality (see n. 17).

If the Stoic account was along these lines, as some have suggested, there would be reason to believe that the Stoics did not use *isotês* in the way that I have suggested, that is to say arithmetic equality as opposed to proportionate equality. The similarity between Aristotle and the Stoics, however, is superficial and in many respects the Stoic account appears to be opposed to that of Aristotle. Indeed John Chrysostom takes it as generally accepted that the Stoics attacked Aristotle (*In Epist. ad Rom. Homil.* 3.23, PG 60.414). The main reason for the comparison is that for the Stoics justice is *aponemêsis* while for Aristotle it is *dianomê* and in both cases this is done according to worth. The similarity in the terms is made more misleading by the translation of both *aponemêsis* and *dianomê* as 'distribution'.[27] This obscures the difference in the use of the two terms. For the Stoics the whole of justice is defined as *aponemêsis* and so any just act involves *aponemêsis*. Aristotle, however, does not consider that any type of justice actually is *dianomê*. Rather, as his text makes clear, he is giving an account of justice which is concerned with distribution, *to en dianomêi dikaion* (*NE* 5.1131b10, 1130b31). *Dianomê* is only important to his account because he is discussing the distribution of common goods; it is not in itself a feature of justice. For the Stoics the situation is quite different. *Aponemêsis* is an integral part of justice, whether the just act concerns the distribution of common goods or the saving of a drowning person. The prefix of *dianomê* implies division and the term is used in that sense by Aristotle, but such an implication is not so apparent in *aponemêsis* and would be inappropriate for many instances of justice. A more suitable translation of *aponemêsis* would be 'rendering'; it is used in this sense by Aristotle when he is considering the obligations due to friends and relatives.[28] Thus since the Stoics are here concerned with justice as a whole, not a particular part of it, they use a more general term and use it in a different way. Because they are defining justice as *aponemêsis*, they are led into a discussion of what is common. For Aristotle, on the other hand, the question of what is common is not important; he is concerned with the question of how such things should be distributed.

This has ramifications for the Stoic use of *axia* and *isotês*. Aristotle

---

[27] Reesor 1951: 13, Griffin 1976: 158-9.

[28] Arist. *NE* 9.1164b23, 65a18, 65a32. Translated as 'render' or 'owe' by Rackham, 'render' or 'assign' by Ross. Pearson 1891: 175 uses 'render' for the Stoic *aponemô* and points out that it is more general in meaning than Aristotle's *to en dianomêi dikaion*.

uses *axia* in the context of a direct relationship between unequal parties; either to describe the differing merits of potential recipients of the same distribution or the differing values of commodities in an exchange (*NE* 5.1131a10-b24, 1133a5-b28). The determination of *axia* would have no purpose if there was only one recipient or one commodity. But the Stoa are applying the term to a much broader range of just acts. These include cases where justice is directed to a single person, for instance in cases of kindness or punishment. So in Aristotle's account of justice the merits of the various parties are decided by reference to each other, not independently. It is on account of this that there is a need for proportionate equality. In the Stoic account, on the other hand, merit is determined by reference to a universal standard, that is to say law or right reason. Our sources preserve an account of punishment which demonstrates this. Punishments are rendered according to worth, *kat' axian*, and are described as 'fixed by law'.[29] The law would be universal law; for it allows no resort to equity or mercy.[30]

If the Stoics had used *isotês* in the sense of proportionate equality, rather than the arithmetic equality which I have proposed, then it would be expected that proportionate equality would be fundamental to their account of justice in exchange, as it was for Aristotle (Arist. *NE* 5.1133a5-b28). Yet for them justice in exchange is the knowledge of conducting exchanges blamelessly with one's neighbours (Stobaeus SVF 3.264, cf. Andronicus SVF 3.273). There is no mention of equality in spite of the fact that it occurred in the definition of *eukoinônêsia* in the previous sentence of Stobaeus. This would suggest that *isotês* was not used to mean proportionate equality, although such an argument from silence should be treated with caution.

Aristotle suggests that such things as wealth, freedom, noble birth and moral worth could be valid criteria for just distributions. The Stoics, even if they were considering the same problem as Aristotle, would have objected to much of this. Their contempt for social status such as nobility and for certain forms of hierarchy, in particular the slave/master relationship, would indicate that they did not acknowledge the validity of those differences in status which Aristotle used as criteria by which just distributions could be made. Indeed the Stoic concept of universal law would have to reject such a relativist assumption that what was just could be affected by the type of constitution one lived under. In this respect they had more in common with Plato and other utopian philosophers. For a school which rejected all divisions within a community and defined a *polis* as a collection of

---

[29] *hai ek tou nomou tetagmenai kolaseis* Stob. *Ecl.* 2.96.4-9, SVF 3.640, cf. *hai epiballousai ek tou nomou kolaseis*, D.L. 7.123, SVF 3.641. *To epiballon* is equivalent to *axia* as used in the Stoic definition of justice, Stob. *Ecl.* 2.84.13-17, SVF 3.125.

[30] SVF 3.640-1, Rist 1978: 267f.

people living in the same place, it is improbable that they would claim that justice demanded the recognition of divisions which they rejected and which had no basis in nature.

Thus it cannot be argued on the basis of the similarity of the terms used by Aristotle and the Stoics that the arguments in which these terms were used were the same or even similar. Their overall context must be considered and what remains of the Stoic context suggests that the arguments were not similar. Indeed there are several respects in which the Stoics seem to be expressing opposition to Aristotle. They abandoned the Aristotelian distinction between general justice and particular justice. For the Stoics all justice is united as rendering to each according to worth. The way in which they used variations on Aristotelian terminology but changed the context and hence the sense also indicates conscious opposition to Aristotle. They used *aponemô* instead of *dianemô* and widened its scope so that it embraced justice as a whole, rather than only applying to distributive justice. Another instance of the rejection of the Aristotelian use of terminology is apparent in their use of *diorthôsis*. In Aristotle's account of justice this refers to the correction of an unjust act, the equalisation of loss and gain, but in Stoic thought it refers also to the correction of the soul that comes as a result of punishment.[31]

So it is possible to see how the Stoic claim that everything is common can be derived from their ideas on justice. Men in so far as they are possessors of reason are equal. Since everything which does not possess reason is for the sake of man, it is only just that as men all should share it equally.

5. Conclusion

Nevertheless, although in theory everything is common, in practice this is clearly not the case. The theme of the injustice of property ownership in contemporary society occurs in a passage of Diogenes Laertius. Here it is said that bad men own their property in the same way that unjust men do; they are only the users of it. In other words they have no right to it because it is acquired by injustice (cf. John Chrysostom), whereas everything belongs to the wise.[32] This is not inconsistent with the claim that everything is common. It is not saying that everything is only the property of the wise, but that only the wise unlike fools appreciate the true nature of community of property. For fools by claiming things as their own personal property are unjustly

---

[31] Clem. Al. SVF 3.332, if it is accepted that Clement is here using a Stoic term.

[32] D.L. 7.125, SVF 3.590, clearly early Stoic, Inwood 1977: 100. Cf. Sen. *De Ben*. 7.4ff, but Seneca is trying to show that the claim that everything belongs to the wise does not affect existing property rights. Injustice does not enter the discussion; instead he argues that there can be dual ownership with the person actually in possession having priority.

rejecting the community of property.

The early Stoa objected to private property, but what they thought should be done about it is more obscure. Cicero does not tell us what their conclusions were, only what was wrong with them. Discussion of property would have entailed consideration of contemporary society with all its failings. Here concessions were made; for instance, the wise man might marry and have children within marriage. Thus, although they did not seek to justify existing property arrangements, it would not be surprising if there was not an outright rejection of property. They did reject slavery, but this was because injustice was involved in the very act of owning a slave. Moderate ownership, *summetros ktêsis*, was considered to be a preferred indifferent, while its opposite was to be rejected (Stob. *Ecl.* 2.81.5-6, SVF 3.136). Presumably the possession of a moderate amount of property is meant by this, the opposite of which would be possession of either too much or too little. This would suggest that they saw an equal or approximately equal distribution of property as desirable, a view which would accord with the conception of justice already proposed. At the same time the phrase could also apply to the common property of the ideal society. It is not specified that this has to be private property. Aristotle could describe *ktêsis* either as common, *koinê*, or as private, *idia* (Arist. *Pol.* 1264a15-16). If this phrase does allow a limited acceptance of private property, it does not contradict the arguments given above. For it is only after it has been argued that existing unequal property arrangements are unsatisfactory that an alternative can be proposed, whether on the basis of common ownership or equal ownership. The former would be more desirable and what would be expected in the ideal society, but the latter would at least fulfil the demands of justice.

Just as the Syracusans in 356 BC, when demanding redistribution of land, had equated freedom with equality and slavery with poverty, that is to say inequality, so too did the early Stoics and both surely had similar ends in mind. One of the major criticisms the early Stoics made about contemporary society was the prevalence of inequality in the form of subordination within it (see Chapter 2). Thus equality in property rights, whether by communal ownership or equal distribution, would have seemed an appropriate goal to them. It would alleviate in some way the existing inequality and perhaps provide a suitable framework in which to improve society.

So some idea of the approach of the early Stoa to property can be formed. While they rejected individual property ownership completely in the ideal society where there would be communal ownership, in contemporary society they may have been prepared to make concessions. Their conception of justice and their belief in the desirability of equality may have led them to argue, at the least, for the equal distribution of property, that is to say the produce of nature which was common to all men and for their sake. There could be no justification of existing property rights, so they may have accepted that a state could legitimately redistribute property on the basis of equality. For reasons that will become apparent in the next two chapters, these arguments were not attractive to later Stoics and were consequently rejected. The early Stoic arguments on property provide an interesting contrast with earlier writers. Such writers as Plato and Phaleas advocated common or equal ownership of property for its consequences, such as harmony in the state. For the Stoics, on the other hand, such a position was not only a means to an end but also the natural outcome of certain other principles which they held.

6

The Spartan Revolution

In earlier centuries Sparta had been the arch-exponent of oligarchy, the spiritual homeland of the Greek upper classes. Now in the third century BC, proclaiming a return to the Sparta of Lycurgus, it gained the support of the impoverished masses of the Peloponnese. Such a bizarre and anomalous situation deserves attention. This revived Sparta proved a threat to the Achaean League on two levels; its military strength led to the erosion of Achaean superiority within the Peloponnese, while its ideological stance threatened to undermine the established social order. Aratus, the leading politician of the Achaean League, denounced the Spartan king, Cleomenes, above all for the abolition of wealth and the correction of poverty, *anairesis ploutou kai penias epanorthôsis* (Plut. *Cleom.* 16.6-7). Military reforms and a talented general may help to explain Cleomenes' success on the field but not the social unrest he provoked among those classes most likely to be suspicious of Sparta. It will be argued here that it was Stoicism which gave the Spartan revolution its coherency and potency. It was because the revolution was seen to be founded on ideals that had a universal attraction that its impact was so widespread.

1. The revolutionary reigns of Agis and Cleomenes

When Agis IV came to the throne in 244 or 243,[1] Sparta had long been in decline, a decline which was exacerbated by the loss of Messenia and the economic effects of Alexander's conquests. The explanation for this is much debated and need not concern us here, but its symptoms were clear enough. The division between rich and poor grew wider and wealth became confined to fewer and fewer people. In consequence many Spartiates could not afford to make their contributions to the *sussitia* (common messes) and simply disappeared from the citizen body, relegated to the status of *hupomeiones*, inferiors. Aristotle had considered the extreme inequality of property-holding and the

---

[1] For dates in Agis' reign: Tarn 1928: 734-5, Beloch 1925: 623-8, Walbank 1933: 181-3, rather than Ferrabino 1921: 280-1, who dates all events two years earlier, rejected by Walbank.

resulting diminution of the citizen body to be important features of
Sparta's decline (Arist. *Pol.* 1270a15ff). By the time of Agis' accession
there were, it is said, only seven hundred citizens left of whom about
one hundred were very wealthy, possessing both their *klêros*
(traditional allotment) and other estates, the rest with just enough
land to maintain their citizenship.[2] Additionally the presence of those
who had lost their citizenship or who were descendants of those who
had would have increased social tensions (cf. Plut. *Agis* 6-7).[3] Among
these groups debt would have been a problem, particularly for those
struggling to stay within the citizen body. Alongside and not
unconnected with this decrease in the numbers of citizens went
Sparta's political decline, which had continued unchecked since
Leuctra in 371, punctuated by occasional futile attempts to regain
Messenia or tackle Macedon. By the 240s it was the Achaean League
under the leadership of Aratus which was becoming the major force in
Peloponnesian politics.

Thus it was scarcely a satisfactory state of affairs that faced the
youthful Agis when he acceded to the throne of the Eurypontid house
and so became one of the two kings in Sparta. His brief reign was
marked by revolutionary disturbances that culminated in his own
death in late 241 or early 240. The most prominent of his associates
included his uncle Agesilaus and the ephor Lysander (*Agis* 6.3-5, Cic.
De Off. 2.80). These were all involved in an intense power struggle
within the Spartan elite, during which the Agiad king, Leonidas, was
deposed and in his place a more amenable king, Cleombrotus, was
installed. Subsequently the board of ephors too was deposed and
replaced (*Agis* 11-12). This attempt to monopolise power in Sparta
collapsed after Agis had led a fruitless expedition to assist Aratus
against the Aetolians and Agesilaus had meanwhile begun alarming
everyone with his increasing megalomania (*Agis* 13.5-16).[4] In the
ensuing discontent their opponents brought back Leonidas from exile,
took control of the situation and quickly had Agis executed. Meanwhile
the leading supporters of Agis fled into exile.

Agis' reign is not represented simply as a struggle for power; there
was also a social aspect to these disturbances. Agis proposed and
carried through a cancellation of debts, a measure designed to alleviate
some of Sparta's social problems and increase his support (*Agis* 8.1).
Plutarch, who is virtually our only source for Agis, also attributes to
him a much more extensive programme of reform, a programme which
was never carried out. In addition to the cancellation of debts, the

---

[2] Plut. *Agis* 5.6-7, Fuks 1962 (*Athenaeum*).

[3] Plutarch's *Life of Agis* will be cited as *Agis*, his *Life of Cleomenes* as *Cleom.* and the
comparison between the Spartan kings and the Gracchi as *Comp.*

[4] Although perhaps our source attaches more blame than necessary to Agesilaus in
order to excuse Agis' lack of political acumen.

whole land was to be redistributed into 4,500 allotments. This land was to be distributed among the citizens whose number was to be augmented by a process of *anaplêrôsis*, a filling up of the citizen body, in other words an extension of citizenship. The beneficiaries were to be those *perioikoi* and foreigners who were considered suitable and presumably also the ex-Spartiates who had become *hupomeiones*. The *perioikoi* were non-Spartan inhabitants of semi-independent communities within Laconia. The common messes and education system (*agôgê*), which had fallen into neglect, were to be restored, along with the Spartan way of life in general (*diaita*). A further more obscure proposal affected the territory of the *perioikoi*; this was to be divided into 15,000 allotments for those of the *perioikoi* capable of bearing arms (*Agis* 8, 4.2). According to Plutarch it was this programme which elicited the vigorous opposition of the wealthy grouped around Leonidas. The authenticity of this programme and the ideology that went with it will be considered below.

Cleomenes III succeeded to the Agiad throne in 235. In his early years he seems to have established himself firmly as king and achieved some military success against the Achaeans. Then in 227 he pre-empted any action by those who were likely to oppose him by staging a coup.[5] At least fourteen, including four ephors, were murdered, while eighty citizens were sent into exile. This may have effectively eliminated the wealthy opposition whose number was given as about one hundred by Plutarch (*Agis* 5.6). Only at this point did Cleomenes introduce and implement his reforms; no opposition is recorded. From what we know of these reforms they were remarkably similar to the programme attributed to Agis. Debts were cancelled and land redistributed equally. It has been convincingly argued that this redistribution of property was to be total and even extended as far as movable property. Then there were 'the social aspects of equality as envisaged by the reformers'.[6] These included the restoration of the *agôgê*, achieved with the assistance of the Stoic philosopher, Sphaerus of Borysthenes, and the revival of the gymnasia and common messes. The revolutionaries claimed that the new Sparta was modelled on the Sparta of Lycurgus, traditionally the creator of the Spartan system.[7] Cleomenes appears also to have made other constitutional changes apart from the elimination of the ephorate, limiting the power of the *gerousia* (council of elders) and creating a new magistracy, the *patronomoi*, whose role may have been to oversee the new 'Lycurgan' Sparta.[8]

---

[5] Cleomenes' accession is dated to 235 by *Cleom.* 38.1 where it is said that Cleomenes died after being king for 16 years. Even when he was in exile the Spartans still considered him to be their king, Polyb. 4.35.8. Tarn 1928: 753, however, dates it to 237. Date of coup and reforms: Beloch 1925: 702.

[6] Fuks 1962 (*CPh*).

[7] Coup and reforms: *Cleom.* 8-11, 18.2, *Aratus* 38; Lycurgus: *Cleom.* 10, 18, *Comp.* 2.4

[8] Paus. 2.9.1, Shimron 1972: 39f, Oliva 1971: 245; Chrimes 1949: 143-55 attributes them to Cleomenes and traces their later history.

The revolution stirred up social unrest throughout the Peloponnese and increased Sparta's military strength. As a result Cleomenes detached numerous cities from the Achaean League until Aratus could see no option but to seek help from Antigonus Doson, the Macedonian king. Even a revitalised Sparta could not compete with the resources of Macedon, and Cleomenes was eventually defeated at Sellasia in 222. As he fled to Egypt, Antigonus moved into Sparta.

This was not the end of revolutionary activity in Sparta. A few years later a claimant to the throne, Cheilon, sought popular support for a rebellion by copying Cleomenes and proposing redistribution of land. Making more of an impact was Nabis, who came to power in 207. In spite of a fairly long reign, the details of his internal policy are obscured by uniformly hostile sources, but even so similarities to Cleomenes are evident. Land which had been confiscated was redistributed and mercenaries, foreigners and at least some helots were enfranchised.[9] The international situation, however, was changing. When Cleomenes had come to the throne in 235, Macedon was the influential power in Greece, but by the time of Nabis' murder in 192 Macedon had suffered a serious defeat and a new non-Greek power was emerging, Rome.

2. The sources and their interpretation

The main extant sources for this period of Spartan history are Polybius and Plutarch in his *Lives* of Agis, Cleomenes and Aratus. It is Plutarch who provides the main narrative for the reigns of the two Spartan kings and the only detailed account of their reforms. In considering the sources it is useful to look at the two kings separately. The reign of Cleomenes is better documented, being covered both by Plutarch and Polybius. It is generally agreed that Plutarch's main source for the lives of both kings was Phylarchus, a contemporary of Aratus. Phylarchus had written a history in twenty-eight books which began with the invasion of the Peloponnese by Pyrrhus in 272 and ended with the death of Cleomenes (*Suda*, s.v. *Phularchos*). As an ardent admirer of Cleomenes (Plut. *Arat.* 38.12) he did not endear himself to Polybius who was intensely critical of him and devoted several chapters to explaining his shortcomings as an historian.[10] Plutarch augments Phylarchus' account with Aratus' *Memoirs* and Polybius.[11] Aratus

---

[9] Cheilon: Polyb. 4.81.2; Nabis: Shimron 1972: 79-100.

[10] Phylarchus, cited by Plutarch: *Agis* 9.3, *Cleom.* 5.3, 28.2, 30.3. Plut. *Cleom.* 13 is clearly Phylarchean, cf. Athen. 4.141f-42f, FGH 81F44. As Plutarch's main source: Bux 1925: 413ff, Gabba 1957, Africa 1961; Macdowell 1986: 20-1 is more cautious. As contemporary of Aratus: Polyb. 2.56.1. Polybius' attack: Polyb. 2.56-63, Walbank 1957: 259ff. For a defence of Phylarchus: Africa 1961.

[11] Use of Aratus: Plut. *Cleom.* 16.4-5, 18.4, 19.4-6. Also used extensively in the *Life of Aratus*, cited *Arat.* 3.3, 32.5, 33.3, 38.6. Use of Polybius: Plut. *Cleom.* 25.4, 27.11,

provides valuable confirmation of the nature of Cleomenes' revolution. For he alludes to the equalisation of property in his denunciation of 'the abolition of wealth and correction of poverty' in Sparta. If the reference to Spartan barley bread and short cloaks derives from Aratus, this implies knowledge of the Lycurgan propaganda of the revolution (*Cleom*. 16.6-7). Aratus may also be included amongst those contemporaries who mocked Cleomenes' attempt to imitate Lycurgus and Solon in the cancellation of debts and the equalisation of property (*Cleom*. 18.2).

Polybius in his own account gives a fairly full picture of Cleomenes' military operations, but he makes only oblique reference to the social reforms of Cleomenes, giving no explanation for Sparta's sudden appearance as a militarily forceful power. He was certainly aware of the revolutionary changes in Sparta. When discussing Achaea's war with Cleomenes, he reports that the king overthrew the ancestral constitution at Sparta and turned the monarchy into a tyranny (Polyb. 2.47.3, cf. 4.81.14). He compares Cheilon's plans for the redistribution of property with those of Cleomenes a few years earlier (Polyb. 4.81.2, 81.13). Indeed he had read Aratus' *Memoirs* and Phylarchus' history, both of which mentioned the Spartan reforms (Polyb. 2.56). Polybius may have wished to play down the fragility of the socio-economic structure of the Achaean League which was exposed by its vulnerability to the revolutionary propaganda of Cleomenes and was inconsistent with his eulogy of the League.[12]

For the reign of Agis we have to rely almost completely on Plutarch's *Life of Agis* and this in turn seems to be more heavily dependent on Phylarchus.[13] The only point where Plutarch clearly uses other sources to expand on Agis' rule is on a question of foreign relations, whether Agis refrained from attacking the Aetolians at his own or Aratus' suggestion (*Agis* 15). Plutarch cites the differing opinions of Aratus and Baton of Sinope. Agis would only have been incidental to Aratus' memoirs and it is unlikely that Baton had any particular interest in Sparta.[14] It is possible that Phylarchus did not know much about Agis himself; for although the idea for the reforms is said to have been developed by Agis, much of the action is in the hands of others,

---

referring to Polyb. 2.64.2, 65.1-7 respectively.

[12] Polyb. 2.37.7ff, 2.42; Mendels 1981: 95-104.

[13] Pausanias gives an account of a battle at Mantinea between Agis and Aratus in which Agis died, Paus. 8.10.5-10, cf. 6.2.4, 8.8.11, 27.14. The account is clearly confused, Habicht 1985: 101-2.

[14] On Baton, Walbank 1933: 16. Ziegler, RE Plutarchos col. 912-13, believes that Plutarch used Baton at second hand. Jacoby, commentary on FGH 268F7, suggests that he was used elsewhere in the *Lives* of Agis and Aratus, but this is based on unsubstantiated speculation about what Baton may have written. Plutarch also notes that some writers were at variance with Phylarchus over the genealogy of Pasiphae, *Cleom*. 9; these need not have been writing on Agis, but only on mythology.

especially Lysander and Agesilaus. Whereas Cleomenes dominates his own *Life*, Agis does not really make an impact until his dramatic death scene.[15] Polybius does not mention Agis at all, although he does note, in passing, the deposition of Leonidas and an attempt by the Aetolians to restore exiles in 240 or 239.[16] This gives credence to Plutarch's account of revolutionary upheaval at the time of Agis although it does not confirm its nature.

Here a non-Phylarchean tradition about the reform programme of Agis is needed and Alexander Fuks has argued that such a tradition can be found in three passages,[17] Polybius 4.81.12-14, Cicero *De Off.* 2.80 and Teles *On Exile*. Closer examination shows that they provide little to corroborate Phylarchus' version of the reforms. Polybius refers to the problems caused by banishments, civil conflict and the division of land in the period prior to Nabis. But Polybius had read Phylarchus, so this might not be a non-Phylarchean tradition. Even if it was, Polybius need not have meant that all three occurred at the time of Agis. Rather they would represent an amalgam of the troubles that beset Sparta prior to Nabis, including the disturbances caused by Cleomenes and Cheilon. So this rather rhetorical passage hardly justifies the interpretation placed on it. Cicero says that Agis and the tyrants who followed him ruined Sparta by redistribution of land and cancellation of debts. Merely because Cicero is hostile and Phylarchus is favourable to the Spartan kings it does not follow that Cicero must have acquired his information from a non-Phylarchean source, especially when what he says is so brief.[18] Unlike Polybius and Cicero, Teles could not possibly have been influenced by Phylarchus; *On Exile* is believed to have been written after the fall of Agis and before 229.[19] He remarks on Sparta's lack of prejudice to foreigners and in support of this he cites the Spartan *agôgê*; all who complete this, even if they are foreigners or helots, are considered equal to the best. Fuks' belief that this is a reference to Agis' proposal to increase the citizen body has been now convincingly refuted.[20] Indeed since Agis' alleged proposal

---

[15] Gabba 1957: 193-4; Beloch 1925: 623-8 brings Agesilaus into prominence and suggests that Agis was the tool of Agesilaus, no doubt because Agis only plays a minor part in his own *Life*.

[16] Polyb. 4.35.11, 4.34.9; Walbank 1957.

[17] Fuks 1962 (*CQ*): 118-21. The edition of Teles *On Exile* (*Peri Phugês*) is *Teletis Reliquiae*, ed. Hense (Tübingen 1909²).

[18] This passage is further discussed in Chapter 7, where it is argued that it derives from a Stoic tradition, but the Stoics may still have relied on Phylarchus for their information. Cicero also provides evidence not in Plutarch that Lysander went into exile.

[19] Wilamowitz 1881: 330ff. Reference is made by Teles, p. 23, to Hippomedon's exile from Sparta which occurred after the fall of Agis, *Agis* 16.5. For additional confirmation of his period as a general in the Ptolemaic service, SIG 502.

[20] Teles pp. 28-9, Mendels 1979: 111-15. Porter 1937: lxiii accepts that Teles is referring to Agis' reforms, but recognises that, as it was written after Agis' death, there is a problem and so concludes that Teles ignored the counter-revolution.

was said to have been violently rejected, it makes it all the more peculiar that Teles should adduce this as evidence for his case. If Teles is not referring to Agis' proposal, then this casts doubt on the historicity of the proposal itself, because its rejection would contradict Teles' argument about Sparta's attitude to foreigners. That he mentions in the same diatribe Hippomedon, who went into exile after the fall of Agis, indicates that he was aware of events in Sparta.

So any examination of Agis has to rely almost exclusively on Plutarch and consequently on Phylarchus, but this *Life* presents serious problems. The existence of upheaval in Sparta at the time of Agis is not in doubt and is supported by several sources. Nevertheless, for the details of Agis' reign there is a lack of corroborative material. Two factors in particular must be taken into account when assessing the value of this *Life* as evidence for Agis' reign.

First, Plutarch's biographical approach in the *Parallel Lives* needs to be considered. He was not writing self-contained biographies, but drawing comparisons between Greeks and Romans, in this case between Agis and Cleomenes on the one hand and Tiberius and Gaius Gracchus on the other. This may well have affected his treatment of Agis. In order to make a satisfactory pair which will sustain the comparison with the Gracchi, Agis must not only be seen to have shared the same aims as Cleomenes,[21] but should also be seen as sufficiently important to merit comparison with Tiberius. Due to the requirements of the comparison, therefore, it is possible that the picture of Agis became distorted.

The problem of distortion stems not only from Plutarch but also from Phylarchus himself. For it is likely that Phylarchus' perception of Agis was affected by his evident familiarity with Cleomenes' career. It was earlier suggested that Phylarchus did not have much information on Agis, an impression supported by the beginning of the *Life of Cleomenes*, where it is said that after Agis' death nobody spoke about him or the things associated with him (2.1). This sounds like an apology for lack of information. Since the reader would want to know how Cleomenes found out the details of his reign if nobody spoke about them, the answer is supplied by certain private conversations that Cleomenes had with his wife, Agiatis, formerly the wife of Agis, and his friend, Xenares. Yet, Plutarch tells us that Xenares never revealed the nature of his conversations with Cleomenes (*Cleom.* 1, 3). This lack of information on Agis would make it all the more probable that Phylarchus would use his knowledge of Cleomenes' revolution to interpret the reign of Agis.

---

[21] Similarly Plutarch attributes to Tiberius Gracchus unfulfilled proposals that bear a strong resemblance to reforms actually carried out by Gaius. Tiberius is said to have proposed a reduction in the duration of military service, appeal to the people from judicial decisions and mixed juries of senators and *equites*, Plut. *TG* 16.1, cf. respectively

In many respects the *Life of Agis* duplicates the *Life of Cleomenes*. If Agis did not actually do those things which Cleomenes did, he at least intended to do them.[22] The similarity in the programme of reforms proposed by both kings has already been noted above. Worthy of attention, too, is the impact of these reforms on the rest of the Peloponnese. When Agis marched his army to assist Aratus against the Aetolians, the common people of the cities through which he passed were full of admiration, but the rich feared that this revolutionary activity would set an example to the masses everywhere (*Agis* 14). Cleomenes' military activity causes a similar impression and this time the fears are justified (*Cleom.* 17-18, cf. *Aratus* 39). Plutarch's remark that the loyalty of Agis' soldiers was inspired partly by the expectation that they would receive allotments of land on their return seems to owe more to a Roman tradition than a Greek one. Agis' expedition itself should not be questioned, but the interpretation of it should be treated with extreme scepticism.

Further similarities occur on the more abstract level of ideology. Both kings model themselves on Lycurgus and justify themselves in terms of Lycurgus (*Agis* 10, 19.7, *Cleom.* 10, 16.6, 18, *Comp.* 2.4). In both cases the establishment of equality is seen as a fundamental tenet of the revolution which could be traced back to Lycurgus (*Agis* 6.1, 7.3, 9.4, *Cleom.* 2.1, 7.1, 18.2). Each seeks to assert the authority of the king over the ephors, for which Cleomenes provides a justification based on Lycurgus (*Agis* 12, *Cleom.* 10). Thus not only are the reforms themselves similar, but they are supported by a consistent ideology, manifested in the revolutionary propaganda. In spite of being spread across two *Lives* the ideology that underpins the revolutions presents a coherent whole, the details and originality of which are discussed below. Given this ideological unity it is highly probable that it stems from only one of the two revolutions. Since it would be hard not to interpret past disturbances in the light of what happened later, it is reasonable to believe that it represents the standpoint of the revolution of Cleomenes. Justifications and objectives are particularly likely to reflect those that are current, all the more so in a period when events in Sparta were so confused.

There are other problems in accepting Plutarch's picture of Agis' reign. If Cleomenes was resurrecting Agis' programme of reform, one would expect a greater degree of connection between the two kings, for instance that Cleomenes made use of some of Agis' supporters. Yet, the only link between the two is the rather forced one of some private conversations that Cleomenes had about Agis. There is no mention of the return of any exiles, except for Archidamus, the brother of Agis,

---

CG 5.1, 4.1, 5.3-4. These proposals of Tiberius are not mentioned in any other sources.

[22] Gabba 1957: 199 suggests that Agis is modelled on Cleomenes.

who was murdered. Some, including Polybius, charged Cleomenes with this murder and Phylarchus can only manage a weak defence of the king; he knew of the plan but was unable to stop it.[23] Further, why did Cleomenes wait about eight years from his accession in 235 until his coup in 227 to introduce a programme of reform with which he was already familiar? Plutarch (or Phylarchus) appreciated this problem and supposed that he deliberately kept his scheme secret for all this time while he became established and waited for his opportunity. It is a problem which has also vexed modern scholars.[24] If Cleomenes' ideas for Sparta were different from and independent of those of Agis, this is no longer a problem. They would take time to develop.

Thus, although there were revolutionary disturbances in the time of Agis which involved the cancellation of debts and maybe even a proposal for some form of redistribution of land, we cannot be clear as to the actual character of these disturbances.[25] For they would have been interpreted under the influence of Cleomenes' career and propaganda. Therefore the ideology which permeates both the *Lives* should be understood as being that of the Cleomenean revolution.

3. Philosophy and the reforms of Cleomenes

It is frequently said that the Spartan revolution can be explained in terms of Spartan tradition and consequently there is no need to introduce philosophy.[26] But is this really so? It certainly tried to use Spartan tradition to explain itself, but this was for propaganda purposes. Many revolutionaries seek to make themselves more acceptable by claiming an area or person of the past for themselves.[27] This was a shrewd move which could legitimate a wide variety of actions. For, as Plutarch remarked at the beginning of his *Life of Lycurgus*, nothing could be said about Lycurgus which was not disputed.

Too often writers seek to explain why the reforms took place but fail

[23] Plut. *Cleom.* 1.1, 5, *Comp.* 5.2, Polyb. 5.37.1-6, 8.35.3-5. Both writers seem to reflect a general opinion that Cleomenes was in some way implicated in the murder, but they differ greatly on the detail.

[24] Shimron 1972: 30-1 believes that Cleomenes kept his intentions about reform secret from at least the time he succeeded to the throne. Gabba 1957: 37-41 suggests that up to 227 Cleomenes followed the conservative policy of Leonidas, but then split with the ephors.

[25] Even the one reform that seems certain, the cancellation of debts, may be derived from the Spartan custom of cancelling debts to the king and treasury on the accession of a new king, Herod. 6.59.

[26] Aalders 1975: 78, Will 1979: 375. It is anyway doubtful whether Spartan tradition can be explained without recourse to philosophy.

[27] Skinner 1974: 294-5 argues that if an ideologist accepts the need to legitimate his own revolutionary behaviour, he has to try to show that his actions can be described by 'some of the *existing* range of favourable evaluative-descriptive terms'. In this way a revolutionary has 'to march backward into battle'.

to account for the form that they took. Various factors are cited to explain their occurrence, all of which could have played a contributory role. There are Sparta's military needs, brought about by a desire for hegemony in the Peloponnese or merely to protect Sparta against the expanding Achaean League. In combination with this there is Cleomenes' desire for self-aggrandisement. Plutarch stresses his love of honour, *philotimia* (*Cleom.* 1.4, 2.3, 6.2). Further, it was necessary to resolve social discontent in Sparta. Nevertheless, it is not at all obvious that any of these factors required the reforms to take the form that they did. None of these accounts for such a radical solution. A degree of equality would perhaps be reasonable and Spartan tradition pointed that way, but the reforms themselves emphasised and strove for absolute equality, albeit of a limited number.[28] It is of a type unknown in earlier writings on Sparta. In the Spartan revolution Lycurgan Sparta was being moulded to fit and justify a conception of contemporary Sparta. As W.G. Forrest says, 'much was being done in Lykourgos' name that would have astonished him'.[29] Whether philosophy played a part in the development of this conception will need to be examined.

Since Phylarchus is our main authority for the Spartan revolution, it is necessary to consider whether he should be regarded as the adherent of any particular philosophical school. For, if he was, any philosophical colouring may have originated not with the revolution but with himself. Although arguments have been put forward in favour of both Cynicism and Stoicism,[30] there is little to support either case. The only guides are likely to be his vocabulary and the ideas expressed by it.

We have little idea what vocabulary Phylarchus used. It is clear that Plutarch did not simply copy out his source, but reorganised it and changed the vocabulary.[31] This can be seen if Plutarch's description of Cleomenes' dining habits (*Cleom.* 13) is compared with the passage on the same subject, quoted from Phylarchus by Athenaeus (Athen. 4.141f-42f, FGH 81 F44). The epithets that Plutarch uses to describe Agis and Cleomenes do sometimes appear in Stoic writers, but they seem to be his own and not borrowed from Phylarchus. For instance Agis is described as *philanthrôpos* (humane) and *praos* (gentle) (*Agis* 20.5, 21.5), both characteristics that Plutarch considers to be important in a statesman.[32] Other writers using Phylarchus may have been more faithful to his vocabulary, but these fragments seem to betray no special philosophical bias (FGH 81).

---

[28] Fuks 1962 (*CPh*).

[29] Forrest 1980: 147.

[30] Cynicism; Africa 1961: 18-22; Stoicism: Ollier 1943: 91-3.

[31] Gabba 1957: 49 n. 1.

[32] Aalders 1981: 46. Stoic use of *praos*: Plut. SVF 3.255, Stobaeus SVF 3.632; *philanthrôpos*: Clem. Al. SVF 3.292, although this seems to be more characteristic of the later Stoa, see Chapter 8.4-5 below.

When his ideas are examined, it is similarly difficult to find any that are definitely attributable to a particular school of philosophy. At least this is the case if the reforms and any justifications that are made for them are ignored, both of which are rooted in the revolution and not its interpretation. Often it may be difficult to distinguish the justification from the interpretation. If a statement is consistent with what is integral to the revolution, it is reasonable to believe that it reflects the stance of the revolution rather than of Phylarchus. Nevertheless, it may not have occurred in the same context. For, as has been said above, some material of this sort is probably the product of the later revolution of Cleomenes, but it is used to interpret the disturbances that took place under Agis.

Those aspects picked out to show that Phylarchus was a Cynic are very general.[33] This is unavoidably so, partly because we know so little about the content of Cynic thought and partly because what we do know suggests that it was a rather imprecise doctrine. Austerity and moralism need have no particular connection with any philosophical school and may just be the consequence of an idealisation of Sparta. As Ollier has shown, Phylarchus was clearly a Spartophile, quite independently of the revolutionary reforms.[34] There is, for example, his account of the heroic response of the Spartan women to Pyrrhus in 272 (Plut. *Pyrrhus* 27). While one scholar considers Phylarchus' description of Cleomenes in chapter 13 to be Cynic, another can see the same passage as having Stoic roots.[35]

Nevertheless there are two passages the Stoic content of which is more generally accepted,[36] Plut. *Cleom.* 22.7 and 31, but it would be unwise to impute Stoicism to Phylarchus on the basis of these. Both are in quotations that are attributed to important figures associated with the reform movement and indicate a Stoicism not apparent elsewhere in Phylarchus' work. The first of these is Cratesicleia's remark about fate. Before her departure for Egypt she consoles her son Cleomenes by telling him that they should not let anyone see them crying or doing anything unworthy of a Spartan. For this alone is attributable to us (*eph' hêmin*), but for the outcome of fortune (*tuchai*) we are dependent on what God grants us. The phrase *eph' hêmin* is common in Stoic discussions of fate (cf. SVF 2.979, 984, 1007) and the statement as a whole recalls the Stoic distinction between our response to circumstances which is attributable to ourselves and the circumstances themselves which are fated.[37] The second passage is the

[33] Africa 1961: 18-22.
[34] Ollier 1943: 89ff.
[35] Cynic: Africa 1961: 20-1; Stoic: Gabba 1957: 48-9.
[36] Ollier 1943: 92, Babut 1969: 19, Flacelière and Chambry 1976: 13. Tigerstedt 1974: 68, 338 n. 104 accepts the Stoic content of Plut. *Cleom.* 22.7, but not of chapter 31.
[37] The translation of *eph' hêmin* is from Long 1971: 183.

discussion between Therycion and Cleomenes about whether or not to commit suicide after the defeat at the Battle of Sellasia. Therycion's argument is essentially that suicide is the only honourable, or perhaps least shameful, course to follow. Cleomenes replies that suicide should not be negative, an escape from action, but positive, an action in itself. A man should not die for himself alone. While there is still hope for his country, he will live, but when there is no hope, that will be the time for suicide. This argument accords with what we know about Stoic views on suicide.[38] There is a right time for suicide, as can be seen in the story of the death of Zeno (D.L. 7.28). The wise man will normally commit suicide for the sake of others (e.g. country, friends), not for himself alone unless he is suffering extreme bodily pain (D.L. 7.130). A suitable time would be when he has lost all hope of action, *elpis tês praxeôs* (Clem. Al. SVF 3.765).

Since these quotations are unlikely to be authentic, one has to ask why they contain such Stoic overtones. Either Phylarchus, aware of a Stoic influence on the revolution, tried to add a Stoic colouring to their speeches, which seems improbable, or he·obtained them from a Stoic source and thus imported these elements of Stoicism into his history. It has been suggested and seems likely that Phylarchus made use of the writings of Sphaerus, the Stoic philosopher present in Sparta during Cleomenes' revolution.[39] Both the quotations concern fate and fortune in one way or another, particularly Stoic preoccupations; Sphaerus himself wrote a work, *Peri Tuchês, On Fate* (D.L. 7.178, SVF 1.620). It is possible that Sphaerus wrote the work to reconcile himself with the failure of the Spartan venture, using the protagonists as examples. Certainly the quotations read like text-book examples and have an overly philosophical tone in comparison to other speeches in the *Lives* of Agis and Cleomenes, such as that of Chilonis to her father Leonidas (*Agis* 17.4-10). Since nothing is known of the contents of this book, this must remain hypothetical. Whichever explanation is most likely, both tend towards the belief that Stoicism played some part in the revolution.

One further passage could be cited to show Phylarchus' Stoicism. At the end of the *Life of Cleomenes* we are told that Sparta showed how in time of crisis virtue could not be violated by fortune (*Cleom.* 39.1). Although this idea does have Stoic antecedents and reminds us again of Sphaerus' book on fate, it is an idea well-used by Plutarch and suits his moralising purpose.[40]

[38] Seneca's obsession with suicide must not be allowed to distort the views of the early Stoa on suicide. As Rist 1969: 233-55 argues, the subject of suicide was in no way central to early Stoic doctrine. Yet, as people do commit suicide, 'what they are interested in is when it is reasonable (*eulogon*) to commit suicide', Rist 1969: 239, cf. D.L. 7.130, SVF 3.757. It is just this question that Cleomenes and Therycion are debating.

[39] Ollier 1943: 105, although his view is too extreme, Gabba 1963: 361-3.

[40] Babut 1969: 19 n. 5, cf. Plut. *CG* 19.4, *Otho* 13.5.

Ollier's theses that Phylarchus was a Stoic and that the Stoic Sphaerus played a major role in the revolution do not co-exist comfortably.[41] For Phylarchus made very little mention of Sphaerus, which is difficult to explain unless a rivalry between the two men is invented. He might be expected to emphasise the contributions of a fellow Stoic to the revolution. Yet if the idea that Phylarchus was a Stoic is abandoned, it becomes no longer surprising that Sphaerus should be neglected. For Phylarchus emphasises the role of Cleomenes and plays down the other males.[42] It is only the women who receive a lot of attention, as they tend to in the rest of his work.[43] Phylarchus had a great affection for Spartan women. The argument that Stoicism, and Sphaerus in particular, did play a major role still needs to be considered.

The presence of Stoic thought on fate in some of the speeches in the *Life of Cleomenes* has already been remarked upon and it was suggested that these might have originated with the Stoic Sphaerus. Plutarch refers to Sphaerus in two passages of the *Life of Cleomenes*. In the first he writes that Sphaerus had taught Cleomenes while the Spartan was still a *meirakion* (*Cleom.* 2.2-3, SVF 1.622). This implies that Sphaerus had been in Sparta before the revolution of 227. Some scholars have suggested that this was during the reign of Agis, but this seems unlikely; Plutarch would surely have mentioned such a visit if it occurred then.[44] The term *meirakion* referred to a young man round about twenty years old, but it was not strictly defined. Plutarch uses it as a description of Aratus when he captures the Acrocorinth at the age of almost thirty.[45] He could also use it of a married man; Agis, when he goes to the aid of Aratus against the Aetolians, is said to be a *meirakion* (*Agis* 14.3). There would have been no difficulty describing Cleomenes in this way in the early 230s. Indeed immediately after the fall of Agis he was considered too young to marry. So Cleomenes' familiarity with Sphaerus would have stemmed from his earlier period as Sphaerus' pupil.

According to the second passage Sphaerus helped Cleomenes with the restoration of the *agôgê*, which had become neglected (*Cleom.* 11.3-4, SVF 1.623). This is important evidence for Sphaerus' role,

[41] Ollier 1943, who discusses the Stoicism of Phylarchus pp. 91-3, the role of Sphaerus pp. 99-123.

[42] In this respect the contrast with the *Life of Agis* is significant. It may be due to Phylarchus' greater admiration for Cleomenes, but it also suggests that Phylarchus had less material at his disposal for Agis.

[43] Africa 1961: 43-7.

[44] Ollier 1943: 103, Legrand 1901: n. 2 believe in a visit during the reign of Agis; Michell 1952: 323, Piper 1986: 43-5 are more sceptical; Oliva 1971: 216f, 231f, Tigerstedt 1974: 70, 347 n. 156 reject it. Jacoby, Commentary on FGH 585, thinks that there may have been a visit before 242.

[45] *Cleom.* 16.4. Walbank 1957: 235 puts Aratus' birth in 271. If the arguments of Beloch 1927: 228-30 were accepted, Aratus would have been even older.

because the *agôgê* was fundamental to the reformed Sparta. The *agôgê* was the Spartan educational system and has been described as the 'most distinctive feature of the constitution and customs of Sparta'.[46] The *paidonomos* who had been in charge of running the old *agôgê* was a highly respected man in Sparta.[47] To pass through it was part of the education of all Spartan citizens and hence its restoration was not something to be entrusted to a minor figure. Rather he had to be someone whose outlook was very close to that of Cleomenes. In 188 the Achaeans, who had endured the revolutionary activities of both Cleomenes and Nabis, abolished the *agôgê* along with much of the Spartan system (Plut. *Philopoemen* 16, cf. Livy 38.34, 39.36). Clearly the *agôgê* was perceived as fundamental to revolutionary Sparta.

Seeking to minimise Sphaerus' role, Thomas Africa suggests that Plutarch has added Sphaerus as a 'pendant for the Stoic Blossius' who appears as an influential teacher in his *Life of Tiberius Gracchus*.[48] Although *'legetai'* (it is said), by which Plutarch introduces the first passage about Sphaerus, may imply a different source, it is unlikely that this source was Sphaerus himself, exaggerating his role, as Africa believes. For Plutarch does not normally give the place of origin and biographical details for a writer he is using as a source.[49] The reference here contrasts with his use of Sphaerus as a source in his *Life of Lycurgus* (Plut. *Lyc*. 5.12).

Sphaerus' writings demonstrate his interest in Sparta. He had written at least two works on Sparta, *On the Laconian Constitution* and *On Lycurgus and Socrates* (D.L. 7.178, SVF 1.620), both of which are particularly relevant to the issues of the revolution, dealing as they do with the constitution and with Lycurgus. The latter title suggests that he examined some of the principles behind Lycurgan Sparta and may have tried to give Lycurgus some philosophical authority. It is futile to try to reconstruct the texts, but we do know that the work on the Spartan constitution discussed the *sussitia* (Athen. SVF 1.630). Sphaerus' remark on the original number of the *gerousia* will have come from one of these two works (Plut. *Lyc*. 5.12, SVF 1.629). Whereas Aristotle had said that Lycurgus had originally had thirty colleagues, two of whom dropped out through cowardice, leaving twenty-eight, Sphaerus held that the number was twenty-eight from the beginning. The Pythagorean explanation of this number which follows in Plutarch is probably also from Sphaerus and would be consistent with a view that linked Lycurgus and philosophy.[50] It does

[46] Shimron 1972: 20.

[47] Plut. *Lyc*. 17, Xen. *Lac. Pol*. 2.2, 2.10, 4.6; Ollier 1943: 118.

[48] Africa 1961: 18.

[49] Babut 1969: 194 n. 2.

[50] Kessler 1910: 32, Ollier 1943: 112, Jacoby, Commentary on FGH 585F1 (though it does not appear in his text). This does not require one to accept Ollier's opinion that Sphaerus himself was influenced by Pythagoreanism, merely that he used it to interpret

not represent Plutarch's opinion, because he considered thirty, the twenty-eight *gerontes* and the two kings, to be the significant number (Plut. *Lyc.* 5.14).

On the basis of these writings alone it would not be unreasonable to imagine that Sphaerus assisted Cleomenes, at least in matters of historical research. That he did so is already apparent from his role in the restoration of the *agôgê*. Historical justifications that were both detailed and innovative were produced for several of the actions in the revolution. Their nature suggests that they were not the work of the Spartan revolutionaries themselves. There are two arguments to justify the treatment of the ephors (*Agis* 12, *Cleom.* 10) and one to show that Lycurgus would have approved of filling up the citizen body with non-Spartans (*Agis* 10). It has been suggested that the reformers would have had to turn to an expert once knowledge of ancient Sparta was getting dim.[51] It is not possible to tell whether Sphaerus was approached because he was an expert on the constitution or he became an expert because he was approached. Both cases indicate a sympathy with his views, but the latter more strongly. Such sympathy would not be unlikely because he is believed to have played a part in Cleomenes' education. Thus Cleomenes would have been familiar with his ideas, whether or not he had already written on Sparta.

Stoic influence can be detected in the Lycurgan justification for the reforms. In some ways it is hard to draw a clear line between this and the reforms themselves. The one would have influenced the other. There was no generally accepted picture of early Sparta and Lycurgus' role. Ephorus criticised the fifth-century writer, Hellanicus, for failing to mention Lycurgus at all (Strabo 8.5.5, FGH 70 F118). Anyone researching into Spartan history on behalf of the revolution would have had to sift through the folklore, make deductions from poets, such as Tyrtaios, and evaluate the conjecture of recent writers, generally from the fourth century onwards. Herodotus has little detailed information on early Sparta, while Thucydides complains of Spartan secrecy (Herod. 1.65, Thuc. 5.68). So while Sphaerus would have provided expert knowledge of the past, it is also clear that the information on old Sparta which he gathered was the result of careful selection of appropriate traditions and the rejection of others. This selection would have been based, in part, on certain criteria, whether conscious or unconscious, derived from his philosophy and his conception of the revolution. Yet, there would not be complete fabrication, unconnected with previous tradition. The arguments had to be plausible to their audience, who would have certain

---

Lycurgus.

[51] Michell 1952: 321-5, cf. Cartledge 1979: 169-70. Michell has in mind both Agis and Cleomenes, but I am concerned here only with Cleomenes. It has been argued above that justificatory arguments attributed to Agis reflect the Cleomenean revolution.

preconceptions about Lycurgus, however vague. The 'Lycurgus' of the revolution had to be sufficiently consistent with these preconceptions to gain general acceptance. The greater the popular support for Cleomenes' aims, the more readily the revolutionary picture of Lycurgus would have been accepted. Moreover it is not reasonable to suggest that these historical arguments to support the Lycurgan stance of the revolution were produced after the event, for instance by Phylarchus.[52] For the revolutionaries, who claimed to model themselves on Lycurgus, would have been rather unconvincing if they could give no Lycurgan precedent for their actions.

4. The extension of citizenship

The Stoic influence can be seen if the least Lycurgan of all the reforms is examined, the replenishment of the citizen body with *hupomeiones, perioikoi* and foreigners. According to Plutarch after Agis proposed it Leonidas protested that Lycurgus who had advocated *xenêlasia*, the expulsion of foreigners, would never have approved of this (*Agis* 10). Sparta certainly had a reputation for hostility to foreigners. This objection is said to have been countered by Agis who replied that Lycurgus would rather have had foreigners than men who were unsuited to Spartan life. He proceeded to produce a list of three foreigners who were respected in Sparta, Thaletas, Terpander and Pherecydes. The teachings of these men were in harmony with those of Lycurgus. Since two of these men were musicians, he extends the argument and draws an analogy between his own objectives and music. His aim is to get rid of luxury and extravagance in the city and promote harmony.

Whether or not the reforms were Lycurgan would have been a matter of controversy at the time of the revolution. A debate such as this certainly reflects the concerns of the revolution and provides contemporary evidence of the arguments that were current in this turbulent period of Sparta's history. Nevertheless the attribution of the debate to Agis and Leonidas must be questioned. It is so detailed that it is highly improbable that it was ever said by them and recalled many years later. The analogy between a city and musical harmony occurs again in the *Life of Cleomenes* (16.6). Given the degree of detail and the musical analogy the subject matter of such a debate is more appropriate to the later revolution of Cleomenes with which Phylarchus clearly had greater familiarity. Indeed the passage of Teles' *On Exile*, discussed above, implies that Agis had not put forward a proposal for increasing the citizen body at all. The attribution of such a debate to Agis and Leonidas would have been brought about by the

---

[52] A possibility put forward by Africa 1961: 14.

tendency to perceive Agis' reign in terms of Cleomenes and consequently assume that the issues were the same.[53] No doubt the disturbances of Agis and Cleomenes' reigns were responses to similar conditions, but it should not be assumed that the responses themselves were the same.

An examination of the argument attributed to Agis produces some interesting evidence of Stoic influence. For out of all those who are alleged to have visited Sparta, the three selected in this argument all have Stoic connections.[54] Thaletas, the musician, said to have been a friend of Lycurgus, came from Crete to put an end to civil upheaval in Sparta by means of his music which induced *eupeitheia* (obedience) and *homonoia* (unity) (Plut. *Lyc.* 4.1-3). Terpander, another musician, also managed to resolve civil conflict at Sparta by means of his musical virtuosity (Plut. *De Mus.* 1146b). He brought together the Spartans with his harmonious song, *tês harmonias têi ôidêi* (Diod. 8.28). Thus these musicians are found promoting *homonoia*, which has a familiar Stoic ring to it.

This would be of little value on its own if it was not for a work of the Stoic, Diogenes of Babylon, who wrote in the first half of the second century BC. Diogenes wrote a book, *On Music*, much of which is preserved and attacked in Philodemus' own work on music (SVF 3 Diog. 54-90). Diogenes sought to show the influence that music could have on character and politics; he appears to be following to some extent the fifth-century Athenian musician, Damon (SVF 3 Diog. 56). Diogenes cites the examples of Thaletas, Terpander and Stesichorus as musicians who resolved civil conflict and *dichonoia* (disunity) in Sparta (SVF 3 Diog. 83-5). Here we find a Stoic recounting these same stories as evidence for his thesis. Moreover, he emphasises that they put an end to *dichonoia*, the opposite of *homonoia*. This is a Stoic term, unknown before the Stoa (see Chapter 2). Its application here suggests that the Stoics had a role in developing the stories of these musicians and in particular the association between the musicians and *homonoia/dichonoia*. Thus not only are the actions of these musicians described by a non-Stoic, Plutarch, in terms that could be construed as Stoic, but they are also described in this way by a Stoic. Diogenes was writing a short time after Sphaerus, but there is no reason to believe that Sphaerus would not have held similar views.[55] Indeed Plutarch, who makes the connection between Thaletas and *homonoia*, may even have been using Sphaerus directly in his *Life of Lycurgus*.[56]

[53] For a discussion of this, see §3 above.

[54] Cf. Ollier 1943: 10-11.

[55] This is not to suggest that it was Sphaerus who originated the link between *homonoia* and Sparta. Ephorus, who had stressed the kinship between Crete and Sparta, had earlier believed *homonoia* to be an important feature of both constitutions, Strabo 10.480, FGH 70F149, Diod. 7.12. Cf. Xen. *Mem.* 3.5.16.

[56] Babut 1969: 194.

Pherecydes of Syros, the third foreigner listed, was not a musician but a sixth-century philosopher, or more accurately a mythographer and theogonist.[57] Theopompus said that it was Pherecydes who recommended that Sparta should ban gold and silver after learning this in a dream, a story also attributed to Pythagoras.[58] The Stoics were familiar with him, as a reference to his illness shows (Plut. SVF 3.762). While they may have approved of his attitude to money, their interest in him was primarily philosophical. Various of his ideas about creation appear to have been subjected to a Stoic interpretation.[59] According to Damascius (KRS 50) Pherecydes held that Chronos' seed produced fire, wind and water (*pur, pneuma, hudôr*). For Pherecydes to have argued that Chronos' seed was cosmologically creative is not implausible, but the introduction of three elements of fifth-century four-element theory seems anachronistic. Scholars have suggested that this is a rationalising Stoic interpretation;[60] the Stoics held that sperm was *pneuma meth' hugrou*, breath with moisture (SVF 1.128) and that *pneuma* was a combination of fire and water (Alex. Aphrod. SVF 2.786, 310). Sphaerus himself was interested in sperm (D.L. 7.159) and even wrote a book about it (D.L. 7.178). Another passage (KRS 54) reports Pherecydes' belief that Zeus, before creating, turned into Eros, but it adds a note of explanation, that 'he brought the world which he had formed out of opposites into agreement and friendship (*philia*) and sowed sameness in all things and unity which permeates everything'. This explanation has been described as a 'palpably Stoic interpretation'.[61] Moreover the conception of Eros as a unifying element and the relationship with *philia* has already been seen to be present in Zeno's *Politeia*.

All three of the respected foreigners are men with whom the Stoa would feel an affinity. The teachings of all of them are said to have been in agreement with that of Lycurgus. Sphaerus' book on Lycurgus and Socrates may well have emphasised Lycurgus' association with philosophers and other learned men. It is clear, at least as regards Thaletas and Terpander, that Agis considers them to be politically important and that he is alluding to their resolution of civil conflict. For he discusses the value of music in eliminating discord. The original stories of their intervention in Sparta, however, appear to have been non-political.[62] Thaletas is reported to have put an end to a plague (Paus. 1.14.4, Plut. *De Mus*. 1146c) and Terpander introduced the first organised music (Plut. *De Mus*. 1134b). It has been argued by W.G.

[57] Kirk, Raven and Schofield 1983: 48f. KRS refers to the fragment numbers in this work.
[58] D.L. 1.117, Tigerstedt 1953: 8-13.
[59] Following Kirk, Raven and Schofield 1983: 56-63.
[60] Ibid. 58.
[61] Ibid. 62.
[62] Forrest 1963: 163.

Forrest that there developed an anti-Spartan tradition which represented a divided Sparta relying on foreign aid to save it from various crises.[63] For Sparta has a disproportionate number of foreigners giving assistance. In addition to those under discussion there were such men as the Aegeidai from Thebes, Teisamenos of Elis and Cimon of Athens. As a result stories of musicians such as Thaletas, Terpander and Stesichorus were politicised. It was a tradition which probably began in democratic Athens in the last half of the fifth century. Forrest puts forward the hypothesis that it was Damon, the musician and associate of Pericles, who first linked music and politics, the same man whose work had been used, whether directly or indirectly by Diogenes of Babylon. Interestingly Philodemus is scornful of these stories and attributes them to musicians and those who made up stories about the past (Philod. SVF 3 Diog. 83). If it is correct that this is part of an anti-Spartan tradition, originating in Athens, it is curious to find it being utilised by the Spartan revolution. Someone educated in Athens, such as Sphaerus, could be expected to be more familiar with this particular political tradition about these men.

Thus, if this argument which is attributed to Agis is examined, some striking points emerge. It begins by ascribing to Lycurgus a view with philosophical implications, that there is no inherent difference between people of different states. Foreigners could be just as valuable as Spartans; in fact it is better to have a good foreigner than a bad Spartan. This recalls the Stoic, although not exclusively Stoic, belief that morality is the only valid distinction between men. The argument proceeds to bring forward historical evidence to support this assertion about Lycurgus' beliefs. This evidence seems to come from a Stoic source, following an Athenian or at least a non-Spartan tradition. For Agis' justification we can speak fairly confidently of a Stoic influence. For the *anaplêrôsis* itself it can be said that it is consistent with Stoicism, both in its attitude to foreigners and in its concern with extending the franchise, although still on a relatively small scale. The reality did not quite match up to the justification. In practice the main emphasis in the selection of new citizens was to be on their youth and physical strength (*Agis* 8.3, *Cleom.* 10.11). For they were to make up the Spartan army.

5. Equality and property

The purpose of increasing the citizen body is not difficult to see; it provided Sparta with a large and much needed citizen army. The property reforms do not allow such a straightforward explanation. It is true that the new citizen body would need to be furnished with a

---

[63] Ibid. 162-5.

certain amount of property, but the reformers went beyond this.
Instead of proposing that all citizens should have a minimum level of
landed property, they sought absolute equality. This emphasis on
equality was fundamental to the revolution; the task was to make
Spartan citizens equal (*Agis* 6.1, 7.3, 9.4, *Cleom.* 7.1, *Comp.* 2.4). The
whole of the Spartan land was to be put in the common stock and
distributed equally among the new and old citizens (*Agis* 8, *Cleom.*
10.11, 11.1, esp. 18.2). There was full equalisation of landed property,
that is to say no Spartan could possess land in addition to his *klêros*,
whether within or without Spartan territory. Further equalisation of
property was to affect not only land, but also 'money and other forms of
moveable property'.[64] In the case of Agis we are told that he proposed
to put at the disposal of the revolution his property, which included
arable and pasture land and six hundred talents in money (*Agis* 9.5).
Cleomenes did likewise with his property and in both cases the rest of
the rich were expected to follow suit. (*Agis* 9.6, 10.1-2, *Cleom.* 11.1).
The cancellation of debts formed an integral part of such a programme
of equality (*Agis* 8.1, *Cleom.* 10.11). The reforms would also have had
an effect on the *perioikoi*, a point that will be considered below.

So Cleomenes achieved a radical change in the distribution of
property which would have created extensive domestic upheaval while
it was being implemented. Since the exigencies of the moment did not
demand such an extreme solution, it might seem that the explanation
lies in Spartan tradition. For the revolution emphasised its links with
Sparta of old. Yet there is little evidence to indicate that those who
wrote in the centuries preceding the revolution believed that Lycurgus
or the early Spartans were the proponents of such extreme equality. In
fact earlier evidence for any form of equality of property in Sparta at
all is scarce, surprisingly so since it is later considered such an
important element of the Spartan system. It will be argued here that it
was the revolution itself which was responsible for elevating the
equality of property into its central position[65] and that in this respect
the revolution reflected contemporary Stoic ideas about equality. As
with the extension of citizenship the revolution again justifies itself in
terms of the past and again Stoic ideas are apparent.

What then do the prerevolutionary writers say about property
ownership in Sparta? Herodotus briefly notes the reforms of Lycurgus,
but has no mention of equality of property (Herod. 1.65). In the fourth
century there are a couple of allusions which occur in Plato. These
would seem to imply the knowledge of some tradition by the audience,
but their brevity could lead us to misconstrue completely the nature of

---

[64] Fuks 1962 (*CPh*).
[65] This was suggested as early as Grote 1872: 311-33 (4th edition); cf. Jones 1967: 40-3
who believes the 'myth of Lycurgan land' reform and equality of property arose in the
fourth century.

this tradition. Plato remarks that a division of land took place at the time of the Dorian invasion, but it was not the result of any revolutionary redistribution. Apparently this was into equal allotments, but this is not made clear, nor is it clear what land was divided (Plato *Laws* 3.684de, 5.736c).[66] No connection is made with Lycurgus. Such a tradition would place the distribution before Spartan expansion and the conquest of Messenia; hence any equality would soon have been swamped by surplus land. Division of land was, anyway, a commonplace occurrence during colonisation. In the classical period division into equal allotments seems to have been the norm; this is likely to have influenced perceptions of early Sparta.[67] Isocrates, on the other hand, complains of the inequality and injustice of the Spartan settlement at the time of the Dorian invasion; later in the same speech he notes that there has never been any revolution, redistribution of land or cancellation of debts in Sparta (Isoc. *Panath.* 178, 259). Aristotle in his lengthy discussion of the equality of property in the *Politics* makes no mention of any equality of property in Sparta, rather he emphasises the gross inequality which existed in his own day (Arist. *Pol.* 1270a15ff). The matter is similarly absent from Xenophon's book on the Spartan constitution, in spite of his familiarity with Sparta. It might be objected that it was not relevant to these works; this seems doubtful and, even if it were the case, one would expect an allusion to something so important. Even the Spartan *klêros* is elusive in these fifth- and fourth-century writers. Aristotle, however, in a fragment of his *Spartan Constitution*, did note that it is shameful to sell land in Sparta and not possible at all to sell the ancient allotment (*archaia moira*) (Arist. Frag. 611.12 Rose, cf. *Pol.* 1270a19ff).

Such silence is mystifying, even with Spartan secrecy. The evidence only allows us to say that there appears to have been a belief in some form of traditional allotment and, to judge by Plato's remarks, presumably equal. Nevertheless, there is no indication that it was thought to be an especially significant feature of Sparta, nor that it embraced all the land. Several writers do comment that the rich and poor had a similar way of life, at least as regards education and the common messes (Arist. *Pol.* 1294b25ff, Xen. *Lac. Pol.* 7, Thuc. 1.6.4). It is possible that this and the fact that Spartan citizens had to contribute an equal share to the *sussitia* (Xen. *Lac. Pol.* 7.3) could have led to the belief that there were originally equal allotments. It is clear from these writers that full equality as it is found in the third century

[66] MacDowell 1986: 89-94 considers Plato to be important evidence, but concedes that it is 'brief and vague' and needs to be supplemented by Polybius and Plutarch. Yet both these are writing after the Hellenistic revolution.

[67] The evidence for the actual practice in earlier periods is, however, ambiguous. The literary tradition indicates equality, but the archaeological inclines in the other direction, Graham 1982: 151-2. Writers in the classical period were more likely to have been influenced by contemporary practice and the literary tradition.

revolution was unknown for early Sparta.[68] 'Equality', as it is found in the term for the Spartan citizens, the *homoioi* (peers), is only used loosely; it is 'unreal'.[69] There was equality as citizens, possibly with an equal *klêros*, but there was always public political privilege for the few and additional, often large, estates for the rich.[70]

The tradition before the revolution shows that it might be possible to claim Lycurgan authority for some kind of redistribution of land into equal allotments, but not for such radical changes which included redistribution of all land and the equalisation of movable property. Yet the revolution did seek to do just that (cf. *Agis* 9.5-6, *Cleom.* 18.2). The only detailed account which gives Lycurgus such extreme aims is preserved by Plutarch in his *Life of Lycurgus*, chapters 8 to 9.2. It is totally out of keeping with all the accounts from before the revolution and has so many links with that revolution that it surely derives from their propaganda. Lycurgus' aim is said to be to eradicate inequality (*to anison*) and unevenness (*to anômalon*) in all forms (Plut. *Lyc.* 9.1). He had intended to divide up movable property, but due to opposition he tried to achieve the same end by banning the use of gold and silver as currency. Instead iron was to be used (Plut. *Lyc.* 9.2). The unsuccessful intentions of a near-mythical figure would have been very hard to ascertain. Since this is so similar to the aims of the third-century revolution as regards movable property, it is reasonable to believe that to justify the revolutionary policy Cleomenes, or more probably Sphaerus, derived Lycurgus' intention from the more well-known assertion that he changed the currency (cf. Xen. *Lac. Pol.* 7.5-6). Thus it was argued that, although Lycurgus had not done this, he would have done so if he could. The revolution was merely carrying out his plans.

If we return to the *Life of Lycurgus*, chapter 8, here too there are close similarities with the Hellenistic revolution as well as evidence of Stoicism. It opens with a review of the problems facing Sparta before Lycurgus. There is great inequality in land distribution, a gulf between the many poor and the few rich; arrogance, envy, crime and luxury are prevalent; the state is afflicted by the diseases, poverty and wealth. This is remarkably similar to the condition of third-century Sparta

[68] The theory that the fourth-century historian Ephorus referred to the equality of property in a now lost work must be rejected, as it is by Gabba 1957: 202-14. Polybius' statements about property for which he gives no source reflect the propaganda of the third-century revolution rather than Ephorus, 6.45.3, 6.48.

[69] Forrest 1980: 51

[70] The existence of a few very rich Spartans in the fourth century is apparent from Arist. *Pol.* 1270a15ff, but there is evidence for wealthy Spartans earlier, cf. Herod. 7.134.2. From the mid-sixth century the Spartan rich often displayed their wealth in chariot racing; on their many victories at Olympia and elsewhere, De Ste Croix 1972: 354-5. Such victories were costly and conferred prestige, Xen. *Ages.*, Isoc. *Archid.* 55, Davies 1971: xxv-vi.

before the revolution. Cleomenes, too, compares poverty and wealth to diseases (*Cleom*. 10.7). Therefore Lycurgus put all the land into the public domain and redivided it, just as Agis and Cleomenes proposed (*Agis* 9.5, *Cleom*. 10.11, 11.1). For pre-eminence should not come through property but virtue. No difference or inequality exists between man except that which is determined by the criterion of blame for bad actions and praise for good ones. The Stoic sentiment recalls the similar one which appeared in the argument for the extension of citizenship discussed above. Finally, the figures given for the number of allotments distributed by Lycurgus are exactly twice those attributed to Agis – 9,000 for Spartan citizens and 30,000 for *perioikoi* – a discrepancy that is made intelligible if one takes into account the loss of Messenia.[71] Since Plutarch did use Sphaerus for his *Life of Lycurgus*, whether directly or indirectly, his account here in chapters 8 to 9.2 may well have derived from him. In addition to the evidence of Stoicism, it is perfectly suited to act as a Lycurgan justification for the extreme equality which was present in the revolutionary reforms of the third century.

The idea of equality was clearly a fundamental tenet of the revolution, but why did they put so much emphasis on it and seek to achieve such an extreme version? It had no basis in earlier conceptions of old Sparta. Rather it was developed by and for the revolution. Shimron believes the philosophical education of the kings was a factor, but he also argues that by a total equalisation of property Cleomenes could deprive his opponents of their property, thus making his own position more secure.[72] This last suggestion is improbable; Cleomenes' opponents were all in exile (*Cleom*. 10.1) and he could easily have confiscated their property without going to such lengths. Unconstitutional action was not beyond him, as his killing of the ephors demonstrates.

The proposals for equality were responses to the economic problems which beset Sparta, but responses conditioned by the Stoicism that Sphaerus had introduced to Sparta. His influence on the historical justifications for the reforms has already been shown. The desire for

---

[71] The figures given in Agis' *rhetra* are contradictory, *Agis* 8. It proposed to divide the land into 4,500 allotments, which fits neatly with the Lycurgan figures, but is inconsistent with the provisions for the *sussitia*. There were to be 15 *sussitia*, some made up of 200 citizens, others of 400 citizens. It is impossible to match these up with the 4,500 allotments if that means 4,500 citizens. This casts doubt on the authenticity of Agis' programme. Cleomenes' reforms produced an army of 4,000 citizen-soldiers. If this is taken to mean that there were 4,000 allotments, it would be compatible with the figures given for Agis' *sussitia* (10 x 200, 5 x 400). However the number of citizen-soldiers might not be equivalent to the number of allotments. It might not include the old and the exiles, who were alloted land, though these are unlikely to make a significant difference. I would suggest that the 4,500 represented the objective and 4,000 the result. The 4,000 citizens were then divided into 15 *sussitia* on the lines given above.

[72] Shimron 1972: 41.

full equality cannot be explained by the immediate military or political aims of Cleomenes. It was consistent, however, with the Stoic ideas on equality and property outlined in the previous chapter, although here it is for a limited number. There it was argued that inequality of property holdings could not be justified, because ideally all property should be common. The produce of nature should be equal for all. Moreover their theory of justice placed great emphasis on equality within the community, an emphasis which recurs in the Spartan revolution (cf. *Agis* 6.1, 7.3, 9.4, *Cleom.* 7.1, 18.2, *Comp.* 2.4) According to Plutarch these Spartans sought to revive a noble and just society (*Agis* 2.10).

The chief concern of the reformers was equality within the citizen body, but it is likely that these ideas about equality were also applied to the *perioikoi*, at least in respect of property holdings. The measures for land redistribution to Spartan citizens must have affected the territory of the *perioikoi*. For many wealthy Spartans, including the kings, had estates in the territory of the *perioikoi*, which were relinquished as a result of the egalitarian nature of the revolution.[73] Additionally many *perioikoi* would have lost land there in order to take up Spartan citizenship. Consequently some degree of redistribution was necessary there too. Plutarch reports that Agis proposed 15,000 allotments for the *perioikoi* in their territory (*Agis* 8.1). This proposal is likely to have formed part of the programme of Cleomenes. Since the land redistribution among Spartan citizens was taking place on the basis of equality, it would be odd if it did not follow the same pattern among the *perioikoi*. The rest of the Peloponnese believed that Cleomenes would introduce reforms outside Sparta (*Cleom.* 17.5), a belief that was unlikely to have gained acceptance if the measures concerning the *perioikoi* contradicted it.

What does it mean for allotments to be equal? If Cleomenes simply divided the land into equal-sized allotments, there would still be a wide range of inequality. For some areas of land would be more fertile than others and no doubt the better land would go to those who had previously been rich and influential. It is a measure of the seriousness with which the reformers treated the promotion of equality that they did not do this. In the account of Lycurgus' land reforms which was developed by the revolution (Plut. *Lyc.* 8, see above) it is said that each lot had to be capable of producing 70 medimni of barley for a man and 12 for a woman and a proportionate amount of wine and oil. So it was not the size that was important but the capacity for production. Since it is likely that this was done by the reformers of the third century, it demonstrates that the equality was not superficial but thorough.

---

[73] Cf. Fuks 1962 (*CPh*).

6. Conclusion

The ideology of the Spartan revolution, although it was rooted in a mythical Lycurgan past, was not an anachronism; rather it was a conception of the past based firmly in the present. Under the influence of Sphaerus and his Stoicism various disparate elements were taken and made into a unity. The contemporary slogans of social revolution, the cancellation of debts and the redistribution of land, were introduced into a Spartan context where they were provided with Lycurgan justifications. Rather than being haphazard this was given a coherency by the Stoic emphasis on equality (*isotês*) which permeated the revolution and its ideology. This was a response to the problem of excessive wealth and poverty and the social unrest inherent in it. Instead of suppressing the unrest the revolution sought to remedy the problem. Some years later Nabis' revolutionary measures were supported by a similar ideology; equality was a theme and the name of Lycurgus was still invoked.[74]

Regardless of whether the Spartan kings intended their revolution to be for export to the rest of the Peloponnese, there is extensive evidence that people believed that it was. This was surely because the ideology of the revolution was not purely Spartan, but was expressed in general terms that, although applied to Sparta, need not have particular reference to it. The reformers did not profess to be simply recreating Lycurgan Sparta. They attacked wealth and advocated equality, a point of view that many Peloponnesians would and did sympathise with. If they had witnessed an equalisation of property among the *perioikoi*, they would have more readily believed that it was intended for them as well. The ruling class of the Peloponnese had no doubt that the Spartan revolution could undermine their position. Aratus is said to have sought the Macedonian alliance to avoid the Spartan barley bread and short cloak and the most appalling things for which he denounced Cleomenes, namely the elimination of wealth and the correction of poverty (*Cleom.* 16.6-7). Clearly they feared not only Spartan hegemony, but the social revolution which they believed would accompany it and whose targets they would be. Hostility to the reform movement is evident, too, in a poem of Cercidas, the Megalopolitan politician and Cynic. He apparently attacked Sphaerus for degeneracy.[75] While the rich were in fear, the poor were restless, awaiting revolution and expecting the redistribution of land and the cancellation of debts (*Cleom.* 17.5). Although this all comes from Plutarch, it cannot be dismissed as wishful thinking on the part of Phylarchus. For he also recorded the frustrated expectations of the

---

[74] Livy 34.31.16-18, 34.32.4, cf. 38.4, 39.33-7, Plut. *Philopoemen* 16.
[75] Powell frag. 8 and 9, Dudley 1937: 82, 93, Walbank 1943: 11.

Argive lower classes (*Cleom*. 20.6). Moreover Aratus' denunciations
probably derive from his own *Memoirs* (*Cleom*. 16.4-7). In the *Life of
Aratus* we hear of the popular support that exists for those leading
Corinthians who were in favour of Cleomenes and opposed to Aratus
(Plut. *Aratus* 40). The tone of the passage suggests that it was not from
Phylarchus. Polybius provides confirmation of the extent of Cleomenes'
support if not the reason for it. Cleomenes had supporters in every city
except Megalopolis and Stymphalia (Polyb. 2.55.8).

The Achaean ruling class was right to be alarmed about social
unrest. Even before Cleomenes' revolution there had been signs of
unrest. At Cynaetha there had been demands for the redivision of
lands (Polyb. 4.17.4) and 'a great massacre', apparently perpetrated by
its opponents, took place some time between 241 and 229.[76]
Nevertheless it might be argued that the unrest that followed
Cleomenes' revolution was based on a misconception of Spartan
intentions. The ideology of the revolution was formulated, on one level,
in general terms which were attractive to the lower classes of the
Peloponnese, but there is no statement in the sources that Cleomenes
did intend to introduce social and economic reforms outside Sparta,
only that people thought that he would. Argos is normally taken as
decisive for the argument that he did not intend it.[77] For the Argives,
after being disappointed in their expectations for an abolition of debts,
revolt from Cleomenes (*Cleom*. 20.6). But this does not tell us that
Cleomenes did not intend to introduce reform there, only that he did
not carry it out. Aratus was concerned about Cleomenes' influence with
the lower classes; he would not allow the king to address the common
people of Argos lest he win them over (*Cleom*. 17.1-2), surely because
what Cleomenes would say to them would particularly appeal to them.
This suggests advocacy of social and economic reform. Moreover, he is
said to have captured some cities by persuasion and others by threats
(Polyb. 2.52.2). Given Aratus' anxiety, it is likely that 'persuasion'
entailed promises of some such reform. So the revolution of Cleomenes
stirred up the lower classes of the Peloponnese both by its example and
by suggestion that the revolution would not be limited to Sparta. There
is, however, no evidence to suggest that revolutionary reforms were
implemented outside Sparta by the Spartans. Nabis, on the other
hand, did make positive efforts to spread revolution. In Argos he
introduced, according to Livy, cancellation of debts and redistribution
of land (32.38).

The Spartan revolution highlights briefly the increasing polarisation
that existed between rich and poor in third-century Greece. The
revolution exacerbated the antagonism and produced a situation in

[76] Cf. Shimron 1972: 46.
[77] Africa 1961: 26; against is Shimron 1972: 45-6.

which change seemed a real possibility. These were the conditions in which Stoic political thought was formulated and the Spartan episode reveals something of their response to them. In the second century Stoics, writing in a different milieu and with different sympathies, were embarrassed by the affiliations and political activities of their predecessors. As the next chapter will show, they sought to distance themselves from the Stoic involvement in Sparta and attacked the land reforms. It was Aratus who deserved praise for attention to property and by implication Sphaerus who should be condemned.

7

The Gracchi

1. Change in the Stoa

The Spartan revolution had widespread repercussions, not only on the international scene, but also on the Stoa itself. It ultimately helped to bring about a division within the Stoa between those more sympathetic to the radical ideas of their predecessors and those who wished to distance themselves from this heritage. Signs of this only became apparent in the second century BC. Cleomenes' revolution itself may not have been sufficient to cause this, but with the emergence of his more radical imitator, Nabis, still espousing the same ideology, certain Stoics became concerned to dissociate themselves from such movements. This led to a revision of Stoic views on property.

The events in Sparta and the ensuing instability would have caused a general loss of confidence among Stoics, which made them more prepared to change their ideas. Such a loss of confidence cannot have been helped by the attacks on the Stoa that emerged from the sceptical Academy during much of the second century. Carneades, in particular, launched a vehement attack on the doctrines of Chrysippus. As a sceptic he was especially concerned with their theory of knowledge, but his attack also embraced their arguments on justice. Thus the Stoics found themselves in a position where it was necessary to defend and reassess their doctrines. In the field of political thought it would have pushed them further in the direction that the reaction against Sphaerus had begun.

But there were also changes in the international situation. At the time of the reign of Nabis a new power, Rome, was establishing its authority over Greece and this was to have an effect on the development of the Stoa in a variety of ways. It is likely that the Stoic reaction against the Spartan revolution, which will be discussed in detail below, was in part a response to increasing Roman involvement in Greece. For in 195, after defeating the Macedonian king Philip V, the Roman commander T. Flamininus fought a war against Nabis; before fighting this he ensured that he had Greek public opinion on his side by calling an assembly of Greek states to Corinth to vote for the war (Livy 34.22-4). Two years later Nabis broke his peace treaty with

Rome, but his subsequent assassination prevented him causing any more problems for Rome. In such a political climate the Stoa would have felt it all the more necessary to dissociate itself from the revolutionary ideology which had permeated this phase of Spartan history and to which Sphaerus had contributed. If Stoics were already attracted to Rome by the latter's hostility to Macedon, they would have been even less willing to run the risk of alienating it.

More important, it was contact with Rome that gave these developing conservative tendencies within the Stoa their lasting influence. For they were in sympathy with the political outlook of their Roman patrons; in contrast Stoic radicalism rapidly disappears from the records. In the second century both these groups of Stoics had their representatives; Panaetius of Rhodes could be described as one of the dissenters, while Antipater of Tarsus and Blossius of Cumae were more traditional Stoics. The emergence of this new power had a considerable impact on Greek intellectuals. Their varying responses to the tribunate of Tiberius Gracchus and to Roman imperial expansion will be discussed in this and the next chapter respectively.

2. Sparta and the Gracchi

During a highly controversial tribunate in 133 BC Tiberius Gracchus, the elder of two brothers from a noble family, proposed and carried an agrarian law. This law limited the size of holdings of *ager publicus* (public land) and arranged for the distribution of the remaining *ager publicus* in allotments to poor Roman citizens. In order to ensure the passing of the law, Tiberius had to arrange the deposition of another tribune, M. Octavius, who had persisted in using his veto to block the measure. A *popularis* politician, relying heavily on the support of the People, he aroused such hostility in the Senate that in the same year he was murdered in a riot by a group of senators and their supporters led by P. Scipio Nasica. Tiberius' brother Gaius was a tribune from 123 to 122 with similar but wider-ranging interests and in 121 he too died violently.

Plutarch made a detailed comparison between these two Roman tribunes and the Spartan revolutionaries. In his *Parallel Lives* he paired the *Lives* of Agis and Cleomenes with the *Lives* of Tiberius and Gaius Gracchus. Yet the comparison did not originate with Plutarch; it already existed as early as Cicero (*De Off.* 2.80) and may even have stemmed from Panaetius himself, at least in respect of Tiberius. Certainly comparison between Sparta and Rome had been made even before this; in the mid-second century Polybius had compared their constitutions (Polyb. 6.10), something which may also have been done by Cato the Elder (Cic. *De Rep.* 2.2). Later Cicero, too, was to compare the basic principles of these two constitutions (Cic. *De Rep.* 2, esp. 42).

These comparisons are with traditional Sparta. As long as the Roman constitution fared better, conservative Romans were happy to make such a comparison, but they had no wish at all to associate the Roman constitution with revolutionary Sparta. For them these revolutionaries were akin to those who destabilised the Roman constitution (cf. Cic. *De Off.* 2.80), a comparison which may have appealed to the more *popularis* Roman. Livy, possibly following Polybius, gives a pair of speeches by Nabis and Flamininus (Livy 34.31-2).[1] In defence of his actions Nabis is alleged to have contrasted revolutionary Sparta with Rome; in Sparta the lawgiver had arranged an equal distribution of wealth and position (*aequatio fortunae ac dignitatis*), whereas Rome was the rule by the few rich over the poor (Livy 34.31.16-19). Flamininus, in response, attacks Nabis' arguments and concludes by describing his speech as a *popularis oratio* (Livy 34.32.20). Nabis' ideas are echoed without reference to Sparta in a slightly corrupt passage of Pseudo-Sallust, discussing a proposed electoral reform of the *popularis* Gaius Gracchus. This is said to have aimed at equalising wealth (*pecunia*) and position (*dignitas*) in the Roman system of electing magistrates (Ps. Sall. *Ep. ad Caes.* 2.8.1-2). It will be suggested here that the comparison between the Spartan kings and the Gracchi, whether justified or not, was the outcome of Stoic arguments which began by debating Sphaerus' activities in Sparta and ended up being applied to Tiberius Gracchus, both attacking him and in support of him. Before discussing the tribunate of Tiberius Gracchus, therefore, it is necessary to examine the development of these Stoic arguments.

3. Justice and equity

In about the mid-second century BC or a little earlier the nature of justice came under scrutiny within the Stoa.[2] Previously what was just (*to dikaion/iustum*) was independent of the laws of any city. In such a system where justice was perfect and absolute, there was no place for equity (*epieikeia/aequitas*). For justice was distribution according to worth (Stobaeus SVF 3.125, 262, 280, Andronicus SVF 3.266), see Chapter 5.2. Therefore an appeal for equity can only be a demand that someone gets more or less than he deserves, because the wise man, who will be perfectly just, cannot be mistaken about such matters. To yield to such a demand would be an example of injustice (Stobaeus SVF 3.640, D.L. 7.123, SVF 3.641).[3] For Chrysippus and the early Stoics all existing laws of cities were in error (Eusebius SVF 3.324; cf. Cic. *Acad. Pr.* 2.136, SVF 3.599; Plut. *St. Rep.* 1033f). In the second century,

---

[1] Briscoe 1981: 97-104.

[2] The argument concerning *iustum* and *aequum* presented here develops some suggestions put forward by Nicolet 1965: 154-7, cf. also Smuts 1958: 106-16.

[3] Cf. Rist 1978: 266-8.

however, there was an attempt to tie justice more closely to the laws of the city. Since such laws are not perfect and do not cover every situation it becomes necessary to resort to equity. This attempt is epitomised in the debate between two leading Stoics, Antipater of Tarsus and Diogenes of Babylon, which appears in Cicero's *De Officiis* (3.50-7, 91-2).

For Cicero the debate is concerned with the conflict between morality and expediency, although it is not clear that this was particularly relevant to the positions of either Antipater or Diogenes. Cicero has already noted that such questions had seldom been discussed in any depth by the Stoics before his own time and he seeks to remedy this omission (*De Off.* 3.8, 10, 34). Such an omission is hardly surprising as the Stoics believed that what is good is always expedient (e.g. Stobaeus SVF 3.86). Book 3 of the *De Officiis* is devoted to this conflict between morality and expediency, and thus Cicero would appear to be interpreting their positions to suit the requirements of his own argument. This claim does not entail the belief that they did not disagree, only that the object of their disagreement was something else. Diogenes' position has often been considered rather shocking; it has been said, for instance, that for Diogenes 'moral virtue was simply obedience to existing regulations'.[4] Since Cicero virtually everyone has tended to side with Antipater against Diogenes.[5] This consensus should lead us to wonder whether Diogenes might have been misrepresented. Since in such a disagreement the person with the most interest in discrediting Diogenes is Antipater, I am inclined to think that Cicero is reporting Diogenes' position via Antipater. There is also the possibility that Cicero did not understand what he was writing about and consequently saw a disagreement where there was none, but I believe that an interpretation of this passage can be produced without charging Cicero with complete incompetence.

The debate is about business ethics, a subject which for the Stoics came within the scope of justice and which was described by them as *eusunallaxia*, justice in exchange. This was the knowledge of how blamelessly to conduct transactions with one's neighbours (Stobaeus SVF 3.264, cf. Andronicus SVF 3.273). Antipater holds to the old Stoic conception of justice; the laws of a city may not instruct the seller to reveal information to the buyer which it would be in the buyer's interest to know, but his obligation to his fellow man demands that he

---

[4] Reesor 1951: 25.

[5] E.g. Sandbach 1975: 128. Annas, 'Cicero on Stoic moral philosophy and private property', in a detailed discussion of this debate defends Diogenes, arguing that his views have been misrepresented, but her interpretation differs from that presented here. She argues that Diogenes and Antipater are concerned with different questions, so their answers are not necessarily incompatible, although Cicero imagines that they are.

does. It would be unjust not to do so (*De Off.* 3.54-5). Diogenes takes a
different position; for him it is only *necesse* or *oportere* (necessary) to
reveal what the law demands (*De Off.* 3.51, 52, 53, 91). No doubt he
would reveal more if he was asked. He is not saying that he should not
tell, but that it is not necessary to do so.

Diogenes' position contains a distinction between what is *iustum*
(just), or a formal definition of *iustum*, and what is *aequum*
(equitable).[6] The seller must do what is *iustum*, that is act in
conformity with the law, but, although it might be *aequum* to reveal
what the buyer needs to know, he is not under the same kind of
obligation to do this. In a sense *iustum* entails legal obligation which is
augmented by *aequum*, a moral obligation. This is where he differs
from Antipater, who ignores the laws of cities and sees obligation only
in terms of universal justice (*De Off.* 3.52-3). Diogenes' view is one
which takes seriously the city's claim to be the arbiter of justice. It is at
odds with the position of early Stoics such as Chrysippus, but
consistent with the emphasis which Panaetius was later to place on
the unwise man. In this debate the role of *aequum* is not made clear,
only implied, but another passage, to be examined shortly, will make
such an assumption valid.

The key to the problem of why such a conception of justice should be
adopted lies in Diogenes' accusation that Antipater's position would
undermine property rights (*De Off.* 3.53). I would suggest that this is a
response to the Stoic involvement in the Spartan revolution. There
Stoic theory had been adopted to justify an equal distribution of
property; claims of justice had overridden legally established property
rights. Resort to a more orthodox approach to justice would tie it to the
law of the city and allow it to be emended by an appeal to equity, as one
finds in Aristotle (*NE* 5.10, 1137a 31-38a3). In this way these later
Stoics could now dissociate themselves from the radical activities of
Sphaerus. Such a position would conform with other information
which we have on Diogenes' thought. From a rather fragmentary
passage of Philodemus it would appear that he attacked rhetors for
their use of the theoric fund and for distributing public money, *ta koina*
(Philodemus SVF 3 Diog. 115). The more legalistic approach of
Diogenes is noted elsewhere by Cicero; in the *De Legibus* (3.13) he had
pointed out that the only Stoic prior to Panaetius to consider
magistrates was Diogenes. He is also known to have written a book
called the *Laws* (Athenaeus 12.526c, SVF 3 Diog. 53).

Diogenes was not the only Stoic to have used this distinction
between legal justice and *aequitas*. It was adopted by his pupil
Panaetius, a contemporary of Tiberius Gracchus. Many of Panaetius'

---

[6] Cf. Nicolet 1965: 154, although he seems to leave the exact relationship between
iustum and *aequum* slightly obscure.

views are known through Cicero, who used the Greek's work, *Peri Kathêkontos* (*On Appropriate Acts*) as the basis for his own *De Officiis*. To what extent this can be said to reflect the views of Panaetius has always been a matter of controversy. Yet Cicero does describe Panaetius as his source more formally than in any other work. Most important is *De Off*. 2.78-84, where the connection with the Spartan revolution is clear.[7] Agis IV of Sparta and the 'tyrants' that followed him are condemned for their attitude to property, but Aratus of Sicyon, his contemporary and Cleomenes' opponent, is praised. When Aratus ousted the tyrant, Nicocles, he was faced with a dilemma. It would be unjust not to let exiles reclaim property which was legally theirs, but it would not be *aequum* to evict the present occupiers, the *possessores*, although they had no legal right to it. Aratus, while not ignoring legal rights, found an equitable solution and offered fair compensation. As a result Aratus had a united state, but Agis' actions led to years of discord. The reference to Agis' several tyrannical successors indicates that Nabis as well as Cleomenes provoked this change in Stoic thinking.

These examples are introduced by a passage that condemns the inequity of laws for the redistribution of land and the cancellation of debts, both themes of the Spartan revolution (Plut. *Agis* 8, *Cleom*. 10.11). There is no *aequitas* in depriving a *possessor* of land he may have held for generations (Cic. *De Off*. 2.79). Diogenes' argument, which was followed by Panaetius, sought to uphold the law and thus Cleomenes, due to the illegality of his coup, acted wrongly. Agis presented more of a problem; he had tried to find a legal way of carrying out his proposals (in spite of removing the ephors). Hence, although Cleomenes made a greater impact, it is the example of Agis which is emphasised in the *De Officiis*. In this case the *iustum/aequum* distinction is relevant. For Agis' proposal may have been legal, but it was not *aequum*; he was evicting existing land-holders. Aratus, on the other hand, was concerned about both – he compromised. And so did the second-century Stoa. Van Straaten has pointed out another passage of Panaetius where the city and consequently its laws are closely linked with property rights: 'The chief reason for the formation of states (*respublicae* and *civitates*) was that private property might be maintained. For although men gathered together with nature's guidance, it was in the hope of keeping private possessions safe that men sought the protection of cities' (Cic. *De Off*. 2.73, Panaetius F.118). So for Panaetius the main function of the state, indeed its reason for coming into being, is the protection of private property.

[7] On Cicero's use of Panaetius: Cic. *De Off*. 2.60, 3.7, *Ad Att*. 16.11.4, Van Straaten 1946: 282. Cic. *De Off*. 2.78-84, based on Panaetius: Schmekel 1892: 45, Pohlenz 1934: 118, Fuks 1962 (*CQ*): 120, Nicolet 1965: 154-5. The stress on Greek examples seems to confirm that it is Panaetius.

The concern with legal justice, something alien to the early Stoa, is also present in Panaetius' account of *iustitia* (justice) as a virtue, where much emphasis is placed on legality and contracts, too much and too integral to be Cicero's contribution alone (*De Off.* 1.20-41). Thus the basis of justice is good faith, *fides*, which is essentially keeping to agreements and contracts one has made (*De Off.* 1.23). There is the question whether it is ever right to ignore an agreement; sometimes it is necessary to do so when circumstances arise which it was not possible to take into account when the agreement was originally made (*De Off.* 1.31-2). We are told that one should not go to extremes in sticking to the letter of the law, not an injunction to disobey the law, merely to conform to its spirit (*De Off.* 1.33). Slaves should be treated as if they were employees, i.e. as parties to a contract with their master, although they are not (*De Off.* 1.41, cf. Sen. *De Ben.* 3.22). This is a strangely legalistic conception of *iustitia* as a virtue. It should be made clear that *iustitia* is not to be equated with doing what is lawful, but it does seem dependent on it. In the discussion of *fortitudo* (courage), a virtue described as fighting on behalf of *aequitas, aequitas* too is seen as an essential feature of *iustitia*:[8] 'When you are very eager to attain pre-eminence over others, it is difficult to preserve *aequitas*, which is such an important element of *iustitia*.' This remark could be an allusion to the Spartan revolutionaries or possibly even Tiberius Gracchus. Thus to do what is *iustum* would be to act in accordance with the law and no more, but *aequitas* would demand honesty, fairness, what the law itself does not demand. *Iustitia*, the virtue, would entail paying attention to both. A further passage, which may have Panaetian origins,[9] states that only someone with the virtue of Socrates or Aristippus can ignore the city's rules, but they are rare (also they have to be dead before it is decided that they are such). Panaetius elsewhere shows an interest in Aristippus (D.L. 2.85, 87) and the passage goes on to express the developing Stoic concern to dissociate the Stoa from the Cynics.

So the general line of argument from Diogenes to Panaetius is that it is necessary (*necesse*) to do what is required by the law of a state, but one can go beyond it if *aequitas* demands it. One is not restricted to the requirements of the law, as, for instance, in the case of Aratus, but it will only be in exceptional circumstances that *aequitas* actually overrides the law. The emphasis on legality and contracts seems particularly Roman the result of a union between Greek philosophy and Rome. It is unlikely that these philosophers felt that they were jettisoning the old Stoic approach to justice; rather they were making it suitable for those who were not wise. If fools went round behaving

---

[8] Cic. *De Off.* 1.62-4, probably based on Panaetius, Schmekel 1892: 32.
[9] Panaetian origin: Schmekel 1892: 43, Pohlenz 1934: 83.

like wise men it led to chaos. Sparta was proof of this.

A conflict exists, therefore, between the more orthodox Stoic position of Antipater and the legalistic approach of Diogenes and Panaetius. The latter was an approach which not only held that laws should be complemented by *aequum*, but also that obedience to these laws is an element of *iustitia*. This difference also appears in their careers. Diogenes, the teacher of Panaetius (*Suda*, s.v. Panaitios), had had Laelius as his pupil (Cic. *De Fin*. 2.24) and later in his career in 155 he took part in an embassy to Rome along with Carneades and Critolaus (SVF 3 Diog. 6-10). Panaetius was from a prominent Rhodian family, which probably favoured Rome. He spent many years in Rome and was an intimate of Scipio Aemilianus and Laelius (Cic. *De Fin*. 4.23).[10] His sympathy with Rome will be examined in more detail in the next chapter. Antipater, on the other hand, appears to have spent most of his adult life in Athens and there is no record of any association with Romans (for Antipater's life, SVF 3 Antip. 1-15). One would expect any significant contact to be remarked upon. Moreover, according to Athenaeus there were several groups of Stoics in Athens, the Diogenists, the Antipatrists and the Panaetiasts (Athen. 5.186c, SVF 3 Antip. 14). Since the period of influence of Diogenes and Panaetius never overlapped, their followers need not have been in opposition to one another. Antipater, however, overlapped with both and so the existence of such groups may reflect a division between Antipater and the other two. Such divisions should not be overstressed; Panaetius is also said to have been the pupil of Antipater (Cic. *De Div*. 1.6, Panaetius F.6).

Elsewhere there are signs that arguments concerned with legality were current. Polybius provides important contemporary evidence. He gives a fairly lengthy discussion of the causes of the Second Punic War (218-201), a discussion that is provoked in part by the legalistic arguments going on in Rome in his own time.[11] These arguments made use of various treaties between Rome and Carthage to demonstrate that Carthage had been responsible for the war. For the Carthaginians had broken the treaty with Lutatius by attacking Saguntum and broken the agreement made with Hasdrubal by crossing the Ebro. Here the emphasis on what is legal is evident. But, argues Polybius, if the earlier Roman seizure of Sardinia was the cause of the war, not the destruction of Saguntum, then such legalistic arguments carry much less weight (Polyb. 3.30). There could be no justification for the Roman

[10] For further details on Panaetius and his family, see Appendix.

[11] The arguments about the treaties which were current in Rome appear in Polyb. 3.29. Polybius explicitly says that these arguments were not used at the time of the fall of Saguntum. Earlier he has given a history of treaties between Rome and Carthage from the first one, Polyb. 3.22-7. On these and the contemporary debate, Mommsen 1859: 320-5, Walbank 1957: 336-7, 356, Derow 1979: 9-10.

seizure and it was this action, believed Polybius, that was the most
important cause of the war (Polyb. 3.28, 3.10). Thus even though
Polybius accepts the Roman interpretation of these two treaties, he
implicitly frees the Carthaginians from responsibility for the war and
sees the justice of their case.[12]

A similar form of argument is found in the remains of the
thirty-sixth book of Polybius' history. He reports four different views
which were expressed by Greeks about the defeat of Carthage in 146
BC. An attack on the morality of Rome's actions is matched with a
lengthy answer justifying Rome's conduct. Rome had committed no act
of impiety (*asebêma*), because they had not wronged the gods, their
parents or the dead; nor an act of treachery (*paraspondêma*), because
no agreements had been broken by them; nor an act of injustice
(*adikêma*), because they had violated no laws or customs nor good
faith. There is here a shift from morality to legality,[13] but it is a shift
that also appears in the Stoic debate examined above. I would like to
think that the Greeks Polybius had in mind were those Stoics who
sympathised with Rome, such as Panaetius. Even if he did not mean
these, the emphasis on legality here indicates that the Stoic arguments
reflected contemporary intellectual concerns. Polybius' views on
Roman imperialism and rule will be discussed at greater length in the
next chapter.

Again in Polybius there is an interesting anecdote with a similar
theme about Scipio Aemilianus, the friend of Panaetius, and his
financial arrangements. Scipio was to pay to each of his two adoptive
aunts fifty talents of their dowry; according to the law the first
payment was due within ten months and the rest was to be paid in
instalments over three years. Scipio caused astonishment by paying it
all within ten months. He explained that when dealing with strangers
he observed the letter of the law, but he treated friends and relatives
differently if he could (Polyb. 31.27).

4. Panaetius and anti-Gracchan propaganda

Thus the debate within the Stoa had led to the development of an
argument directed against proposals for the redistribution of land and
which could be applied to any act which sought to overrule the law in
the interests of some universal justice. At the same time a law that
might harm certain members of the community should be tempered by
aequitas, a course followed by Aratus. Such arguments could also be
applied to Tiberius Gracchus. After examining examples of them in
action against Tiberius, the question of whether or not Panaetius

[12] Derow 1979: 9-13.
[13] As noted by Walbank 1965: 9.

himself applied them to Tiberius will be considered.

The clearest case of this distinction being used is not in fact with reference to the agrarian laws but the deposition of Octavius. Plutarch condemns the deposition as being neither lawful nor equitable, *ou nomimon oud' epieikes* (Plut. *TG* 11.4), probably echoing the arguments of its opponents, but Tiberius claimed that such a move was just, *dikaion* (Plut. *TG* 15.7). T. Annius, who delivered a vigorous attack on the deposition, is described by Plutarch as *ouk epieikês*, a further indication that this theme was important (Plut. *TG* 14.5-9, Livy *Per.* 58). The implication originally would have been: how could such a man judge?

As regards Tiberius' agrarian law the justice of his case receives considerable emphasis in our sources (e.g. Plut. *TG* 9.2, 9.4, 11.5, 15.7, Appian *BC* 1.11). The opposition's response follows very much the argument outlined above. They do not attack the law as being illegal, but what they do say is that it is not *aequum* that *possessores* (occupiers) be dispossessed from property that they may have held for generations or even inherited. This argument is put forward in an interesting passage of Florus with reference to both the Gracchi (Florus 2.1):[14] 'In everything they did there was the appearance of equity (*species aequitatis*). What could be more just than that the people (*plebs*) receive what is their own from the Senate, so that a people (*populus*) victorious over nations and possessor of the world should not be exiled from their altars and their hearths?' Then follows the counter-argument of those who believe that Tiberius' law is not *aequum*: 'How could the people (*plebs*) be returned to the land without turning out the occupiers who were themselves part of the people (*populus*) and who for a long time possessed as if by right estates left to them by their ancestors.' Both these arguments are attributed elsewhere to the protagonists (in favour of the law: Plut. *TG* 9.4-6, Appian *BC* 1.11; against it: Appian *BC* 1.10), but in Florus the argument of the earlier Stoic debate about *aequitas* is also introduced. This passage particularly recalls those of the *De Officiis* which stress the inequity of evicting those who have occupied land for generations (Cic. *De Off.* 2.79, 81). The argument that occupancy justifies possession occurs in Cic. *De Off.* 1.21 and goes back as far as Panaetius (see Chapter 5 above).

This debate had clearly been in progress since Diogenes, but when did Panaetius write his version of it? Did he refer to the tribunate of Tiberius Gracchus? The stress on the examples of Sparta and Aratus indicate the source of the debate and these were no doubt standard examples. In the *De Officiis* the comparison is made between the Spartan revolutionaries and both the Gracchi; Panaetius may have

[14] Nicolet 1965: 155-6.

referred to Tiberius alone and Cicero updated it in the light of Gaius' subsequent tribunate. It is odd that Cicero should attribute Gaius' death to his agrarian legislation, certainly not the most significant aspect of his tribunate. If Panaetius did make this comparison, it would strengthen the case that Stoic arguments were used against Tiberius.

There are, however, two views on the dating of Panaetius' *Peri Kathêkontos*. Posidonius said that it was written thirty years before his death (Cic. *De Off.* 3.8). One argument holds that, since Panaetius was no longer head of the school in 109 (Cic. *De Orat.* 1.45), he must have been dead by then. Therefore he wrote this work before Tiberius' tribunate and so could not have had Tiberius in mind. On the other hand Max Pohlenz has argued that, since the *De Oratore* shows only that he was not head of the school, he could have retired, as, for instance, Carneades had. He then proceeds to argue on the basis of internal evidence from the *De Officiis* that the work was written after the death of Scipio in 129.[15] Pohlenz' argument seems the most persuasive. Books 1 and 2 of the *De Officiis*, which Cicero based on Panaetius, contain seven references to Scipio Aemilianus (*De Off.* 1.76, 87, 90, 108, 116, 121, 2.76), whereas the third book, for which Panaetius was not used, contains none. Almost all the references involve praise of Scipio in some way and, if written during Scipio's lifetime, seem to be taking sycophancy too far, at least for Rome in the second century BC. There is an eulogy of Scipio in Polybius, but this too was probably written after its subject's death.[16]

Moreover there are several passages in the *De Officiis*, mentioning Tiberius, which have a very contemporary feel. At *De Off.* 1.76 Scipio Aemilianus' service to the state in destroying Numantia in Spain is described as no greater than Scipio Nasica's in destroying Tiberius Gracchus. Therefore the two branches of this family are seen as simultaneously ridding Rome of threats to its security, both external and internal, a remark that has greater potency if it is remembered that by 129 both had just died. Another passage (*De Off.* 2.43) discusses true glory, *vera gloria*; to achieve *vera gloria* one has to perform the *officia iustitiae*, duties required by justice. It is no good appearing to be just; one must actually be just (a theme which also appears in the account of *fortitudo*, again with reference to glory, Cic. *De Off.* 1.62-3). As an example a contrast is drawn between the elder Tiberius Gracchus and his sons, unfavourable to the latter. This discussion brings together three different themes associated with the Gracchi. First there is the contrast between Tiberius and his father, which was first known to have been used in 133 by Q. Metellus

[15] Early: Van Straaten 1946: 23-5; later: Pohlenz 1934: 125, followed by Walbank 1965: 1, cf. Philippson 1929: 338.

[16] Date of eulogy: Walbank 1967: 594, 1979: 492-3.

Macedonicus, probably in the speech against Tiberius recorded by C. Fannius (HRR 1 Frag. 5). Secondly it has been argued that *vera gloria* was claimed by the Gracchi.[17] Sallust refers to the Gracchi as nobles who preferred *vera gloria* to *iniusta potentia*, unjust power (*Jug.* 41.10-42.1). Similarly there is the claim of C. Gracchus that he does not seek financial benefit from the People, but a good reputation and honour, *bona existimatio et honor* (ORF p. 188, Frag. 44). Finally the idea that one cannot achieve *vera gloria* by a pretence of justice, as the Gracchi tried to do, echoes the criticism of their laws in Florus as having only the appearance of *aequitas*. The Gracchi are described as justly killed, *iure caesi*, an allusion to Scipio's famous remark in 131 that Tiberius was *iure caesus*.[18] None of these themes appear in combination elsewhere, yet here in the *De Officiis* they are all succinctly expressed to elucidate the notion of *vera gloria* and simultaneously make clear that Tiberius' claim to it was as unfounded as his claim to justice. The casualness of the way these themes are combined suggests immediacy to the events in question.

So the Stoic arguments which had developed as a reaction to the Spartan revolution were adopted in Rome to counteract the Gracchan propaganda. Panaetius shows how such arguments were applied to the Peloponnese and, if the date for his work suggested above is accepted, how they attempted to undermine Tiberius' claims. Florus, too, would seem to support this. Yet the arguments are far from compelling. Posidonius, a later Stoic, believed that Tiberius got the punishment he deserved, but he still acknowledges that on the agrarian issue at least Tiberius had the law on his side.[19] The opposition could only complain, as they did, that the eviction of existing occupiers of *ager publicus* was not fair or *aequum*. One has to ask why these arguments were taken up by those opposed to Tiberius. No doubt it was partly because they seemed relevant, but also because one of the prominent associates of Tiberius was the Stoic philosopher, C. Blossius. If, as seems likely, Tiberius was using ideas derived from Stoicism to justify his policies, then there was all the more reason to look to dissenting Stoics to furnish the responses. Thus the debate, which for some time had been pursued in the Stoa, took on a new form. Their differences, which had previously been confined to theory, were now translated into the political arena and found expression in the controversy surrounding Tiberius' tribunate.

5. Blossius and the pro-Gracchan tradition

Before examining in what way Blossius and Greek philosophy in

---

[17] Nicolet 1965: 156-7.

[18] For the texts containing them, see Astin 1967: 264-5.

[19] Diod. 34/35.6.1. Posidonius as the source for Diodorus here, Reinhardt RE Posidonios.

general might have influenced Tiberius, it is necessary to consider Blossius himself. C. Blossius was a Stoic philosopher from Cumae in Campania; he was said to have influenced or even to have led Tiberius and subsequently committed suicide after the failure of Aristonicus' struggle in Asia against Rome, which he had joined. He was a close friend of Antipater of Tarsus, who had even dedicated several philosophical works to him (Plut. *TG* 8.6). Such an affinity with Antipater would lead one to expect to find him opposed to Panaetius, at least in matters of political thought. He is often linked by modern scholars to the more radical wing of the Stoa and this seems to have been the case.[20] Apart from his relationship with Tiberius very little is known about him with any certainty. He is sometimes thought to have been Tiberius' tutor, as the rhetorician, Diophanes of Mytilene, was (Cic. *Brutus* 104),[21] but there is no evidence for such a belief. As a *hospes* of the family of P. Mucius Scaevola, he must have been a member of a prominent Cumaean family and thus was unlikely to have been in Rome as a tutor to the *nobiles* (Cic. *Laelius* 37).

His Campanian background has been examined by D.R. Dudley.[22] He argues that he was a descendant of the Blossii of Capua, who had followed a democratic, anti-Roman policy at the time of the second Punic War. In 216 Marius Blossius, a *praetor Campanus*, had been involved in an agreement with Hannibal whereby Capua revolted from Rome (Livy 23.7.8-9). Six years later the *Blossii fratres* were the leading members of a conspiracy to burn down the huts of the Roman soldiers outside the walls of Capua (Livy 27.3.3ff). At some point, he believes, some of the family may have moved to Cumae. Dudley, however, draws the conclusion that Blossius' activities with regard to Tiberius and Aristonicus can be explained by his Campanian background which was democratic and anti-imperialist. Such views, he says, have little to do with Stoicism. While accepting Dudley's account of Blossius' background, I would suggest that it was this that led him into Stoicism. For such an approach to political matters is consistent with that of the early radical Stoics of the third century, who had supported democracy in Athens and independence from Macedon. Such a philosophy would provide him with the ideological justifications for the position which he already held and doubtless strengthened it. Moreover, if his reasons for adopting Stoicism were political, it would also explain the fervour with which he applied it.

According to Plutarch most authorities believed that Blossius, together with Diophanes, had been a major influence on Tiberius in his agrarian proposals (Plut. *TG* 8.6). Cicero claimed that Blossius 'did not obey the rashness (*temeritas*) of Tiberius Gracchus but rather he took

[20] Ferguson 1975: 138, Aalders 1975: 80, Smuts 1958.
[21] Katz 1942: 66.
[22] Dudley 1941: 94-9.

charge of it; he did not offer himself as a companion of Tiberius' madness (*furor*) but the leader' (*Laelius* 37). Both the account of Blossius' activities in Plutarch and the one in Cicero are often dismissed as deriving from hostile sources, attempting to blacken Tiberius' reputation and show him as the tool of obscure philosophers.[23] Although those opposed to Tiberius probably did seek to use Blossius in this way, it does not undermine the validity of the claim. For there were two rival traditions about Blossius, the one hostile, the other friendly; it is unlikely that those hostile to Tiberius would offer an account that sought to treat Blossius with sympathy.

Cicero and Plutarch give different accounts about Blossius and the *quaestio* set up after Tiberius' murder (Cic. *Laelius* 37, Plut. *TG* 20.5-7) and it is useful to compare them. Another of less interest here appears in Valerius Maximus, stressing Blossius' loyalty to Tiberius (Val. Max. 4.7.1). According to Cicero's version Blossius appealed to Laelius, who was advising the consuls on the matter. When Blossius said that he would have done whatever Tiberius had wanted him to do, Laelius asked whether he would have set fire to the Capitol, if Tiberius had wanted it done (an allusion, suggests Dudley, to the arsonist tradition in Blossius' family). Blossius denied that Tiberius would have made such a request, but he acknowledged that, had Tiberius done so, he would have carried it out. Subsequently Blossius, out of his mind and afraid of the *quaestio*, fled to Rome's enemies in Asia; there he was justly and heavily punished. In Plutarch's account this questioning seems to take place at the *quaestio* itself and is conducted chiefly by P. Scipio Nasica. A further justification is added; Tiberius would not have instructed anyone to burn down the Capitol, if it had not been in the interests of the People, *ei mê tôi dêmôi sunepheren*. Then Blossius flees to Aristonicus in Asia and when this project fails he commits suicide. Apart from the replacement of Laelius with Nasica, there are several other important differences. Cicero's account is openly hostile to Blossius, who makes a rather discreditable appeal to Laelius to use his influence on his behalf. No explanation is given of Blossius' views or actions. Instead opposed to the reasonable attitude of Laelius is the mindless frenzy of Blossius; he is described as governed by *amentia* (insanity) and inciting the *temeritas* and *furor* of Tiberius. Finally he meets a just end with Rome's enemies in Asia. In Plutarch, on the other hand, his behaviour is represented as a reasoned course of action following set interests. Blossius justifies Tiberius' actions in terms of the interests of the People; he supports Aristonicus against Rome and only after this fails does he deliberately take his own life. Thus each account gives a completely different impression of Blossius. What is the height of irrationality in Cicero is

[23] E.g. Astin 1967: 195, Bernstein 1978: 47.

reasonable conduct in Plutarch.[24]

Plutarch's approach to Blossius displays a consistency which shows that his account of Blossius' interrogation is not an isolated anecdote. For on the day of Tiberius' final assembly there was a series of bad omens, as there always were on such days. Blossius encourages the hesitant Tiberius that as champion of the Roman People (*prostatês tou Rômaiôn dêmou*) he should not be dissuaded by such occurrences from obeying the summons of the citizens (Plut. *TG* 17). Here again Blossius is found using the *dêmos* as a justification for Tiberius' actions: as champion of the Roman *dêmos* he should not ignore the will of the People. Moreover, there is nothing in this anecdote to indicate that it is from a hostile source.[25] Indeed it explicitly seeks to counter charges levelled against Tiberius by his opponents. They claimed that Tiberius was a disgrace to his father and that he was using the People to become a tyrant (e.g. Cic. *Laelius* 41; Plut. *TG* 14.3). Yet here Tiberius is told by Blossius that by obeying the summons of the citizens, the will of the People, he would be living up to the reputation of his father, Ti. Sempronius Gracchus, and his grandfather, Scipio Africanus, and not to do so would be shameful. To respect the wishes of the People is correct, but to ignore them is a sign of tyranny. Tiberius then goes to the assembly and therefore shows himself to be neither a disgrace to his father nor a tyrant.

Thus there was a tradition favourable to Blossius which must have been part of a pro-Gracchan tradition. As a result we should not be over hasty in dismissing Blossius' influence on Tiberius as anti-Gracchan propaganda. In both these anecdotes from Plutarch defences of Tiberius are ascribed to Blossius. We may reasonably doubt the historical authenticity of the anecdotes, but a pro-Gracchan tradition cannot have viewed Blossius as Tiberius' apologist and adviser with no reason, especially if those opposed to Tiberius could take advantage of it. The position attributed to him is significant for its consistency with its emphasis on the role of the People. The circumstances in which he expressed these arguments were probably different and less interesting, but there is no reason to believe that he did not hold similar ones. For such an attribution to succeed it must at the very least have been plausible. The tyranny charge may have appeared only after Tiberius death, although the view that it was contemporary does have modern adherents.[26] For the pro-Gracchan tradition to claim that he did support Tiberius with such arguments he can scarcely have been a minor figure with little influence on Tiberius.

How Blossius came to know Tiberius is not clear. It could have been through P. Mucius Scaevola, whose *hospes* Blossius was and who is

---

[24] This is pointed out by A. Müller 1971: 141-3.
[25] Hadot 1970: 139.
[26] Such as Boren 1961.

alleged to have advised Tiberius on his reform (Plut. *TG* 9.1). The Sempronii Gracchi, however, may have had links with Cumae for a long time. For in 215 Ti. Sempronius Gracchus (RE 51) as consul had endured a lengthy siege in Cumae against the forces of Hannibal. It is possible that an association with the town had been maintained since then (Livy 23.35.2ff).

Therefore there was a pro-Gracchan tradition which assigned to Blossius a significant role in Tiberius' tribunate. It represented him as advising Tiberius. It has often been contended that Tiberius had no need of Blossius' advice in drawing up his agrarian legislation,[27] for he had the assistance of two eminent lawyers, the brothers P. Mucius Scaevola and P. Licinius Crassus Dives Mucianus (Plut. *TG* 9.1). This should be matched with the more cautious statement of Cicero. He comments that it was the practice of seditious politicians to produce the names of distinguished men to justify their case. As examples he gives Crassus and Scaevola, who were said to be supporters of Tiberius' legislation, but only Crassus' support was open; Scaevola was suspected to have supported him more secretly (Cic. *Acad. Pr.* 2.13). Such advice need only have concerned the legal side on which Blossius was unlikely to have been adept. If Blossius did advise Tiberius on the law, it could have been on the nature of the reform or its justification or both.

There is a problem in trying to assess the arguments put forward by Tiberius. It is difficult to determine to what extent our information has been contaminated by later propaganda, whether pro or anti-Gracchan. For instance, C. Gracchus had an interest in his brother's image and in stressing the continuity of policy (e.g. Cic. *De Div.* 1.55). In a pamphlet he wrote that Tiberius developed his policy after seeing the number of slaves in the fields in Etruria, while on his way to Numantia. Possibly the claim which dates Tiberius' motivation before the Numantia episode was a response to the charge that Tiberius' actions resulted from the snub to his *dignitas* inflicted by the repudiation of the treaty with Numantia (pamphlet: Plut. *TG* 8.9; the charge: Cic. *De Har. Resp.* 43). C. Gracchus also showed concern about his ancestors in general (Cic. *De Div.* 2.62), perhaps trying to bring their mother into prominence to counteract unfavourable comparisons with their father.[28]

Nevertheless the speeches attributed to Tiberius by Plutarch and Appian probably contain at least the substance of what he said, although not necessarily his words.[29] For the speeches of Tiberius would appear to have been preserved until at least the first century

[27] E.g. Astin 1967: 195.
[28] Taeger 1928: 8.
[29] Plut. *TG* 9.4-6, 15, Appian *BC* 1.9, 1.11, also in ORF pp. 149-52, F.13-16; Badian 1972: 677-8.

AD; Cicero knew them and Pliny the Elder said that he had seen documents in the hands of Tiberius and Gaius Gracchus (Cic. *Brutus* 104, Pliny *NH* 13.26). So it is plausible to believe that they would have been used by those writing on Tiberius.[30] In Plutarch there is a speech of Tiberius in which he complains that those who fight for Italy and are described as masters of the world do not even have an ancestral altar (Plut. *TG* 9.4-6), themes that recur in Florus (2.12) and in Appian (*BC* 1.10). Ernst Badian has argued for the authenticity of Tiberius' defence of Octavius' deposition (Plut. *TG* 15), on the grounds that the reference to the destruction of the Capitol and the shipyards could be an allusion to the work of the Greek architect, Hermodorus of Salamis, who was active in Rome at the time.[31] Moreover, much of the material given by Appian and Plutarch to provide the background to Tiberius' reforms may have derived from Tiberius' own speeches; it is clearly favourable to the reforms. The themes which appear in his speech at Appian *BC* 1.9, the poverty and scarcity of the Italians, the problems of excessive numbers of slaves, the old law limiting the holding of *ager publicus* all occur in greater detail in the previous chapters (Appian *BC* 1.7-8). What is striking is that there is nothing in Tiberius' speech which has not been said earlier. Similarly the complaints of the poor which would have been voiced by Tiberius simply repeat the background material (Appian *BC* 1.10). The same topics reappear in Plutarch, although with a different chronology and less emphasis on the Italians (Plut. *TG* 8.1-5). Thus there is little reason to doubt that historians did make use of Tiberius' speeches. They certainly had the opportunity. Therefore we should treat seriously, but cautiously, the arguments attributed to Tiberius in these speeches especially where there is external evidence to suggest that the ideas expressed in them were current.

It is these speeches and Tiberius' political actions that we must examine to assess what, if any, Greek philosophical influence there is. It has recently become fashionable to argue that there was no such influence; Tiberius was acting in accordance with Roman tradition. While the unprecedented nature of his approach can be overstated, claims for orthodoxy go too far.[32] There is a modern struggle to find precedents for the actions of Tiberius, but often, at best, it can only be shown that there were trends leading this way.[33] The deposition of

[30] Fraccaro 1912: 426-33 believed that the speeches recorded by Plutarch were fragments of Tiberius, but was hesitant about those found in Appian.

[31] Badian 1972: 708.

[32] E.g. Badian 1972, Earl 1963, Bernstein 1978. Badian p. 711, for instance, points out that C. Gracchus describes his brother as *optimus*, but omits to mention that this is in contrast to the nobles who killed him, the *pessimi*. So Gaius is in fact reasserting the idea of morality implicit in the term *'optimus'* and certainly not claiming that his brother was *optimus* in any sense that would be understood by the optimates, his *pessimi*.

[33] Taylor 1962.

Octavius and the commandeering of the legacy of Attalus caused an outcry in the Senate (Livy *Per.* 58, Plut. *TG* 14-15.1); yet the sources offer no clear precedents, only justifications. This would suggest that there were none; for Gracchan supporters would surely have found them. Particular precedents will be considered in more detail below. It will be convenient to examine the two main aspects of Tiberius' tribunate separately, first his agrarian legislation and secondly his attitude to the tribunate itself.

6. The agrarian legislation

What prompted Tiberius' agrarian law (*lex agraria*) is still the subject of much debate and it is perhaps unwise to continue this speculation here. The law contained both traditional and novel aspects; it is the origin of the latter that is of particular interest here. *Viritim* settlements on *ager publicus* were not unprecedented, but to be presented in the form of a law was unusual. There were no known examples of such distribution by legislation in the second century prior to Tiberius.[34] There were, however, *senatus consulta* (decrees of the Senate); in 173 *viritim* settlements were made in Liguria and Gallia by *senatus consultum* (Livy 42.4). The only certain example of a settlement by means of a law is that of C. Flaminius as a tribune in 232 (Polyb. 2.21.7-8, Cic. *De Sen.* 11). This applied only to a limited area of land, probably just the *ager Gallicus*, although Cicero adds the *ager Picenus*.[35] Other earlier instances of such legislation appear to be anachronistic; the account of the agrarian law, alleged to have been proposed by Spurius Cassius in 486 BC, looks as though it is modelled on the career of Tiberius Gracchus.[36]

Thus there was a precedent for *viritim* settlement, if only on a small scale, and also by a tribune, although almost one hundred years previously. Whether Tiberius was the first to propose such a measure in this period is debatable. There is an infuriatingly vague reference in Plutarch to a proposal of some sort by Laelius, who abandoned it when there was opposition from the powerful, *hoi dunatoi* (Plut. *TG* 8.5). It is unclear what the problem he was trying to correct was; the preceding passage discusses increased poverty, landlessness and military problems. No clearer is the date or content of the proposal. It has been suggested that it was a law for the redistribution of land,[37] but it may only have demanded that the limit on holdings of *ager publicus* be more strictly enforced. It may have nothing to do with the land. This is

[34] Badian 1972: 696.

[35] Walbank 1957: 192.

[36] Gabba 1964; Dion. Hal. 6.68-80; Badian 1972: 701 n. 100 points out that it seems to be modelled on Gaius as well.

[37] Scullard 1960: 64-5.

the only reference to the proposal and it could have derived from a speech of Tiberius, reinterpreting an action of Laelius to emphasise the general popularity of his own proposal, a practice mentioned by Cicero (Cic. *Acad. Pr.* 2.13). For it follows Plutarch's account of the background which, it has already been suggested, may have originated with Tiberius.

Tiberius' law differed in several respects from all previous known measures. First it differed in scale; the area of *ager publicus* was not limited, but embraced all *ager publicus*.[38] This difference in scale also marked a difference in conception, which can be seen in the arguments brought forward to support the new law. It was not simply more *ager publicus* that was to be affected, but all. Previously no justification for the distribution of *ager publicus* would have been required; it was the state's land to be distributed by the Senate, the embodiment of the state, in a piecemeal fashion as it saw fit. This would have been done on the basis of what seemed necessary at the time, although there may have been dispute over what was necessary. For Tiberius it was very different. He is re-interpreting the meaning of *ager publicus Romani populi* (the public land of the Roman People). Thus he claims that it is just that what is common is divided in common, *dikaion ta koina koinêi dianemesthai* (Appian *BC* 1.11; cf. Florus 2.1.2, Plut. *TG* 9.4-6). Such an argument represents a different approach, not the state's right to allocate those areas which it want to allocate, but the People's right to allocate the whole *ager publicus*. It is common land, which they themselves had fought to acquire and they had been robbed of it by the rich. Tiberius' argument does not impose a limit on land to be distributed, whereas previous distributions had specified a particular area. Flaminius usurped the role of the Senate, but he did not take this to the conclusion that Tiberius did. He only aimed to distribute land in a limited area. Flaminius was of course acting at a time when there was less *ager publicus* and conditions were very different.

[38] The *ager Campanus* is sometimes believed to have been exempted under Tiberius' law, e.g. Earl 1963: 25. This is based on Cic. *De Leg. Ag.* 2.81, cf. 1.21: *nec duo Gracchi, qui de plebis Romanae commodis plurimum cogitaverunt, nec L. Sulla ... agrum Campanum attingere ausus est*. But Cicero is not writing a piece of straightforward historical narrative and has good reason to be partial. He is delivering a vehement attack on the *lex agraria* of the tribune, Rullus, who does include the *ager Campanus* in his bill. The speech is addressed to the People and it obviously suits Cicero's purpose to demonstrate that the Gracchi as popular heroes of the past would have not have done this. In fact Cicero only says that they did not dare to touch it. This can be taken to mean that it was not distributed, but it cannot be assumed from what Cicero says that it was explicitly exempted by the law. In fact there are signs that preparations at least were made for distribution. Two *termini Gracchani* have been found in the *ager Campanus*, ILLRP nos. 467-8. Badian 1972: 705 withholds judgment on whether it was exempted or not. Unlike some other areas where *ager publicus* was acquired, it was still occupied by Campanians, who had never been removed from it after the fall of Capua in 211 in spite of a *senatus consultum*, Toynbee 1965: 2.117-28, 229-33, Briscoe 1973 on Livy 31.29.10-11. Consequently it may not have been given first priority for distribution.

This radical difference of approach to *ager publicus* needs an explanation. The People's role in politics may have undergone a change in the previous twenty years or so, but this is not adequate to explain a change in the conception of *ager publicus*. We have, however, come across Tiberius' argument before, that it is just that what is common is distributed in common. It is one of the key features of the Stoic theory of justice, which was discussed in Chapter 5. The theatre analogy was produced to prove that such a conclusion is not a consequence of Chrysippus' arguments on justice (Cic. *De Fin*. 3.67). Diogenes is keen to show that Antipater's views on justice would undermine private property. Panaetius, too, was aware of this position: it is one of the principal tasks of justice 'to ensure that men use what is common for common purposes and what is private for their own' (Cic. *De Off*. 1.20, Panaetius F.105). But Panaetius limited *communia*; he did not mean by the term the same things that Blossius, Antipater or the early Stoics meant. For him *communia* are those things which are inexhaustible, such as water, fire, light or anything which it would cost nothing to give (Cic. *De Off*. 1.51-2).[39] Perhaps it is no coincidence that Tiberius complains that the poor and the landless have a share of nothing but air and light (Plut. *TG* 9.5). Tiberius' proposal does not go to the extremes that theory does, but the justification has clear Stoic origins and is connected with the debate within the Stoa which has been examined above. It was in this way that Blossius influenced Tiberius, although it does not mean that he was the instigator of the reform. This conception of the *ager publicus* as the common property of the People to be used by the People is later extended by Tiberius to cover gifts to the People, as in the treatment of the legacy of Attalus, king of Pergamum. Similarly it recurs in the justification of C. Gracchus' subsidy on corn, that a people in need should be maintained from their own treasury.[40] The notion of popular control implicit in this will be considered in the next section.

Thus the Stoic ideas on social justice and property which had found expression in the Spartan revolution reappear in the tribunate of Tiberius. Circumstances and environment may have produced a different emphasis, in Sparta on equality, in Rome on justice, but they are compatible and represent the same underlying theme. It is not enough to object that Tiberius' activities were different from those of Cleomenes. That is only to be expected. Nevertheless, contemporary opinion does seem to have linked the two. Blossius was adopting a traditional Stoic stance, which had already been seen to have undesirable consequences in Sparta. Yet Tiberius was not as extreme as Cleomenes who had redistributed all land; Tiberius was only

---

[39] Accepted as Panaetian by Pohlenz 1934: 34, against Schmekel 1892: 32.
[40] Haepke 1915 suggests that this may reflect Gaius' own words.

distributing *ager publicus*, but this was *de facto* redistribution, as some of it was occupied by wealthy land-holders (cf. Plut. *TG* 9.3 which describes it as *gês anadasmos*). Thus the arguments of the dissident Stoics were mobilised against Tiberius. These were developed to counter wholesale redistribution, arguing the inequity of evicting existing land-holders. Against Tiberius they had less validity, but it was an argument that had been developed before Tiberius and not in consequence of him. Tiberius proposed only to distributed *ager publicus*, not all of which would have been occupied by large land-holders anyway.

One of the most distinctive features of Tiberius' *lex agraria* was the requirement that no allotment made by the commission should subsequently be sold (Appian *BC* 1.10, 1.27). An inalienability clause was probably contained in the law itself and not merely implicit in the small rent that was payable.[41] This has been explained as due to the need to increase the numbers available for military service. One scholar has suggested that the recipient would consequently have the necessary property qualification for military service for as long as he lived. He need not even go to his farm; he could go straight into the army.[42] The manpower shortage, however, is a modern construct to explain the Gracchan land reforms and has little basis in the ancient sources. The reluctance to serve is attested by the problems with the levy for Spain in 151 and 138, but shortage of manpower need not be the only explanation of such problems. Spain may have been unpopular, but there was no lack of enthusiasm to serve against wealthy Carthage.[43] Indeed it is likely that the prohibition on sale and the rent excluded the land distributed by the commission from counting towards a person's property status. It has been argued on the basis of the *lex agraria* of 111 BC (FIRA 8) that land distributed as a result of the land reform was not taken into account by the censors as part of the assessee's property, although anything over and above this, such as buildings, would be.[44]

The combination of such an inalienability clause and the rent had several functions. First and most important, it showed that the land distributed was still in some sense public land. Confirmation of this status can be found in the *lex agraria* of 111 BC, by which the *ager publicus* distributed by the land commission became private land. That the distributed land was meant to remain public land would be consistent with the argument that it was the common land of the

---

[41] Bauman 1983: 260-5, based in part on an analysis of later laws. Livius Drusus in 122 proposed to abolish the rent on distributed land, a rent that had probably been in force since the original distribution, Plut. *CG* 9.4.

[42] Earl 1963: 30-40.

[43] Rich 1983 has a full discussion of the alleged manpower problem, cf. Shochat 1980.

[44] Shochat 1980: 42-3, 87, FIRA 8, section 8, cf. 12-13.

People. Appian believed that the prohibition on sale was to prevent the land return into the hands of the rich (Appian *BC* 1.10). This is not the same as being given security of tenure for life. It cannot be sold, but presumably it could be requisitioned, for instance if it fell into neglect. The rent may have acted as a guide to the success of the project. Finally, and less interestingly, it ensured that applicants were serious and did not intend to claim their land and then sell it to large land-holders.

Such a prohibition on sale was unprecedented in known Roman tradition.[45] Indeed it was rare elsewhere, but it does appear in Greece, in particular in the Spartan tradition, where Aristotle attributes such prohibitions to the Spartan lawgiver.[46] According to a story in Plutarch, which may originate from the propaganda of the third-century revolution, a law of the otherwise unknown Epitadeus abandoned some of the restrictions on the transfer of property (Plut. *Agis* 5.3). Whether or not one believes in the authenticity of this law, the story implies that there was a tradition that there were such restrictions. No doubt this tradition received added emphasis at the time of the revolutions of Agis and Cleomenes. A more detailed comparison between the Spartan and Roman measures cannot be made, because the intricacies of the Spartan land system elude us; for instance, exactly what was the status of occupied land? Nevertheless, since the Stoics provide an ideological link between the two events, it is plausible that Tiberius' Stoic adherent played a role in the adoption of such a proposal.

7. The tribunate and popular sovereignty

It is not so much for his agrarian legislation that Tiberius is important; rather it is for changing perceptions of the tribunate. The argument was developed by him that the tribune must be accountable to the People; he cannot act contrary to their will, but must seek to further their wishes. Such a position need not seriously undermine senatorial control, so long as the decisions which the People could make independent from the Senate are limited, albeit only by convention. But it would pose a threat if the areas in which legislation could be passed by the popular assembly (*concilium plebis*) without the prior approval of the Senate were increased. This is what Tiberius did by introducing his *lex agraria* directly to the popular assembly and by

[45] Badian 1972: 680.

[46] Finley 1968: 25-32 discusses inalienability in Greece and gives examples from the Hellenistic period. Cretan refugees who received land and citizenship in Miletus in 228/27 were not allowed to alienate in any way at all, *Milet.* I.3.333. When Orchomenus was admitted into the Arcadian League in c. 233 the decree prohibited anyone receiving a house or allotment in Orchomenus from alienating it for twenty years, SIG 490. Aristotle on Sparta: *Pol.* 1270a19-20, Heracl. Lemb. *Pol.* 2.7 = Arist. Frag. 611.12 (Rose).

having the question of Attalus' legacy and the Asiatic cities debated there first. His stance was more threatening than that of previous tribunes, however disruptive they might have been, because they were working within an accepted framework, not extending it. He aroused greater hostility than the other tribunes who had opposed the Senate in the previous twenty years, because he produced a coherent justification of popular sovereignty. In the process he redefined the role of the tribune and the People in the constitution.

Tribunes had become more disruptive and clashed with the Senate in recent years, but such disputes were in areas where tribunician influence was acknowledged, even if they involved the abuse of existing conventions. They fell mainly into two categories. First there were those cases which arose from the tribunician *ius auxilii* (the right to aid a citizen), in particular conflict with the Senate and consuls over the levy. Since the tribunes had the *ius auxilii*, citizens who were dissatisfied with the levy could appeal to them. Thus there was a case in 171 about the levy for the war against Macedon; former centurions were called up, but they were not to keep their old ranks, so they appealed to the tribunes (Livy 42.31-5). Two tribunes held that the consuls should settle it, while the other eight proposed to bring *auxilium* to those who required it (Livy 42.32.6). Eventually the centurions relented and allowed the Senate and the consuls to discuss their case. Affairs were not concluded so amicably twenty years later. In 151 when many refused to serve in Spain and appealed to the tribunes, the consuls were thrown in jail by the tribunes (Livy *Per.* 48). This situation recurred in 138 when the tribunes, C. Curiatius and Sex. Licinius, imprisoned the consuls because of the levy (Cic. *De Leg.* 3.20, Livy *Per.* 55, *Oxy. Epit.* 55). Whether or not such an act could be considered constitutional has been disputed.[47] The consuls had probably defied a tribunician veto and continued with the levy, hence providing grounds for imprisonment.[48] Although such an extreme step may never have been taken before, it could be seen as a natural outcome of the tribune's role as protector of the People. It stretched the framework to its limits, but it did not assert any fresh powers for the tribunate or for the People.

The second area of dispute was legislation about franchise and voting. Badian has argued that since at least 188 such legislation fell within the domain of the People and thus there was no need for it to be approved first in the Senate.[49] In 188 C. Valerius Tappo, a tribune, proposed that residents in the municipalities of Formiae, Fundi and Arpinum should be given full citizenship. This was vetoed by four

[47] Taylor 1962: 19, opposing Smith 1955: 177 who believes that it was unconstitutional.
[48] Astin 1967: 43.
[49] Badian 1972: 694-6.

tribunes, because it had not been approved first in the Senate. When it was held that the People and not the Senate had the right to decide such matters, the tribunes abandoned their objections (Livy 38.36.7-8). Livy does not give any further information, but it is unlikely that such a dispute was resolved without some kind of concession from the Senate, perhaps a senatorial decree authorising the People to decide the matter.[50] A similar argument is put forward in 148 when the legal restrictions are suspended to allow Scipio Aemilianus to stand for consulship: 'that according to the laws of Tullius and Romulus the People were sovereign in elections and they could set aside or confirm any of the electoral laws' (Appian *Lib.* 112). It is significant that in the second century all laws prior to Tiberius' agrarian law which are believed to have by-passed an unwilling Senate are concerned with franchise and voting. The *lex Licinia de sacerdotiis* in 145 proposed that priests be elected by the People, but was defeated (Cic. *Laelius* 96, *Brutus* 83). The *lex Gabinia* in 139 and the *lex Cassia* in 137 ensured secret ballots in elections and judicial assemblies respectively (Livy *Oxy. Epit.* 54, Cic. *De Leg.* 3.35, *Laelius* 41, *Pro Sestio* 103). There is a fairly lengthy list of legislation passed with the approval of the Senate between 200 and 146, which would suggest that this was the normal practice.[51] There was presumably uncontroversial legislation that was introduced directly to the popular assembly, but this would have been with the tacit approval of the Senate.

So the tribunes were prepared to oppose the Senate in some areas, but they were not prepared to produce legislation without its consent, with the exception of those matters discussed above, which all fall into one category. This reluctance can be seen in the tribunate of C. Curiatius in 138. As a result of a corn shortage he publicly demanded that the consuls propose to the Senate that the state buy corn by means of specially appointed legates (Val. Max. 3.7.3). The consul, P. Scipio Nasica, opposed him, apparently successfully. There is no evidence that Curiatius proposed this legislation directly to the People; he merely pressed the consuls to propose it to the Senate. Yet this is the man who took the 'revolutionary' step of throwing the consuls into jail over the levy and was described by Cicero as the lowest and most obnoxious man there had ever been (Cic. *De Leg.* 3.20). It must be remembered, however, that even if the measure had been passed by the People, the Senate had control of the finance necessary to implement it, a problem which Tiberius himself initially had to face (Plut. *TG* 13.2-3, 14.1).

Thus, while Tiberius may have been just another in a series of disruptive tribunes, his predecessors had remained within certain

---

[50] Astin 1967: 340.
[51] Such a list is given by Earl 1963: 45-6.

limits. Tiberius not only went beyond those limits; he produced
justifications for this. When the passage of the agrarian bill was
frustrated by the veto of Tiberius' fellow tribune, M. Octavius, Tiberius
solved this problem by proposing that the assembly remove Octavius
from office. This it did. Such a step was unprecedented in respect of the
tribunate. Indeed there is only one known case of the abrogation of any
other magistracy; this was the deposition of L. Tarquinius Collatinus,
the consul of 509 BC, but even here the sources are far from
unanimous.[52] Relevant here is the argument that Tiberius used to
justify the deposition of Octavius; it may also have been used to support
his claim to be allowed to stand for re-election, another aspect of his
tribunate which was perhaps in breach of convention. It certainly had
wider implications for the sovereignty of the People.

The argument was produced to counter the charge that he had
violated the *sacrosanctitas* of the tribune. He claims not to be attacking
the tribunate or its sacrosanctity, but upholding it. The main features
are given by Plutarch, but his summary may have blurred the argument
somewhat (Plut. *TG* 15, ORF p. 151 frag. 16). The tribune is sacrosanct
because he acts on behalf of the People, *tou dêmou proestêken*. He is only
a tribune in so far as he carries out the will of the People and it is only by
virtue of being a tribune that he is sacrosanct. Therefore, if he seeks to
wrong the People, curtail their strength or deprive them of the
opportunity to vote, he has in effect deposed himself. To this Tiberius
adds certain points of clarification. For it is only by directly wronging the
People that a tribune can be deprived of office. He may burn the
dockyards or raze the Capitol to the ground, but this in itself does not
affect his status as a tribune. It only makes him a bad tribune: *kai tauta
men poiôn dêmarchos esti ponêros*. But, if he attacks the power of the
People itself, he is not a tribune at all: *ean de kataluêi ton dêmon, ou
dêmarchos esti*. In denying the power of the People, he is denying his
own power, because that is dependent on the People (Plut. *TG* 15.7).
Tiberius' position is essentially an assertion of popular sovereignty;
what the People gives, it can take away. Finally should anyone argue
that the popular will was independent of the sacrosanctity of the
tribune, he draws a distinction between the office and the holder. It is
not the man who holds the office who is sacrosanct, but the office itself.
Holding the office imposes certain conditions on the holder. Failing to
observe these justifies deposition. This argument, although without the
detail, also appears in Appian *BC* 1.12. The issue to be voted on was
whether a tribune who opposed the People could continue in office: *ei
chrê demarchon antiprattonta tôi dêmôi tên archên epechein*. Moreover
Tiberius told Octavius that as a tribune he should share the desires of
the People. For Tiberius a tribune who opposes the People is a

[52] E.g. for: Cic. *Brutus* 53, *De Off.* 3.40; against: Livy 2.2.7f, 4.15.4

contradiction in terms.

It is necessary to ask how new this interpretation of the tribunate is. Tiberius could not have simply imposed new, perhaps Greek, ideas, previously totally unfamiliar in Rome. Rather one should envisage a gradual development, which would make them acceptable in some quarters at least, for instance among Tiberius' influential backers. Yet this may have been the first time that such ideas had been explicitly formulated in the Roman political arena.[53] Signs that the tribunate was becoming tied closely to the notion of popular sovereignty and that the tribunes were the 'executive organ of the *plebs*'[54] are limited. There is, however, a greater recognition of the importance of the People. In 145 C. Licinius Crassus became the first tribune to turn on the *rostra* and face the bulk of the People, probably when proposing his bill about the election of priests (Cic. *Laelius* 96). Outside the confines of the tribunate and its relation to the *concilium plebis*, there are other indications of an increasing awareness of the will of the People, for instance in Scipio's election to the consulship of 147, although here, as has been discussed above, the emphasis is on sovereignty in elections. The series of ballot laws, too, contain the implication that the People should be allowed to exercise their will without restriction; this is not to discount the view that there may have been tactical reasons for proposing such laws.

Yet before Tiberius the tribunate is not considered to be so much the embodiment of the will of the People as the protector of its interests. Thus in 138, when the consul P. Scipio Nasica attacked Curiatius' proposed corn measures, he appealed to *utilitas rei publicae* (interests of the state), while an anonymous tribune, who may have been Curiatius, is described as acting *pro commodis populi* (for the benefit of the people).[55] Tiberius, on the other hand (regardless of what actually prompted him), is seen not only as responding to popular demands, for example, in the form of graffiti (Plut. *TG* 8.18), but also subordinating himself to the wishes of the People. Moreover Octavius is represented as following the tradition of Scipio Nasica, *pro bono publico stans*, defending the interests of the state (Vel. Pat. 2.2.3).

Nevertheless there is one source which does explicitly set out a position very similar to that of Tiberius. Polybius in his analysis of the

[53] Bauman 1983: 46-7, 278 believes that Tiberius' argument for deposition is earlier than both Tiberius himself and Polybius (for Polybius see below). He cites Livy 10.6.4-5, 9.1-2 on the *Lex Ogulnia* which was probably passed in 300. But here the emphasis is on the interests of the People, if anything. Tiberius' argument is based on the will of the People. Moreover, the justification for a law passed as early as 300 must be regarded as suspect and is very likely to have been contaminated by later events, especially by the time of Livy.

[54] Walbank 1957: 692.

[55] Val. Max. 3.7.3, Livy *Oxy. Epit.* 55; Nicolet 1983: 40-1 argues that he should be identified with Curiatius and discusses this incident.

Roman constitution writes that the tribunes must always do what the People decides and especially fall in with its will, *malista stochazesthai tês toutou boulêseôs* (Polyb. 6.16.5). Since the sixth book is generally acknowledged to have been written no later than 150, this passage has puzzled many. Some suggest that it is a later insertion by Polybius, after he had witnessed the activities of Tiberius Gracchus.[56] F.W. Walbank, however, believes that Polybius has misunderstood the role of the tribunate, due to 'Greek schematism'.[57] It is this latter approach which seems the most plausible. For since Polybius was viewing Rome in terms of Greek political philosophy, the product of the Greek *polis*, misconceptions were likely to arise. By identifying the *plebs* with the *dêmos* he is importing, though not necessarily consciously, the connotations that went with it. Unlike the intimate relationship between the Greek *dêmos* and its elected officials, that between the *plebs* and the tribunes was ambiguous. Although elected by the *plebs* the tribunes 'had become increasingly the tools of the *nobiles*'.[58] Polybius gives his own statement on the tribunate little weight, not because all Romans were bound to agree with him, but because as a Greek, versed in Greek constitutional practice, it was obvious to him what the relationship between the tribunes and the People must be.

Although one should not expect one sentence of Polybius to make a major impact on Roman consciousness, his whole analysis reflects the introduction of Greek ideas into the Roman sphere. Greek intellectuals were visiting Rome and some, such as Panaetius, were staying. The Greek conception of the *dêmos* would have permeated those sections of the Roman ruling class which were more familiar with Greek ideas. Such familiarity could be gained through discussions with Greeks in Rome, visits to Greece or simply association with those who had done these things. Polybius' misconception foreshadows the position of Tiberius, but the latter's adoption of it as a working principle may have been a consequence of the prevalence of Greek ideas in Rome at the time.

Tiberius' position reflects long-held Greek views on the *dêmos*. A statement of this position can be found in Aristotle's *Politics* (1317b28-30): 'The assembly (*ekklêsia*) has authority over everything or at least the most important things, the magistracies have authority over nothing or as few things as possible.' It does not follow that awareness of such views about the sovereignty of the popular assembly would lead to supporting it; it was most likely to have alarmed the upper class and hence exacerbated the hostility felt towards Tiberius.

---

[56] Before 150: Walbank in Brink and Walbank 1954: 101, Taylor 1962: 27; later insertion: Earl 1963: 87-9.

[57] Walbank 1957: 691-2. Polybius may also have been influenced by the career of C. Flaminius and the levy problems of 151, Walbank 1967: 646-7.

[58] Walbank 1957: 691, cf. tribunes as *mancipia nobilium*, Livy 10.37.11.

Polybius believed that democracy would lead to the redistribution of land and the rule of a *despotês* and sole ruler (Polyb. 6.9.9). Such accusations were levelled at Tiberius. Aristotle also wrote (*Pol.* 1305a29-32): 'Wherever there are elective magistracies not based on a property qualification and the *dêmos* elect, then those who are eager for office act as demagogues and bring about a situation in which the *dêmos* even have authority over the laws.' While I would not suggest that the Roman upper class had read Aristotle's *Politics*, there is no reason why they should not have had some familiarity with these ideas about the Greek *dêmos* by way of those Greek intellectuals they knew.

It is against such a background that C. Crassus, the ballot laws and the tribunate of Tiberius should be considered. It was Tiberius who went furthest. His assertion of popular sovereignty went so far as to demand the deposition of a fellow tribune. Abrogation of a term of office was unprecedented in Rome, with the dubious exception of L. Collatinus. Yet this was an important feature of popular sovereignty in Greek democracy. In Athens in every prytany officials were subject to a vote on their conduct in office, known as an *epicheirotonia*; if they were rejected, something known as *apocheirotonia*, they were tried in the lawcourts (Arist. *Ath. Pol.* 61.2, 43.2). The most notorious instance of such a vote was the deposition of Pericles (Plut. *Per.* 35, Thuc. 2.65.3-4). In the fourth century there is an example of the deposition of the *thesmothetae* by this process (Ps. Dem. 58.27). The idea that the Roman consuls are accountable to the People at the end of their term of office is found in Polybius' discussion of the Roman constitution, where the term *euthuna* is used (6.5.11). Here in the period before Tiberius Greek political ideas are being used to interpret the Roman constitution.

Thus Tiberius was exploiting a Greek conception of the *dêmos*, introducing notions of popular sovereignty and deposition. It might be argued that it was later propagandists who devised these justifications for Tiberius. Although they may have embellished his position, it is unlikely to have been anything more than this. Such a position would have been consistent with the contemporary intellectual climate. It has already been suggested that the arguments in Tiberius' speech about the deposition, which recur in Appian, are authentic. Furthermore, some of these arguments are also ascribed to Blossius. It is improbable that later pro-Gracchan writers would attribute to Blossius ideas which he did not hold, when they could have concentrated their emphasis on Tiberius alone. This would indicate, as has already been argued above, that Blossius did hold such democratic views and that he influenced Tiberius in this respect. He may not have made Tiberius aware of the Greek conception of the *dêmos*; for such ideas were current. But he may have advised him on it. In the speech justifying Octavius' deposition Tiberius described the role of the

tribune as championing the People, *tou dêmou proestêken*; Blossius
calls Tiberius *prostatês tou Rômaiôn dêmou* (Plut. *TG* 15.2, 17.5). Here
too there is the curiously Greek example of burning the dockyards – an
act which could be a capital offence in Athens.[59] Not only does Blossius
say that Tiberius as a good tribune would only do what was in the
interests of the *dêmos* (Plut. *TG* 20.6), but he also asserts that for
Tiberius not to obey the citizens when they summon him would be to
lay himself open to the charge of acting like a tyrant (Plut. *TG* 18.5-6).
Thus the anecdotes present a Stoic Blossius who believed that the
tribune championed the cause of the People and acted in its interests
and in accordance with its wishes. Such ideas are typical Greek
democratic ones and have nothing exclusively Stoic about them. It has
been argued in Chapter 3 that early Stoic theory was democratic, but
our knowledge of what this entailed in practice is slight. Blossius'
stance would support the case that he was maintaining the traditions
of the early Stoa.

It is necessary to consider briefly an argument which takes a very
different view of Tiberius' actions to that given above. Badian has
stressed the orthodoxy of Tiberius' position, at least until the matter of
Attalus' legacy.[60] It was not Tiberius who first broke with precedent by
introducing legislation directly to the People or by having Octavius
deposed, but Octavius by persisting with the veto. He points out that in
the previous ten years there was only one known instance of a veto on
another tribune and that was withdrawn. This reflects a senatorial
reluctance to use the veto and risk upsetting the *concordia*.[61] In this
ten-year period, however, there were only two laws believed to have
been passed or even proposed without senatorial approval and both
concerned voting which Badian himself believes to have been the
People's domain.[62] If the veto was rarely used, it was not due to
senatorial restraint, but the lack of tribunician initiative. His analysis
of Tiberius' speech justifying the deposition differs from that given
above. For him Tiberius is arguing that, although major crimes, such
as a tribune burning the dockyards, are not catered for by *mos
maiorum*, it must have been legally possible to depose a tribune who
does this. Similarly if a tribune continues to veto a law which the
People want to pass, there is no rule for dealing with this eventuality.
Therefore as such an act is not covered by *mos maiorum*, it is necessary
to return to basic principles, i.e. that the tribune is meant to act as the
champion of the People and in its interests. This was not a new

[59] Cf. the execution of Antiphon for such an attempt on behalf of Philip II, Dem.
18.132-3. Philip V later had Heracleides set fire to the Rhodian dockyards, Polyb. 13.3-5,
Polyaenus 5.17.
[60] Badian 1972.
[61] Ibid. 700-1.
[62] Ibid. 694-6.

position, but the standard interpretation of the tribune's role; for it appears in Polybius, 'a shrewd observer of the Roman scene', a claim that might be doubted. Thus Tiberius was acting properly, in good optimate fashion. But Tiberius is not comparing the man who burns the dockyards with the one who ignores the will of the People; he is explicitly contrasting them. The former is a bad tribune, the latter is not a tribune at all. He is not reverting to basic principles to cope with a situation not catered for by *mos maiorum*, but he is claiming that these were the basic principles in order to justify an unprecedented act. Moreover, not only should a tribune act in the interests of the People, but also in accordance with its wishes. There is nothing in the speech to suggest that a tribune had never persisted with a veto before. It has already been argued that Tiberius' position owed more to Greek political thought than to the traditional view of the tribunate; there are no grounds for believing that it was accepted as orthodox. No other tribune is known to have opposed the deposition, but this does not imply that the rest of the tribunes accepted it as in order.[63] Popular feeling was such that it would have been unwise to oppose it (Plut. *TG* 12.5-6).

Tiberius combined this emphasis on the sovereignty of the People with the extension of their area of decision. Previously, although the *lex Hortensia* of 287 gave all *plebiscita* the status of law, few were passed without the prior approval of the Senate. The main exception, apart from the law of Flaminius in the previous century, appears to have been the legislation on franchise and voting. Tiberius was breaking a long-standing constitutional custom.[64] For Tiberius what was the People's should be decided by the People. The *lex agraria* was introduced directly to the *concilium plebis*, something which had not been done since Flaminius. Attalus' legacy and the fate of the Asiatic cities were to be decided there too (Plut. *TG* 14,1-2). Yet gifts to the state and foreign affairs were traditionally a senatorial preserve.[65]

It is possible to give an explanation of these actions in terms of tactics.[66] Even so, it does not follow from this that Tiberius was unaware of their implications and that it was a coincidence that the role of the *plebs* in Roman politics was enlarged. The choice of tactics will no doubt be determined also by other considerations, which may be conscious and perhaps theoretical or unconscious. §6 of this chapter has shown that he identified what is *publica* with what is common. Furthermore what is common belongs to all the People and can therefore be used by them. If this is combined with his stress on popular sovereignty, it is hard to avoid the conclusion that he argued

[63] Ibid. 707-12.
[64] Earl 1963: 44.
[65] Mommsen 1888: 1112-13, Polyb. 6.13.
[66] Cf. Astin 1967: 201-2, 212.

that what concerned the People should be decided by them. Such an argument is not explicitly attributed to Tiberius, but in Plutarch there is a passage that comes very close, at least in a negative form (Plut. *TG* 14.2): 'About all those cities which were part of the kingdom of Attalus Tiberius said it was not appropriate for the Senate to deliberate but that he would put the proposal to the People.' Here Tiberius does not merely say that the People will decide about the Asiatic cities but that it has nothing to do with the Senate. Attalus' legacy was a matter for the People, because he had made the *populus Romanus* his heir (Livy *Per.* 58; Plut. *TG* 14.1; IGRR 4.289/OGIS 338).

This interpretation of *res publica* occurs in Cicero's *De Republica* 1.48. Scipio has been discussing various interpretations of *res publica* which he defines as *res populi*, the property of the people (Cic. *De Rep.* 1.39ff). He reports the views of those who interpret this as the rule of the People. Nothing is better than when the People are the masters of the laws, the courts, war and peace, treaties and the life and property of every citizen: 'They think that this is the only form of government that can rightly be called a *res publica*, in other words the property of the people. And so the property of the people is often freed from the control of kings and senators but people who are free do not demand kings or the power and wealth of the aristocracy.' Here we find the very Greek idea of the *dêmos* in a thoroughly Roman context.

8

The Justification of the Roman Empire

1. Introduction

Zeno and the early Stoics had characterised all forms of subordination (*hupotaxis*) among the bad as slavery. To exercise despotic authority, whether as a slave-owner or as an imperial state, was unjust. Consequently they condemned not only slavery, but also empire, the exercise and maintenance of power over other states. The main difference between the two was one of scale.[1] In the third century the imperial power had been Macedon; in the second century it was Rome. From the mid-second century, however, the Stoic attitude to both empire and chattel slavery underwent a change. Now when Roman rule was increasingly coming under attack from Greek intellectuals, Stoics emerged not as the opponents of empire, but as its defenders. Correspondingly they were no longer willing to reject the slave/master relationship. Disagreeing with their predecessors they argued that slavery could be in the interests of the slave. It was just that those incapable of governing themselves should be subject to those who were able to govern them, because such relationships were natural and in the interests of the subjects. This theory forms the basis for the justification of the Roman empire and is developed further in the course of the first century BC. While the original argument took the form of an analogy with slavery, it could be suggested that it was made more acceptable to Roman minds by being transmuted into the more Roman concepts of patron and client.

By the beginning of the Principate notions of the justice and benevolence of Roman rule were prevalent. Livy could say that Rome's allies in Campania had remained loyal during the Hannibalic war because of the justice and moderation of Roman rule and because they were prepared to obey their betters, *melioribus parere* (Livy 22.13.11). Virgil celebrates Rome's imperial destiny in the famous lines of Anchises (*Aeneid* 6.851-3):

---

[1] See Chapter 2 for arguments on slavery and empire, Chapter 4 for their application to Macedon.

You, Roman, remember to rule peoples under you, (these will be your skills) to build civilisation on peace, to spare the vanquished and subdue the proud.

tu regere imperio populos, Romane, memento
(hae tibi erunt artes), pacique imponere morem,
parcere subiectis et debellare superbos.

Cicero believed that *patrocinium*, which meant 'patronage' or 'protection', was a more appropriate term for Roman rule than *imperium* (Cic. *De Off.* 2.27). Similarly in his letters he advocates good government in the provinces and stresses the need to take account of justice and the interests of the subjects (e.g. Cic. *Ad Q. F.* 1.127). His vision for the Roman empire verges on pure altruism: 'I think that in all matters those in power must adhere to the following principle, that their subjects be as happy as possible' (*Ad Q. F.* 1.1.24). It might be said that these are merely self-congratulatory platitudes and of no significance; for they were scarcely likely to say otherwise. But, on the other hand, they need not have commented at all. Thus one has to ask when and how such ideas developed.

At this point a distinction must be drawn between Rome's claims that her wars were just and claims that the empire was just. The Romans had long asserted that their wars were just; there were good propaganda reasons for doing so. In 230 BC the Roman ambassador to Queen Teuta the Illyrian is said to have told her that the Romans punish injustices done to individuals and assist the victims of injustice (Polyb. 2.8.10). Polybius notes the concern of the Romans that their wars should appear just; in the mid-second century it is concern for foreign opinion that restrains them from attacking Carthage until a suitable pretext has been found (Polyb. 36.2 cf. Polyb. Frag. 99 B-W). Polybius, however, gives a cynical appraisal of Roman pretensions to justice with his view that Rome had a 'universal aim', a desire to subjugate the known world (Polyb. 1.3.6, 9-10, 3.2.6). The fetial procedure for declaring war was really only an internal policy for ensuring that the gods were favourable and would have little, if any, influence on foreign opinion.[2]

Although there were clear reasons to prompt the Romans into claiming that their wars were just, there were no such reasons to encourage them to consider that their empire was just in itself. War needs to be justified because it is concerned with changing a state of affairs. For the proclamation of a just war has propaganda value directly related to the course of the war which has been undertaken. But empire is the existing state of affairs and therefore it only becomes necessary to justify it when it is threatened. Nevertheless it might be

---

[2] Harris 1979: 168-71; Rich 1976: 58 would limit the scope of the fetial procedure.

seen as just in consequence of a just war, but this would probably be an unconscious assumption.

Such ideas with moral and justificatory overtones often arise when an institution or the *status quo* is being defended against attack. For instance, Aristotle put forward a defence of slavery, but this was a reaction to the criticisms of those who claimed that slavery was contrary to nature and unjust (Arist. *Pol.* 1253b20-23, 1254a17-55b15). First one needs a hostile judgment, then there is a justifying response. In the mid-second century Roman rule was coming under just such an attack. On the one hand there was criticism by intellectuals. Isocrates, an otherwise unknown public lecturer, condemned the Romans for their arrogant commands and unrestrained use of power.[3] Probably writing after the destruction of Carthage in 146, Agatharchides of Cnidos with a clear jibe at Rome wrote that the Sabaeans and their neighbours only preserved their enormous wealth because they lived so far from 'those who turn their arms in every direction'. Otherwise 'they would have become the stewards of the wealth of others, having been masters of their own'.[4] Polybius promises to recount the judgments made by the subjects about the rulers, a further indication that this was a subject of debate at this time (Polyb. 3.4.6). The most thorough attack on Roman imperialism which we possess from this period was voiced by Carneades, the head of the Academy. He presented arguments which demonstrated the injustice of empire with particular reference to Rome (see below, §3). Alongside the intellectual opposition there was practical resistance. In the early 140s there occurred the rising of Andriscus in Macedon against Rome and the revolt of Achaea. Rome reasserted her authority, turning Macedon into a province and razing Corinth to the ground.

2. A contemporary view: Polybius

It is at such a time that one would expect justifications for Roman rule to develop. Since our knowledge of the arguments of Carneades and the Stoics comes from later sources, primarily Cicero's *De Republica*, it is necessary to consider the evidence of a contemporary. Polybius was in Rome at this time as one of the thousand Achaean hostages who came there in 167 after the Romans defeated Perseus, the Macedonian king, in the Third Macedonian War. He established a close friendship with Scipio Aemilianus, who was soon to become one of Rome's most prominent politicians. Although he was not a philosopher, his work reflects current ideas, both Greek and Roman, on the subject of Rome's empire, a subject integral to his account of Roman expansion and its

---

[3] Polyb. 31.33.5, 32.2.4-8, where Isocrates is described as *grammatikos* and *kritikos*.
[4] GGM I pp. 189-90, section 102, Fraser 1972: 1.545, 550, 2.786.

aftermath. Probably a member of the audience for Carneades' lectures in Rome (Polyb. 33.2 = Gell. 6.14.10), he was aware of the contemporary debate about the merits of Roman rule and made his own contribution to it (Polyb. 3.4). Consequently an examination of Polybius' history allows an insight into contemporary perceptions about Rome's role and the degree of interest it aroused.[5]

The original intention of his history had been to explain how in less than fifty-three years the Romans had succeeded in becoming rulers of almost the whole world (1.1.5). This period extended from 220 until 167, that is from the prelude to the Hannibalic War until the dissolution of the Macedonian kingdom which followed Perseus' defeat. In an important passage (3.4), believed to have been written after 146, he tells us why he has decided to extend his history beyond 167 when he regarded Roman expansion as complete.[6] His purpose is to provide the information which will enable the reader to pass judgment on Roman rule; thus, he says, contemporaries should be able to determine whether it should be avoided or welcomed and future generations whether it should be praised or condemned.

This purpose naturally affects his selection of material and therefore he explains what aspects he believes to be important for making such a judgment:

> In addition to these matters I must add (*prostheteon*) an account of what sort of policy the conquerors had after this and how they governed the world, and of the various appreciations and judgments of the rest about their rulers; furthermore I must examine (*exêgêteon*) the tendencies (*hormai*) and ambitions (*zêloi*) which prevailed and were dominant among each, both in their private lives and in state policy (*tous kat' idian bious kai tas koinas politeias*).

Polybius proposes to add to what he has said about proceedings up to Pydna an account of the conduct of the rulers in the period after this, but this will be balanced by presenting what the subjects think about the rulers. In order to make an assessment of Roman rule it is not sufficient to record merely the conduct of the rulers and the judgments of the ruled; one must probe beneath the surface, hence the last part of his programme. He must investigate what were the prevailing and dominant tendencies and ambitions among both the rulers and the ruled in their private lives and in state policy.[7] Whereas the first and second elements of this programme are grouped together, following

---

[5] In this section of the text all references are to Polybius unless otherwise stated. On the date of Polybius' arrival in Rome, Walbank 1979: 497.

[6] On the date of composition of this passage, Walbank 1957: 292-7, 1972: 27.

[7] Following Schweighäuser's translation: '*tum in vitis privatorum, tum in publicis consiliis*'; rather than Paton (Loeb): 'in their private and public life'. For the phrase, cf. Polyb. 5.88.3, 6.48.3.

prostheteon, this last one is treated separately, following *exêgêteon*. Unlike the first two it is concerned with examining both ruler and subject; it is something that must be taken into account when considering the first two elements. We cannot form an adequate evaluation on the basis of actions or judgments alone. To point out that the Romans acted generously in their treatment of subjects is not enough to lead one to commend their empire; that Macedon resented Roman rule does not mean that Roman rule should be condemned. Weighed against this sort of claim must be an examination of the forces that underlay these actions and judgments. If Rome treats her subjects well because this is the best way to fulfil her aim of maintaining her hold on the empire, if Macedon resents Roman rule because of restrictions on her freedom to make war, then these must be taken into consideration.

If Polybius' text is examined, it can be seen that his treatment of the post-Pydna period follows this pattern. First, however, it is useful to look at another passage of Polybius (10.36). Here he digresses from his account of the Spanish wars to discuss the most sensible course of conduct for an imperial power. He begins by repeating the theme expressed in the earlier passage that it is more difficult to use success well than to achieve it (3.4.1-5). The Carthaginians lost the hold which they had gained over Spain in 212, because they treated the inhabitants arrogantly (*huperêphanôs*, 10.36.3, cf. 10.7.3). Moreover they made their subjects (*hupotattomenoi*) enemies instead of friends and allies. Superiority is acquired by those who treat their neighbours well, but it can only be maintained if the rulers continue to pursue such a policy. If, as the Carthaginians had done, the ruling state abandons the considerate policy by which it gained power and governs badly and despotically (*despotikôs*), the attitude of the subjects will change to one of hostility. Thus for Polybius the ruling state should be benevolent towards its subjects, but only because it is expedient, not because it has any moral duty to act in this way. This passage shows an affinity with his analysis of the features which should be taken into account when passing judgment on an empire; it deals with the conduct of the rulers and the reactions of the subjects in relation to the self-interested desire of the rulers to maintain their position.

Whether Polybius' account of the post-Pydna years conformed to his programme is partly obscured by the fact that much of the original text of the last ten books which cover this period is missing. The first five books of his history are complete and together these are more than twice the length of the sum of the extant parts of the last ten books. He divided these years into two sections, the first to enable men to judge Roman rule and the second, from about 151 to 145/4, to examine 'the disturbed and troubled period' that followed (3.4.12-13). But it is difficult to see a clear division between these two sections, and both play a part in the passing of judgments.[8]

It can be gathered from the two passages that have been discussed that Rome's conduct will be a manifestation of its *hormai* and *zêloi*; her conduct may involve treating the subjects well or badly, but for Polybius it is consistently motivated by utilitarian considerations, the desire to maintain the empire.[9] The Senate agreed to the request of the younger Ptolemy that they revise the agreement between himself and his brother, because it was in their own interests. This was typical of many Roman decisions, says Polybius, 'taking advantage of the errors of others they effectively increase and build up their own power, at the same time doing a favour and appearing to confer a benefit on those at fault' (31.10). On the many occasions when the Romans had to arbitrate between Carthage and its Numidian neighbour Massinissa they always judged in favour of Massinissa, not because his claim was just, but because it was in their interests (31.21). Other examples of Roman self-interest in the conduct of affairs can be cited, e.g. 31.2, 32.13.8-9, 36.2. Clemency and magnanimity are shown to the Odrysian king Cotys by returning his son, although the king had fought on the side of Perseus, but this is coupled with the purpose of the action – to bind Cotys to them (30.17). In 10.36 Polybius had noted that it was in the interests of the imperial power to treat its subjects well. It is in this way that one should view a couple of passages in which Polybius represents the Romans as the bringers of peace and order, although no claim of Roman self-interest is explicitly made. The Aetolians had been accustomed to supply their needs by plundering other Greek states, but they were prevented from doing this when the Romans took control (30.11). The Romans bestowed many important benefits on the Macedonian people, whose system of government had been oppressive and whose cities had suffered from civil unrest and bloodshed. The Romans changed this (36.17.13). Polybius had also promised to investigate the dominant tendencies (*hormai*) and ambitions (*zêloi*) in private lives. Perhaps his intention was to enable the reader to judge whether the Romans were fit to rule. About Scipio Aemilianus there could be no doubt; he had *hormê* and *zêlos* for a virtuous life, *ta kala*, but the rest of the young men at Rome displayed only a tendency to immorality, *hê epi to cheiron hormê*. Significantly this interest in debauchery dated from the war with Perseus (31.25).

To assess an empire the judgments of the subjects must also be examined. Here again Polybius follows the same pattern. Any reported judgment is complemented by consideration of the tendencies and ambitions of the proponent, whether a state or an individual. Some judgments will be explicit, but others only implied in the form of acts in

[8] Walbank 1957: 303.
[9] Walbank 1965: 8.

favour of or hostile to Roman rule, although the latter may have been made explicitly in the full text. A clear example of an event which implies a hostile judgment is the revolt of the Macedonians under the leadership of Andriscus in 149 (36.17.13-16). The mutilation of the text at this point prevents us from knowing whether Polybius expressed it any more fully. This revolt should not necessarily lead to the belief that Roman rule in Macedon was reprehensible; Polybius certainly did not think so. The hostile judgment is balanced by the consideration that the Macedonians are impelled by restrictions on their internecine tendencies, for Polybius a totally irrational impulse (36.17.16). Individuals are treated in a similar way. Those Greek statesmen who support Rome, such as Charops of Epirus and Lyciscus the Aetolian, need not be taken as evidence in favour of Roman rule; they are seen to be exploiting their relationship with Rome for personal gain and in order to promote their own position within the state, murdering, robbing and exiling fellow citizens (Charops: 30.13.4, 32.5-6, Lyciscus: 30.13.4, 32.4-5).

There are also cases of judgments which are explicit. When a Roman commission came to Syria in 162 to burn the fleet and hamstring the elephants, there was popular uproar and in Laodicea a certain Leptines assassinated Gn. Octavius, one of the commissioners, claiming that the murder was just and approved by the gods. Isocrates, the public lecturer mentioned above, praised the action and attacked the Romans for their arrogant commands (*huperêphana epitagmata*) and unrestrained use of power. Although the attitudes of these two men, Leptines and Isocrates, towards Rome are very similar, their behaviour and character are sharply contrasted by Polybius. Here there is an assessment of their private lives. Isocrates is self-centred, garrulous, boastful, cowardly and unpopular even with Greeks; he is prompted to make his attack on Rome not through sympathy for the Syrians, whom he despises, but from an arrogant desire to be provocative. Leptines, on the other hand, is courageous, noble and altruistically concerned about the fate of the Laodiceans (32.2-3). In the war between Rome and the Achaeans in 146 Critolaus, the Achaean *stratêgos*, condemned the Romans and put the worst interpretation on everything they said. He asserted that he wanted to be a friend of the Romans, but would not accept them as masters (*despotai*), in other words the Romans were acting as masters, not as friends (Polyb. 38.11.8, 12.8). But for Polybius the aim of Critolaus was tyranny, attained by rousing the masses through demagogy.[10] Nevertheless, although Polybius is virulently hostile to both Isocrates and Critolaus, the views attributed to them are meant to be treated

---

[10] Polyb. 38.11.7-13.7, esp. 13.7, *monarchikê exousia*, Walbank 1979: 708, Musti 1967: 203.

seriously as judgments on Roman rule. If true, they represent major criticisms of the administration of Rome's empire. For Polybius himself had made these same criticisms of the Carthaginians in Spain; they treated their subjects arrogantly (*huperêphanôs*), as enemies not friends, as masters (*despotikôs*) (10.36). Philopoemen, whom Polybius greatly admired, warned that Achaea would become enslaved by the Romans as other states already were (24.13.4).

Thus Polybius puts forward a framework of interrelated factors which should be taken into account when assessing the merits of an empire. He then proceeds to write this part of his history on the basis of this framework. He does not come to a conclusion; he only supplies the information necessary for such a conclusion. Others are expected to do the judging. A similar procedure is followed when he explains the origins of wars. He seeks to pick out the factors which influenced the decisions of the participants, but it is not his concern to assign responsibility.[11] His failure to provide a standard by which empire should be judged seems odd in the light of his belief that there should be some imperial purpose beyond conquest and subjugation.[12] He does not explain what this imperial purpose should be, but the remark may merely reflect his awareness of contemporary arguments about the nature of such a purpose.

In addition to examining the judgments of the subjects on Roman rule, Polybius also includes a long passage giving the views of the Greeks about Roman methods of war and the annihilation of Carthage (36.9). It has already been suggested that the Stoics were responsible for the legalistic arguments here (36.9.12-17; see above, Chapter 7.3). The Stoics, however, did not limit themselves to justifying the acquisition of power; in response to criticism of Roman rule they also justified the maintenance of power, as will be seen from an examination of Cicero's *De Republica*. The arguments found in Book 3 of the *De Republica* fit neatly into the context of the second century BC which has been seen in Polybius. Ideas of empire as self-interest and slavery, as benefiting the subjects, of the imperial power as a bringer of peace and order all appear in this work of Cicero. But, unlike Polybius, the speakers in the *De Republica* are prepared to come to unambiguous conclusions about the merits of Roman rule.

3. Criticism of Roman rule: Carneades

In 155 BC the Athenians sent an embassy to Rome to obtain remission of a fine of 500 talents, which was imposed for a raid on Oropus. The embassy was partly successful, managing to get the fine reduced to 100

[11] Derow 1979: 9-13.
[12] Polyb. 3.4.9, Walbank 1965: 12.

talents (Paus. 7.11.5). The ambassadors were three leading philosophers, Carneades, the head of the Academy, Diogenes, the head of the Stoa, and Critolaus, the head of the Peripatetic school. It was Carneades who made the greatest impression by delivering two lectures on justice. On one day he spoke in favour of justice, on the next he demolished the arguments put forward the previous day. This caused consternation; Cato demanded that they should be sent away as soon as possible, because Carneades was distracting the young men from 'the laws and magistrates' and when he was talking 'it was difficult to discern what was true'.[13]

The third book of Cicero's *De Republica* contains a debate, set in 129, between Furius and Laelius about justice. The speech against justice, which is given to Furius, borrows heavily from the arguments of Carneades' second lecture (*De Rep.* 3.8). It is answered by Laelius. Unfortunately much of this book is missing and the gaps have to be filled from the accounts of later writers, such as Augustine, Lactantius and Nonius.[14] The quotation and paraphrases by Augustine are particularly valuable; he had a thorough knowledge of the text and much of the time he appears to have had the *De Republica* in front of him when referring to it.[15]

Furius' speech attacks both common conceptions of justice and the theories of philosophers. It has been argued that the Stoics were Carneades' principal target,[16] but it is clear that his victims also included Plato and Aristotle (Lactantius *Inst.* 5.14.5, *Epit.* 50 (55), 5-8; Cic. *De Rep.* 3.9-11) and the Epicureans (*De 'Rep.* 3.26). Since the sceptical Academy and Carneades did not believe that Plato was a dogmatist, a refutation of his arguments involved no conflict of loyalties.[17]

The argument of Carneades, as presented by Cicero, begins by arguing that there is no really convincing account of justice. It is not justice that determines men's actions, but self-interest, the Greek notion of *to sumpheron*. As he says at one point, weakness is the mother of justice, *imbecillitas mater iustitiae est* (*De Rep.* 3.23). Nevertheless he continues with a direct assault on the position of Plato, Aristotle and the Stoics, all of whom believed that the good man possessed both justice and *sapientia*, that is practical wisdom or prudence. For even if it is accepted that justice exists, argues

---

[13] Pliny *NH* 7.112-13, Plut. *Cato Mai.* 22, Gell. 6.14.8-10, 17.21.48, Cic. *Acad.* 2.137, *De Orat.* 2.155, *Tusc. Disp.* 4.5, *Ad Att.* 12.23.2.

[14] The accounts of later writers are included in K. Ziegler's Teubner edition of the *De Republica*, Leipzig 1969.

[15] Hagendahl 1967: 540-53, cf. also Testard 1958, vol. 1, p. 195; for list and texts of citations by Augustine from Cicero in the *De Civitate Dei*, Testard, vol. 2, pp. 36-71, 122-4.

[16] Ferrary 1977.

[17] Glucker 1978: 48-52.

Carneades, the demands of justice would be very different from the demands of prudence. A just state should pay attention to the interests of others: 'Justice instructs you to spare all men, to show regard for the human race, to return to each his own, not to touch what is sacred, what belongs to the state and what belongs to someone else' (*De Rep.* 3.24). Yet this is not a sensible policy for a state to pursue. The prudent state seeks to increase its wealth and expand its influence and territory at the expense of other states. Imperialist expansion is only piracy on a large scale (*De Rep.* 3.24). As an example Carneades introduces the Romans who rule the whole world. Did they achieve this by justice or by prudence, *iustitia* or *sapientia*? Clearly they did not achieve this by being just. For justice would entail restoring what was not theirs. Thus they would have to return to their huts and live in poverty.[18] According to Augustine Carneades argued that the slave/master relationship was unjust: *iniustum esse ut homines hominibus dominantibus serviant*; it was exactly this sort of injustice that an imperial power practised (Cic. *De Rep.* 3.36, Aug. *De Civ.* 19.21). Here Carneades is found adopting the analogy between slavery and empire which has already been noticed in the political thought of the early Stoics.

Although there is little doubt that Carneades did deliver two lectures on justice in Rome, it cannot be proved that the remarks about the injustice of Roman imperialism were included in them. Since Carneades published no writings (D.L. 4.65), Cicero could not have had direct access to his arguments. If, as I believe (see below, §4), Laelius' reply is derived from a Stoic source refuting Carneades, this source may have furnished him with the arguments used by Carneades. It is possible, however, that the lectures may have been written up by his pupil, Clitomachus, and that it was this work which Cicero used.[19] Even if the arguments criticising Roman imperialism are Clitomachus' own contribution, they would still be evidence for second-century debate, since he died 110/109 BC.[20] But it is more probable that this is an accurate record of arguments used by Carneades, whether in Rome or in Athens; he was not averse to making contemporary allusions (cf. his remarks on Perseus and L. Aemilius Paullus, Plut. *Tranq. An.* 474F-5A) and the conception of Rome presented in the speech is consistent with current ideas. Nevertheless, since Carneades' lectures made a considerable impact at Rome, there may have been a separate Roman tradition which related how Carneades had accused the Romans of injustice, even if it did not record the arguments used.[21] For there were many prominent

---

[18] Cic. *De Rep.* 3.24, 3.21, Lact. *Inst.* 5.16.2-4, Cic. *De Rep.* 3.36, Aug. *De Civ.* 19.21. Ferrary 1977: 130 rightly argues that the reference to imperialism in Lactantius should follow *De Rep.* 3.24.

[19] Ferrary 1977: 154-6.

[20] Von Arnim RE Kleitomachos 657.

[21] Ferrary 1977: 154.

Romans in the audience, including Cato, C. Acilius, who acted as interpreter, and Postumius Albinus (Plut. *Cato Mai.* 22; Cic. *Acad. Pr.* 2.137). Polybius referred to the lectures in a lost part of his history and they were also mentioned by P. Rutilius Rufus (Gell. 6.14.8-10, Polyb. 33.2).

Polybius provides confirmation that questions of the type said to have been raised by Carneades were current in the second century BC. The justice of Rome's wars was the subject of intense debate among both Greeks (Polyb. 36.9) and Romans (Polyb. 3.29) in the middle of the second century, as was noted in the last chapter. These involved heavily legalistic arguments to justify Rome's wars and such arguments may have been a response to the criticisms put forward by Carneades. Even if they were not a response to Carneades in particular, they indicate that such matters were the subject of contemporary debate. On the question of the justice of empire, it has already been seen that Polybius paid great attention to how Rome's role should be judged.

Thus there are two possibilities, neither of which can be proved beyond doubt. If Carneades did include the example of Roman imperialism in his lecture at Rome, then this would explain the consternation caused there by his lectures. For the Romans laid great stress on their attention to justice in their dealings and so would take such an attack very seriously. A philosophy of empire was now urgently required.[22] Indeed such was the effect of the arguments that Cicero still thought they warranted discussion some hundred years later. Plutarch argues that Cato's hostility to the philosophers derived from his hostility to philosophy in general; he cites various examples of Cato's animosity to other philosophers to support his case, but it is clear that Plutarch is disputing with others who believed that it was Carneades alone to whom Cato objected (Plut. *Cato Mai.* 22). Some scholars do not believe that the remarks on Rome were a significant part of the lecture; for such remarks were hardly tactful in the context of an embassy to the Senate.[23] However, another could argue that it was all part of Carneades' diplomacy; it was a clever, although impertinent, plea for indulgence – Athens had merely done on a small scale what Rome did on a large scale.[24] The reference to Rome was certainly important enough to be picked out of Cicero's version by both Augustine and Lactantius. It is claimed that what engendered the controversy was not the content of the lecture but the method of argument.[25] It is true that Carneades was following his usual and unsettling practice of arguing both sides of a question. Yet Carneades

---

[22] Walbank 1965: 13, though see n. 42 below.
[23] E.g. Astin 1967: 300, Forte 1972: 70.
[24] Martha 1896: 113-15.
[25] Gruen 1984: 342, Forte 1972: 69-70.

did not have to choose justice to demonstrate his skills, nor did he have to give the lectures in the order that he did.[26] Given that he did make such choices, it becomes hard to divorce method from content as a cause of the controversy.

If, on the other hand, this example was omitted from Carneades' Roman lectures (although it may still have been implied), then the circumstances in which the justification of empire emerged could have been different. The arguments critical of Rome would still have been put forward, but in Greece, not in Rome. So initially at least the reaction may have been centred in Greece. The justification would have been developed by those Greeks who sympathised with Rome and sought to justify their own support for the imperial power. Nevertheless Carneades' role should not be over-emphasised. There is no reason to believe that Carneades was the first to apply these arguments to Rome, nor that he needed to visit Rome for the arguments to become known there. No doubt he reflected ideas that had been developing since Pydna, after which Greek subjection to Rome was unmistakable (cf. Polyb. 31.25). Polybius was certainly familiar with this kind of idea; he regularly represents Rome as affecting justice when in fact motivated by self-interest. In the mid-160s there were large numbers of Greeks coming to Rome (Polyb. 31.24.6-7); some would have brought information on debates about Rome current in Athens. What is important about Carneades is not where he put forward these arguments, but that they were put forward at all. The ultimate effect was the same. A justification of empire was formulated.

4. A justification of empire: Panaetius

In the *De Republica* it is to Laelius that Cicero entrusts the task of defending Rome against these charges (*De Rep.* 3.33-41). There were two main charges against Rome: first that her wars were unjust and secondly that the maintenance of the empire gained in consequence was also unjust. On the first point Laelius appears to have made a fairly orthodox reply, stressing the idea of defence whether of allies or of oneself, *aut pro fide aut pro salute* (Cic. *De Rep.* 3.34, Aug. *De Civ.* 22.6; *De Rep.* 3.35, Isid. *Orig.* 18.1). 'Our people has now gained power over the whole world by defending its allies' (*De Rep.* 3.35, Nonius p. 498.18). Rome's wars are also just when fought in revenge or in accordance with the fetial procedure. Wars are only unjust when undertaken without reason, *sine causa* (*De Rep.* 3.35, Isid. *Orig.* 18.1).

It is the argument justifying the maintenance of empire which is novel, for which Augustine is the main authority (Cic. *De Rep.* 3.36-7;

---

[26] Fuchs 1964: 3.

Aug. *De Civ.* 19.21, *Con. Iul.* 4.12.61; Nonius p. 109.2). According to Augustine's summary of the argument in his *City of God*, Cicero said that the rule of subject states was just, because slavery was in the interests of a certain kind of men, *quod talibus hominibus sit utilis servitus*. For this kind of men, if left to their own devices, would only damage their own interests, for instance by robbery and civil war. If, however, the imperial power administers its rule correctly, it will be in the subjects' interests and the opportunity for injustice, *licentia iniuriarum*, will be removed from them. Therefore in such cases subjection is better than independence.

This argument is reinforced by the claim that it is a principle of nature that the best rule the weaker in the interests of the latter. It is in this way that God rules man, the mind rules the body and reason rules the desires, anger and other vicious parts of the soul. The rule of mind over body and the rule of reason over the vicious parts of the soul are to be distinguished; the former is monarchic and constitutional, the latter is like the rule of master over slaves. It is the latter which is analogous to empire. Implicit in this is the notion that it would be an abnegation of responsibility for the imperial power to abandon its empire. Taken in conjunction with this should be a passage of Lactantius which in Ziegler's edition of the *De Republica* is printed at the beginning of Laelius' speech (Cic. *De Rep.* 3.33, Lact. *Inst.* 6.8.6-9). Here we are told that true law is right reason in accordance with nature; such law is eternal and unchangeable; good men obey it and all men should obey it. If it is a principle of nature that the best rule the weaker, then one would expect the best, appreciating their duty to obey the injunctions of nature, to seek to fulfil this role. Thus the argument is that the rule of the best (i.e. Rome) over the weaker (i.e. Rome's subjects) is both natural and advantageous; for the latter are incapable of living in peace and harmony without Rome's assistance. This leads to the conclusion that empire is just so long as it has the well-being of the subjects in mind.

Of course it is still possible to conclude that the Roman empire itself is unjust, but such a conclusion would be far more subjective and hence easier to deny. The argument may have gone as follows: if all Rome's wars have been just, their opponents must have acted unjustly; therefore they need to be subject to their moral betters. It seeks to counter Carneades' objection that the possession of empire is necessarily unjust. Instead the Romans could and did feel reassured in their moral superiority and their role as the world's benefactors. Doubtless the 'lunatic' behaviour of the Greeks in the early 140s provided suitable evidence of their inability to rule themselves.

Laelius' speech is certainly using ideas which had philosophical antecedents, but, as will be seen below, there is good reason to believe that it was not Cicero who originally applied these to the justification of empire. So when was the justification devised and by whom? It fits most naturally into the context of the debate about the merits of Roman rule in the mid to late second century BC. The concept of benevolent empire has already been seen to have made an appearance in Polybius, although for him it is thoroughly self-interested. Apart from the topicality of the subject as a whole, the speech at one point contrasts the death of a person which is natural and often desirable and the annihilation of a state which is neither. Therefore such elimination is a more appropriate punishment for a state than a person (Cic. *De Rep.* 3.34, Aug. *De Civ.* 22.6). This remark would be particularly relevant in the aftermath of the destruction of Carthage, an action which needed some defence in Greece. It recalls the view of those Greeks who held that Rome was justified in its conduct towards Carthage, because they were responding to Carthaginian wrong-doing (Polyb. 36.9.12-17). As was shown in the last chapter, these Greeks were probably Stoics.

Indeed an examination of Laelius' speech demonstrates that its defence of empire was heavily influenced by Stoicism, in particular the ideas of Panaetius. Early in the work Cicero introduces the discussions which Scipio Aemilianus used to have with Panaetius and Polybius on political matters; this implies that Panaetius was in the background to some of the dialogue (Cic. *De Rep.* 1.34, Panaetius F.119). Cicero distinguished Panaetius from the early Stoics, noting that he had a more practical outlook in his work (Cic. *De Leg.* 3.14, Panaetius F.48, 61). His affinity with the Roman ruling class and his arguments against the Gracchan reforms have already been noted. So, if a Stoic was the source, Panaetius is the most likely candidate in this period.[27]

The beginning of Laelius' speech contains an account of law in accordance with nature which is undoubtedly Stoic in origin:[28] 'True law is right reason, in accordance with nature, spread out among all men, unchanging and eternal, which calls to duty by its commands and deters from wrongdoing by its prohibitions.' This passage could be derived from any Stoic writer and there is nothing exclusively Panaetian about it. Moreover, it does not necessarily follow from this that the rest of the justification of empire is Stoic; it is always possible that Cicero amalgamated several different and even inconsistent ideas to create the speech, but the relevance of nature to the justification suggests otherwise. Indeed an examination of the argument in *De Rep.* 3.36-7 will show that it is Stoic and that it is consistent with other aspects of Panaetius' philosophy, aspects which were anathema to the

---

[27] Schmekel 1892: 47-63, followed by Capelle 1932: 94, argued that Panaetius was Cicero's source for the whole of *De Republica* 3, but Van Straaten 1946: 308-13 has rightly argued that Schmekel's argument is inadequate.

[28] Cic. *De Rep.* 3.33, Lact. *Inst.* 6.8.6-9; for Stoic origin, see D.L. 7.88, SVF 1.162, D.L. 7.128, SVF 3.308, Marcianus SVF 3.314. Van Straaten 1946: 309.

early Stoics. For it is in the evidence for Panaetius that the first signs of a change in the Stoic approach to psychology and slavery appear. With this we should expect to see a change in their approach to empire also. The Stoics were regularly targets for Carneades' attacks and the lecture on justice was no exception. Carneades had said 'Without Chrysippus there would have been no Carneades' (D.L. 4.62). Thus the Stoics were likely to have responded to Carneades on this matter as they did on others.[29]

Nevertheless it might be argued that, although the Stoics contended that morality and expediency should not be divorced, the passage from Augustine's *City of God* places too much emphasis on expediency and too little on nature; so a Stoic argument cannot lie behind it. But this ignores Augustine's intention, which was to show that subjection to God was in the interests of men; it was not important to him to prove that it was natural or just. Consequently he may have altered the emphasis of the argument to suit his own purpose.[30] Here *utilitas*, expediency, is the most important word, but the other fragments from this part of the argument concentrate on the natural principle, the rule of the capable over the incapable in various fields. This concern with the natural relationship is what we would expect from a Stoic thinker.

This argument in the *De Republica* compares the relationship between the imperial power and its subjects not only with that between master and slave, but also with the relationship between the rational and the irrational parts of the soul. The Stoics before Panaetius could have accepted the slavery analogy and hence concluded that the maintenance of empire was unnatural and unjust, but they could not have accepted the comparison with the soul. They held that the soul was a unity and not divided into rational and irrational parts. Immoral action was not the result of a conflict between reason and irrational desire, which reason loses, but due to defective rationality. Impulses or desires (*hormai*) are manifestations of the rationality of the soul as a whole. Impulses can be described as disobedient to reason, in which case they are called passions (*pathê*), but this is not with reference to a rational part of the soul; rather it is to a standard of rationality as personified in the wise man, the rationality of whose soul is perfect. The bad man has an unhealthy soul, a condition which is cured by perfecting one's rationality. In this way the passions are not restrained as they are in the divided soul, but eradicated.[31]

Panaetius, on the other hand, sought to divide the soul in some way.[32] He distinguishes two elements in the soul, reason which is in control

[29] Long 1967: 59-90, 1974: 117.

[30] For the tendency of Augustine to paraphrase in this way, Hagendahl 1967: 701.

[31] For a fuller account of the psychology of the early Stoa, Rist 1969: 22-36, Long 1974: 175-8, Gill 1983: 136-49, esp. 138-40.

[32] Rist 1969: 182-4, Pohlenz 1970: 198-9; Long 1974: 213 is more cautious.

and impulse (*appetitus/hormê*) which obeys (Cic. *De Off.* 1.101, Panaetius F.87; *De Off.* 1.132, Panaetius F.88). The impulses are to be made obedient to reason and the passions are to be restrained (Cic. *De Off.* 2.18, Panaetius F.89), not eradicated. Thus the analogy would be consistent with Panaetius' psychology. Cicero in the *De Officiis*, which is heavily dependent on Panaetius, uses two terms to translate *pathê*, *motus animi turbati* and *perturbationes* (Cic. *De Off.* 2.18, Panaetius F.89; *De Off.* 1.66, Panaetius F.106; *De Off.* 1.67, 69). *Perturbationes* appears also in the *De Republica*: the best part of the soul exercises restraint over its own vicious and weak elements such as desires, anger and the other *perturbationes* (Cic. *De Rep.* 3.37, Aug. *Con. Iul.* 4.12.61).

Nevertheless some scholars believe that this justification of empire, rather than being Stoic, is simply Aristotle's defence of slavery rehashed and adapted to cover international relations. Consequently there is no need to introduce any Stoic as a mediator between Aristotle and Cicero. Anybody who was familiar with Aristotle could have borrowed it, including Cicero himself.[33] This view is mistaken. For the argument in the *De Republica* is only superficially Aristotle's defence of slavery and is in fact fundamentally different. Aristotle seeks to show that there is such a person as a natural slave. For Aristotle the rule of the soul over the body is like that of master over slave, because it is absolute and despotic, whereas the rule of reason over desire is monarchic and constitutional. He claims that those men whose function is the use of their bodies rather than their souls should yield to their superiors in the interests of both; for then there is a suitable combination of soul and body. The soul of the man who is a slave by nature is deficient, because he participates in *logos* only so far as to perceive but not so as to possess it. So in Aristotle's analogy the soul instructs the body just as the master instructs the slave. Without this help the slave's reactions would be intuitive like an animal. Thus Aristotle's account requires some form of subhuman man, incomplete because his soul is inadequate (Arist. *Pol.* 1253a17-55a2).

Cicero's version clearly borrows from Aristotle, but it contains significant differences. Most importantly Aristotle's analogies are transposed. The rule of soul over body is no longer despotic, instead it is constitutional and monarchic. Now it is the rule of reason over the passions which has become despotic; reason restrains them like a master a slave. Here there is no notion of an incomplete human being, rather someone who needs control in his own interests. Thus there is a distinction between instruction as in Aristotle, and restraint, as in Cicero. Restraint does not appear at all in Aristotle's account of the slave by nature, but it is present in Panaetius' doctrine of the soul. Yet

---

[33] Strasburger 1965: 45, Astin 1967: 300-1.

there are clearly Aristotelian links. Indeed at one point in the *Politics* Aristotle implies that he considers his argument for the natural slave relevant in international relations. He writes that one of the objects of war is 'to be the masters of those who deserve to be slaves' (Arist. *Pol.* 1334a2). Panaetius is known to have been influenced by both Aristotle and Plato. He is described as *philaristotelês* and *philoplatôn*, terms meaning an admirer of Aristotle and Plato.[34] Cicero says that he got rid of the harshness of the old Stoa and spoke constantly of Plato, Aristotle, Xenocrates, Theophrastus and Dicaearchus.[35] Such a hybrid theory would not be such in implausible result. The imperial power is seen as imposing peace and order on its subjects as reason does on the passions.

So why are there these differences between the arguments of Aristotle and Cicero? Why have the analogies been transposed? Strasburger, albeit unwittingly, supplies the answer, while trying to refute the claim that a Stoic devised the argument in the *De Republica*. He objects that Aristotle's defence of slavery is blatantly inconsistent with the Stoic doctrine of the equality of all men.[36] This is correct. According to Aristotle's argument there are slaves' souls and masters' souls and the *logos* in each is different in kind. The slave by nature is virtually on a level with animals. But the Stoa drew a very sharp distinction between man and the rest of the animals. Although some men were more rational than others they were all constituted the same and all possessed *logos*. It was the possession of *logos* which distinguished them from animals, which have no *logos*. Thus Aristotle's argument was useless for a Stoic unless it was altered. The argument in the *De Republica* makes them all full human beings, but some less capable of self-government. It does not prove that there is such a person as a slave by nature; it only seeks to prove that this relationship between one who governs well and one who cannot is natural and hence good, but not that anyone is by nature suited to either role. There is nothing to require that an individual is permanently in a state of being unable to control himself or defective as Aristotle's slave is. The revision of Aristotle's argument precludes the possibility that Cicero himself devised it; he had no reason to make such changes. A Stoic would have no choice but to change Aristotle's argument.

The use of this argument reveals a different attitude not only to psychology but also to slavery. The early Stoa used an analogy with slavery to show that something was undesirable, but here it is used to show that it is desirable. This change in approach can be seen in the *De*

---

[34] *Stoic. Ind.* LXI, ed. Comparetti 534, Panaetius F.57.

[35] Cic. *De Fin.* 4.79, Panaetius F.55, cf. also Panaetius F.56, 58, 59 for the influence of Plato on Panaetius.

[36] Strasburger 1965: 45.

Officiis. Here advice is given on the treatment of slaves, which presupposes that slavery is acceptable. We are told that even the lowest should be treated with justice; it is slaves whose condition and fortune is the lowest and these should be treated as if they were hired labourers (Cic. *De Off.* 1.41). The comparison with hired labourers recalls and misuses Chrysippus' description of the slave as *perpetuus mercenarius* (Sen. *De Ben.* 3.22, SVF 3.351; Chapter 2.4). If there is no other way of controlling them, one must have recourse to force (Cic. *De Off.* 2.24), just as with the slave states in the *De Republica*. Thus if a slave's behaviour is appropriate to his position, he should be treated well; if not, force should be used. A similar acceptance of slavery can be seen in the writings of later Stoics. Hecaton, a pupil of Panaetius (Cic. *De Off.* 3.63), discussed whether a good man would let his slaves starve when grain was expensive (Cic. *De Off.* 3.89). It is interesting to note that for Hecaton possession of a slave appears to be consistent with being a good man. Posidonius, too, saw nothing wrong with the institution of slavery itself, as his account of the Sicilian slave revolts shows. What he objected to was the harsh treatment of slaves. Revolts would not occur if the slave-owner exercised *philanthrôpia*, humanity (FGH 87F108c, Diod. 34/35.2.33), a virtue that Posidonius thought was important in many fields.

The justification of empire required two conditions to be met; first that the ruling state should be morally better than its subjects and secondly that it should act in its subjects' interests. Rome, it would appear, fulfilled both these conditions. This argument may have been used to justify chattel slavery also, but it would be a very unsatisfactory defence of the institution of slavery; for many cases of chattel slavery will not meet these conditions. Yet slavery was acceptable to Stoics from Panaetius onwards. Posidonius, Seneca and probably Panaetius all believed that men became slaves as a result of fortune.[37] This does not justify slavery, but it does conveniently place it outside men's control, thus freeing men from responsibility for it. In such a situation, therefore, they accept it and advocate merely that one should treat one's slaves well and show concern for their interests.

It might seem that the analogy with slavery involved unnecessary difficulties for an argument which could have been put forward more easily without reference to slavery. This is to neglect the background against which the argument developed. The early Stoa had drawn attention to the prevalence of subordination within society. All forms of subordination among the bad were slavery; this included chattel slavery, empire and other types of subordination within a city. There was no suggestion here that the masters (*despotai*) were in any way

---

[37] Posidonius: FGH 87F108c, Diod. 34/35.2.33; Seneca: Sen. *Cons. Marc.* 20.1; Panaetius: Cic. *De Off.* 1.41.

morally superior to their subordinates. So even before Panaetius the Stoics saw empire as slavery, a characterisation used by Carneades in his lecture. Aristotle had distinguished between government based on force and that which was not, that is between despotic and constitutional forms of government; it was the justice of the former which was controversial as he realised. By arguing that all forms of subordination among the bad were slavery, the early Stoa rendered them all open to the criticism that they were unjust. Panaetius did not accept this claim. He reintroduced the Aristotelian distinction and this freed some types of slavery from the charge of slavery. Empire, however, was based on force and could not be justified as constitutional. So the problem of empire as slavery still had to be faced. If Panaetius had held Rome or any imperial power to be morally good in an absolute Stoic sense, slavery would not have been an appropriate characterisation of the relationship. But he did not choose to do this. His concern was with relationships between men who were not wise, though some were better than others. Panaetius and later Posidonius both use relative terms rather than absolute ones to describe the ruler and ruled in this relationship.

Thus Panaetius follows the early Stoa in identifying empire with slavery, but he rejects the idea that it is necessarily unjust. The early Stoa had claimed that the master used the slave in his own interests and therefore acted unjustly. Panaetius and Posidonius, on the other hand, place their emphasis on the master's concern for the well-being of the slave. In this way they seek to show that the slave-owner and the imperial state do not have to be self-interested. *Philanthrôpia*, which may have been translated as *humanitas*, is often considered a feature of later Stoics, for instance Posidonius.[38] This was not so much the manifestation of an increased concern for mankind; rather it was developed in an effort to compensate for the Stoa's increased acceptance of contemporary society. As a result they argued that one must exercise one's virtue within this framework.

It has been contended that, if Panaetius had been behind Laelius' speech, 'the doctrine of minor peoples which need tutelage' should appear in Cicero's *De Officiis*, but it does not.[39] The *De Officiis*, however, is concerned with moral and expedient conduct, hence the inclusion of a discussion about justice in war (*De Off.* 1.34-8), but empire is a condition or state. The justification of empire is not relevant to the subject matter of the work and so its omission is of no significance. Similarly Cicero has nothing to say about the morality of slavery, but only offers some advice: one should treat slaves well if possible. Comments on the treatment of subject states would be

[38] Strasburger 1965: 48.
[39] Ibid. 45 n. 50.

relevant and they do appear, albeit with a Ciceronian colouring (*De Off.* 1.35, 2.26-7, cf. *De Rep.* 3.41).

Now that the approach of the second-century Stoa to empire has been examined it is useful to return briefly to Polybius. Polybius was certainly aware of the contemporary debate about Rome's empire, but was he also aware of these discussions within the Stoa? If he was, this could account for traces of Stoic thought that occur in his remarks on empire. When he is explaining his intention in continuing his history beyond Pydna, he writes that he wants to enable his contemporaries to determine whether Roman rule is to be avoided or welcomed, *pheuktê* or *hairetê* (3.4.7). These two words have strong Stoic connotations and may reflect Stoic debate about empire, although Polybius need not be using them in a strict Stoic sense. For the Stoa only the morally good is *hairetos* and only the morally bad is *pheuktos*.[40] These two words only occur together in one other passage of Polybius (6.47). Later in 3.4 Polybius argues that conquest and subjugation cannot be an end in themselves. No one sails the sea simply to cross it or takes up the arts and crafts for the sake of knowledge alone; all these things are done for the sake of the pleasure, good or advantage that results from the actions, *charin tôn epiginomenôn tois ergois êdeôn ê kalôn ê sumpherontôn* (3.4.9-11). In this argument the utilitarian conception of knowledge suggests Stoic influence, as do the three motives for action.[41] Elsewhere, when discussing the relationship between the conquered and the conqueror, he is found describing the subjects as *hupotattomenoi*, a word important in Stoic accounts of subordination (e.g. 10.36.4, 36.7, 24.13.2; cf. D.L. 7.122, SVF 3.355; see Chapter 2). After Pydna the Romans are represented as bringing peace and order to Greece; they put an end to civil conflict and massacres in Macedon and restrained the plundering expeditions of the Aetolians. When the Macedonians and Achaeans revolt in the 140s, their behaviour is described as insanity, recalling the Stoic idea of passions that are out of control (*mênis*: 36.17.15; *mania*: 38.11.6, 18.8; *agnoia*: 38.9.5, 10.12, 11.6, 16.2, 16.9; *anoia*: 38.18.7-8).

5. After Panaetius

The justification for the Roman empire which originated in the second-century Stoa was taken up and applied by Posidonius, a pupil of Panaetius.[42] In Posidonius' philosophy the tendency towards

[40] Stobaeus SVF 3.88, 3.118, for further examples see the index in SVF vol. 4; Long 1976 gives a discussion of the meaning of *hairetos* in Stoic thought.

[41] Walbank 1957: 300-1; but the three motives for action also appear in Aristotle *NE* 2.1104b30ff.

[42] Capelle 1932: 98-103, Walbank 1965: 14-15, but Walbank later rejected the view that Panaetius was the originator, Walbank 1972: 181-2 and note. Posidonius as a pupil of Panaetius: Cic. *De Off.* 3.8, Panaetius F.160, Cic. *De Div.* 1.3.6, Panaetius F.6.

dualism becomes more pronounced. He distinguishes a rational and an irrational force in the soul. John Rist argues that this dualism is present not only in Posidonius' psychology, but also in his physics, in which the governing principle of the world is found separated from everything else.[43] His acceptance of slavery has already been noted. Thus the justification of empire is as consistent with his philosophy as it was with that of Panaetius.

W. Capelle has drawn attention to several Posidonian passages in which this approach to subordination is exemplified.[44] Posidonius cited the Mariandyni as a people who recognised that they suffered from weakness of intellect, *to tês dianoias asthenes*, and therefore made themselves the serfs of the more capable Heracleots, an arrangement which benefited both groups (Athen. 263cd, EK F60, FGH 87F8). The connection with Stoic ideas on slavery and subordination is clear also when he uses the verb *hupotattô* to describe this relationship: *Mariandunoi Herakleôtais hupotagêsan*. In Strabo's account of Spain the Romans are represented as imposing peace and order on lawless natives. They put an end to piracy and brigandage; their presence brings peace in the turbulent north-west (Strabo 3.144, 2.5; 154, 3.5; 156, 3.8). Capelle has argued that all these passages of Strabo are derived from Posidonius.[45]

A letter of Seneca is important evidence for Posidonius' position (Sen. *Ep*. 90.4-6, Theiler F.448).[46] Posidonius believed that it was natural that the weaker submit to those more capable than themselves: *naturae est potioribus deteriora submittere*. Among the animals the largest and fiercest rule, as the strongest bull leads the herd. Thus in the Golden Age the wise governed the weaker in the interests of the latter. The Golden Age shows the naturalness of the relationship, but even in more corrupt times it is desirable that those who are better should be in power: *summa felicitas erat gentium in quibus non poterat potentior esse nisi melior*. The Roman rule in Spain and the relationship between the Heracleots and the Mariandyni are examples of this.[47] The conception of the Golden Age as a time when the wise ruled the rest is alien to the early Stoics.[48] Sextus Empiricus noted that later Stoics, of whom Posidonius was presumably one, believed that there were superior, god-like men in the past and thus implies that the early Stoa did not believe this (Sext. Emp. *Adv. Math.* 9.28, Theiler F.305).[49]

[43] Rist 1969: 201-18, cf. Long 1974: 219.

[44] Capelle 1932: 99-103.

[45] Ibid. 100-3; accepted as Posidonian by Walbank 1965: 14-15, Strasburger 1965: 46-7; Gruen 1984: 351 is sceptical.

[46] Capelle 1932: 99.

[47] Walbank 1965: 15 rightly rejects the argument of Seel 1937: 71-2 that only the reference to the Golden Age is Posidonian.

[48] Cf. Baldry 1959: 10.

[49] Theiler, comm. on F.305, believes Sextus must be referring to Posidonius here.

Several features of the justification of empire are apparent in Posidonius' account of Marcellus, the Roman commander who captured Syracuse in the Hannibalic War (Plut. *Marc.* 20.1-2, EK F 257, FGH 87F43). He was the first Roman to show the Greeks that the Romans were more just; hence one can assume that the Romans were better fitted to rule the Greeks than the Greeks themselves. He was a benefactor to cities and individuals, as the imperial state should be. Moreover, if the people of Enna, Megara and Syracuse thought that they had been badly treated by him, it was their own fault and not the fault of the Romans. It has already been seen that Posidonius believed that slave-owners should display *philanthrôpia* in their treatment of slaves; here the importance of *philanthrôpia* for imperial powers in their relations with their subjects is stressed.

H. Strasburger provides evidence to show that Posidonius' attitude to Roman rule was more complex that Capelle suggests. Posidonius did not consider Roman rule to be an unmitigated good and was prepared to demonstrate that Rome's treatment of her subjects was at times unjust.[50] It is necessary, however, to consider Posidonius on two levels. On the one hand there is his general view of Rome as an imperial state whose rule should be in accordance with Panaetius' theory of empire if it is to be justifiable. On the other there is his description of how the Roman empire worked in practice. If he believed any of its conduct to be unjust, this was only in the light of how that empire was viewed by him; the individual action contradicted the essence of its imperial purpose. If he did not take such a view, everything Rome did while performing its imperial function would be unjust and therefore it would be wrong to distinguish between instances. It is only because Posidonius has a conception of an imperial ideal which Rome sometimes lives up to that he can criticise the Romans, implicitly or otherwise, for not living up to it. The alternative is the position put forward by Carneades and the early Stoa that empire is intrinsically unjust.

This conception of empire as the rule of the superior over the inferior for which there was a natural mandate persisted, but the unpleasant analogy with slavery largely disappeared as it became divorced from the philosophical context in which it originated. Nevertheless, its roots in Stoic theories of subordination remain visible; the relationship is still described in the Stoic terminology for subordination, such as *hupotaxis* and *hupotattô*. Dionysius of Halicarnassus, who had some familiarity with Stoic concepts,[51] tells the Greeks that they should not feel aggrieved at their *hupotaxis* to the Romans: 'it is a law of nature, common to all, which the passage of time cannot destroy, that the

[50] Strasburger 1965: 46-9.
[51] Schulze 1980: 14.

superior always rule the inferior.' The Romans are superior to any Greek or barbarian in justice, piety, temperance and war (D.H. *AR* 1.5.2-3). Here is the combination of moral and practical superiority which Posidonius had advocated (Sen. *Ep.* 90.4). The arguments of Panaetius and Posidonius which have been discussed appear also in other contexts. Dionysius argues that it is desirable that the People should be subject to the Senate, just as the body should be subject to the soul. However, his analogy is muddled; for he also compares the rule of the Senate over People to that of reason over the passions (D.H. *AR* 5.67.4). Again the term used for the relationship is *hupotattô* (cf. also Dio Chrys. 2.67-72, where it is used in support of the good king). It may be that the slave analogy of the *De Republica* developed into the more palatable patron/client metaphor, which also indicates a subservient relationship. Cicero describes the Romans as *patroni* and their empire as a *patrocinium* in the *De Officiis*, a work based on Panaetius (Cic. *De Off.* 1.35, 2.27). There is no evidence that the subject states were referred to as clients until Proculus in the first century AD (Procl. *Dig.* xlix 15.7.1).[52] Perhaps the Romans were more willing to see themselves as patrons than see their subjects as clients.

The Stoic theory of empire involved the recognition of obligations which Rome herself had to the subject states. Doubtless this was agreed with and ignored in most cases. Even so there were men such as the Stoic senator, P. Rutilius Rufus, a pupil of Panaetius, who appears to have taken these obligations seriously when he acted as an imperial administrator (Cic. *Brut.* 30.114-15, Diod. 37.5, Quintil. *Inst.* 9.1.2). The Romans disliked thinking ill of their past. Cicero believed that the destruction of Carthage and Numantia was quite warranted, but regretted that Corinth had to go; yet he is sure that Mummius had good reason for doing what he did (Cic. *De Off.* 1.35). Livy could not always resist the temptation to emend the historical records in the interests of Rome's reputation.[53] For such people benevolent empire was an attractive idea, regardless of whether or not it was acted on. It appealed to that fondness for self-congratulation which runs right through the *De Republica* and *De Legibus* of Cicero.

*

These ideas about empire became little more than comfortable platitudes for many, especially for Romans; others, such as Posidonius, were prepared to adopt a more critical, though hardly radical, approach to them. By this time, Rome had been predominant for over a hundred years. This should not lead us to underestimate the intense

---

[52] Harris 1979: 135 n. 2.
[53] E.g. Livy 45.19-20, compared with Polyb. 30.1-3, Luce 1977: 207-8.

intellectual debate out of which these ideas emerged in the second century. To do so would be to underestimate the impact of Roman expansion in Greece and the East. Intellectuals there had to come to terms with a new order. Where previously there had been a balance of power there was now only one power, to which the rest were subordinate. Consequently Roman rule was the important issue in that period. The debate which ensued reflects not only the divergence of opinion amongst the Greeks about Rome, but also the strength of feeling. For these were not banal statements of support for or opposition to Roman rule, but carefully thought out arguments. By his justification of the Roman empire Panaetius guided the Stoa towards Rome, but not all Stoics agreed with him. Blossius made the point clearly enough by going off to join Aristonicus' revolt in Asia. Not unnaturally the Romans themselves were more willing to be influenced by ideas which coincided with their own interests.[54]

---

[54] Such theories have had their modern proponents. Cicero would have approved of the admirable *humanitas* of F.S. Marvin 1922: 7-26, who argues that 'the West must be trustee for the rest of mankind' (cf. Cicero's *patrocinium*) and that their prime duty is to educate the 'backward' races. For this the West is the 'natural' leader.

Conclusion

In the field of political thought, Stoic ideas underwent a considerable transformation. That there should be change during the period from its beginnings under Zeno to the Stoa's emergence in Rome is not surprising, but the differences between the two are pronounced. The early Stoa until at least Chrysippus developed Zeno's political ideas. From the second century BC there appears not development but reaction against these ideas.

This change in the Stoa was perceived in antiquity on both a general and political level. The Epicurean Philodemus noted with some satisfaction the confusion among later Stoics as they tried to explain away Zeno's *Politeia*. Cicero was aware of an increasing tendency among Stoic philosophers such as Diogenes of Babylon and Panaetius towards greater practicality in both subject matter and style. Their predecessors, he said, had dealt with political matters in a much more theoretical fashion. Panaetius was said to have written in a more attractive style than his predecessors, content to be clear rather than precise.[1] Stoic doctrine in the hands of Panaetius was softened and he frequently introduced Plato, Aristotle, Theophrastus, Xenocrates and Dicaearchus into his discussions.[2] The first two books of the *De Officiis* provide some confirmation of this latter point; all these writers are cited, but significantly there is no mention of Zeno, Cleanthes or Chrysippus.[3] As to Posidonius Galen had stressed his differences from Chrysippus, in particular in the matter of the soul, on which he believed that Posidonius was heavily influenced by Plato (EK T96-9, F32-4, 142-6). The political significance of the soul in the work of Plato and the Stoics has been discussed earlier.[4]

---

[1] Cic. *De Leg*, 3.14, Panaetius F.48, *De Fin*. 4.78-9, Panaetius F.55, *De Off*. 2.35, Panaetius F.62, contrast Cic. *De Fin*. 4.7, 4.78 on the stylistic inadequacies of the early Stoa.

[2] Cic. *De Fin*. 4.79, Panaetius F.55, cf. Chapter 8.4, and nn. 34 and 35 there for further references to the influence of Aristotle and Plato on Panaetius.

[3] The references to these in Cicero's *De Officiis* 1 and 2 are as follows: Plato: 1.4, 1.15, 1.22, 1.28, 1.63, 1.64, 1.85, 1.87, 1.155. Aristotle: 1.4, 2.56. Theophrastus: 1.3, 2.56, 2.64. Xenocrates: 1.109 (though the text seems corrupt here). Dicaearchus: 2.16.

[4] Plato had given the soul political sigificance by comparing it to a state. The early Stoa had reacted against him by rejecting the divided soul and replacing it with a unitary one,

This shift in Stoic thinking is apparent in the attitudes of the later Stoics to their predecessors. There was much that they found positively embarrassing, in particular the *Politeia* of Zeno. The approach of the later Stoics to Zeno was different from their approach to other early Stoics, such as Chrysippus. Zeno was the founder of Stoicism and consequently had to be treated with caution. It would not be appropriate to attack the founder of the school.[5] The more unpalatable elements of his thought were excused, disowned or re-interpreted. This has been demonstrated in Chapter 1 as regards the treatment of the *Politeia*. Zeno's career was divided into two parts. While he was young and foolish he produced the *Politeia*; only later did he produce work that merited serious attention. His work could also be re-interpreted; Galen, though not an impartial source on this point, could claim that Posidonius tried to turn Zeno into a Platonist (EK T99).

Yet the political thought of the *Politeia* was continued in later Stoics such as Chrysippus. But Chrysippus was not so immune from criticism as Zeno. He was not the founder of the school, so disagreeing with him did not prejudice one's standing as a Stoic. Seneca, after acknowledging that he was a great man, is quite happy to ridicule him (Sen. *De Ben*. 1.3.8-4.6). If his views were unsatisfactory, they could be seen as misinterpretation of Zeno. According to Diogenes Laertius he disagreed with Zeno and Cleanthes on almost everything (D.L. 7.179, SVF 2.1). This sounds implausibly extreme and is not supported by the evidence. Such an argument probably emanates from Stoics who wanted a more comfortable heritage. According to Galen Posidonius had claimed that Chrysippus disagreed with both Zeno and Cleanthes on the nature of the soul. Yet Posidonius' main evidence for attributing a Platonic conception of the soul to Zeno and Cleanthes appears to be four ambiguous lines of verse written by Cleanthes (Galen *HP* 5.475-6, EK F166).[6] Galen accepts Posidonius' claims about Cleanthes but says that he does not know what psychology Zeno proposed (Galen *HP* 5.477-8), which suggests that Posidonius produced no evidence for Zeno. Posidonius had presumably argued that because Cleanthes held that the soul was divided (at least according to Posidonius' interpretation of Cleanthes) and because Cleanthes was earlier than Chrysippus, Cleanthes must represent Zeno's views on the subject.[7] So Posidonius' treatment of the soul provides an example of a later Stoic concentrating his criticisms on Chrysippus and re-interpreting Zeno.

---

which corresponded to their own conception of the ideal society. See further on the soul, Chapter 1.4, 2.5, 3.2, 8.4.

[5] David Sedley in an unpublished paper has argued in detail that loyalty to the founder was a feature of established Hellenistic schools.

[6] Zeller 1923: 203 n. 1, followed by Rist 1969: 29, has pointed out that these verses are compatible with a unitary soul. In contrast to Posidonius, Plutarch SVF 1.202 says that Zeno, Aristo and Chrysippus all believed in a unitary soul.

[7] Rist 1969: 29-30.

The nature of the change that took place in Stoic political thought has been examined in the preceding chapters, but two questions about the process of this transition need to be faced. How was it that a philosophy which began by challenging existing conventions came to advocate the established order? And what prompted this change?

Ancient political thought was closely tied to ethics, so in an examination of political thought ethics cannot be neglected. In the early Stoa, moreover, ethics was intimately connected with physics and logic. They formed part of an integrated system; the understanding of the one entailed the understanding of the rest. K.V. Wilkes has argued that Stoic ethics were able to change from 'revisionary' to 'reactionary', because in Rome it abandoned this overall context from which it acquired its potency.[8] Physics and logic ceased to be of importance. This is apparent as early as Panaetius who had little interest in logic and appears to have downgraded the role of physics.[9] Panaetius in his definition of the end (*telos*) lays emphasis not on universal nature but on human nature.[10] Thus *phusis* was to be equated not with universal nature but with human nature and the relationship between the two became less important.

Yet the Stoa's capacity to challenge accepted conventions was derived from its stress on universal nature. It was this that demonstrated how far society as it was fell short of the ideal. Man should aim to have his own nature in harmony with the universal nature, with right reason. The man who personifies this harmonisation of human and universal nature is the wise man, but, as Wilkes points out, from Panaetius onwards he becomes less important as a 'standard or model of *aretê*'.[11] Thus there is an evident shift away from universal nature and the ideal of the wise man. It was these that allowed an external standard by which contemporary society and its moral values could be judged. By adopting such a standpoint the early Stoa could question taboos on such matters as incest within the context of a coherent framework. By emphasising human nature while at the same time neglecting universal nature, this capacity to call into question is muted.

The shift from the ideal to the actual can be seen in the increasing respect paid to existing laws and conventions,[12] as has been observed in the arguments about property. It can be acknowledged that private property is contrary to nature, while at the same time it can be

---

[8] Wilkes 1983: 183-8.

[9] Rist 1969: 174-9, Long 1974: 211, Van Straaten 1946: 130-7.

[10] Clem. Al. 2.21, Panaetius F.96, Wilkes 1983: 184, Rist 1969: 186-90.

[11] Cf. Sen. *Ep.* 116.5, Panaetius F.114, Cic. *De Off.* 2.35, Panaetius F.62, Wilkes 1983: 184.

[12] On the extent to which Stoics of the Roman period supported convention, Brunt 1975: 10-16, who writes: 'In general the conventions of the upper-class society to which both Panaetius and Cicero belonged were unquestionably accepted.'

asserted that occupancy justifies possession of it, something which is reinforced by existing laws. Cicero in the *De Legibus* may not be using a Stoic source, but he is clearly influenced by such contemporary Stoic ideas.[13] He proposes a code of law in accordance with natural law; rather than being critical of contemporary laws, he points out that what he is proposing is very similar to the laws of Rome (Cic. *De Leg.* 2.23, cf. 3.12). Chrysippus, on the other hand, condemned all existing law codes as mistaken.

This acceptance of contemporary society is reflected in the resurrection of a psychology which mirrors the structure of society as it is, not as it should be. The development of such a psychology demonstrates that the political perspective of later Stoics such as Panaetius and Posidonius was significantly different from that of the early Stoics.

The change in the Stoa is often believed to have begun with Panaetius and to be due to the Roman context. This obscures the gradualness of the process, which might be said to start once the impetus of the Stoic reaction against the ideas of Plato and Aristotle had subsided. The beginnings of the transformation are apparent as early as Diogenes of Babylon. He had concerned himself with more practical matters such as magistrates and, as was seen in Chapter 7, played an important role in the debate on private property. The change in political outlook should not be explained in terms of a single factor, such as Rome, but rather a variety of factors all contributing to this transformation over a long period of time. The importance of Rome was chiefly that it reinforced and allowed to develop an already existing trend in the Stoa. As a result of the Stoa's anti-Macedonian outlook in the third century, which was discussed in Chapter 4, the Stoa may initially have been attracted to Rome by the latter's anti-Macedonian policy.

It has already been suggested in Chapter 7 that it was Sphaerus' activities in Sparta and their repercussions as late as Nabis which prompted this initial reaction against some of the political ideas of the early Stoa. It resulted in attempts by subsequent Stoics, such as Diogenes, to dissociate themselves from such theories. Thus it helped to lead to a revision of Stoic views on property. Indeed the loss of confidence which this engendered probably led to a more extensive reassessment of doctrines as the Stoics came under attack from a revitalised Academy led by Carneades.

Although Rome may have indirectly affected the political outlook of the Stoics by causing some to wish to emphasise their dissociation from

---

[13] Stoic ideas occur at various points, e.g. *De Leg.* 1.23, the universe as *communis urbs et civitas hominum et deorum* (cf. D.L. 7.87-8), *De Leg.* 1.25, nature has put many things including animals at the service of man (cf. Chrysippus at Cic. *De Fin.* 3.67). Von Arnim prints many extracts from the *De Legibus*, see *Index Fontium*.

Sparta and Nabis, it was the later more direct contact which was to give the developing conservative tendencies within the Stoa their lasting influence. Panaetius was not the first Stoic to visit Rome. Before him Crates, a grammarian influenced by Stoicism, visited Rome in about 168; he had originally come on an embassy from Attalus of Pergamum, but when his stay in Rome was prolonged by breaking his leg he began giving lectures there.[14] In 155 Diogenes arrived on the famous embassy from Athens, although most of the emphasis in our sources is on the controversial Carneades. These and many other Greeks in Rome in the mid-second century would have helped to promote awareness of Stoicism and create an environment in which it would be more readily received.

As a result of Roman predominance in Greece many Greek ideas were entering Rome in the form of literature, art and philosophy. The latter by its nature would have caused questions to be asked which had previously been taken for granted and once asked could not be ignored. Romans who were bothered by these questions were likely to take into their favour the school whose solutions were least threatening to their own society or could be made most compatible. The Academy, even without Carneades' unpalatable arguments on Roman imperialism, would hardly have been popular, given its tendency to undermine traditional values. Of the other main school, the Epicureans, it is not difficult to see why it would not be embraced enthusiastically by such an active city.[15] The unsatisfactoriness of the other schools therefore provided a negative reason for the popularity of the Stoa in Rome.

By patronising the dissident Stoics, Romans such as Laelius and Scipio, no doubt unconsciously, fostered the new conservative outlook that is apparent in the work of such men as Panaetius and Posidonius. Panaetius, after accompanying Scipio on an embassy to the East, had lived in Rome in the 130s (see Appendix). Blossius, on the other hand, in spite of his association with Tiberius Gracchus, was hardly welcome among the Roman upper classes. It might seem odd that Romans should have been attracted to a school with the political heritage of the Stoa, even if some members of the school were trying to disinherit themselves. Political thought, however, was only an element of Stoicism; what appealed to Romans was not this but the strict morality of the Stoa, that virtue is the only good, as Cicero makes the younger Cato point out at *De Fin.* 3.10.

It may be suggested that the change in the political direction, the tendency to support the *status quo* and favour Rome, can be explained

[14] Suet. *Gram.* 2. For Stoic influence, Hansen 1971: 409-18. *Suda*, s.v. *Kratês* describes him as a Stoic philosopher.

[15] Cicero attacked the Epicureans for their non-participation in politics in particular, a snub to the whole political system; the introduction to the *De Republica* is devoted to this, cf. Cic. *De Fin.* 2.75-7.

in part by personal factors. Panaetius came from a wealthy upper-class Rhodian family active in public affairs. At the time of the Third Macedonian War and afterwards they probably favoured Rome. The intensity of the political conflict in Rhodes at that time would have led to an even more pronounced pro-Roman attitude. Thus Panaetius' background could be adduced to explain his defence of private property and support for Rome (see Appendix). Nevertheless, this does not explain change in Stoic political thought. It was not because Panaetius came from a wealthy Rhodian family and was pro-Roman that the Stoa changed.[16] Rather, it was because the Stoa was changing that it could attract a man like Panaetius. Panaetius in turn would draw the Stoa closer to Rome and take it further in the political direction in which it was already going.

The Stoa becomes transformed from a school intensely critical of contemporary society to one which largely accepts it. In the evidence which we have this is most apparent in their treatment of private property and empire, rejected by the early Stoa but justified by their successors. Now it is for the individual alone to change and not society as well. The individual should develop and exercise his virtue within the existing framework.[17] This defence of particular aspects of contemporary society reflects an increasing tendency to defend society as a whole. In the first century BC Posidonius can advocate better treatment of slaves without calling slavery itself into question.[18] Cicero, to whom this Stoic conservatism appealed, could commend moderate benefactions to the distressed, yet argue against agrarian laws and cancellation of debts on the grounds that they undermined the foundations of the state.[19] He can express doubts about the morality of those governing the empire, but not about the institution of empire itself.[20]

---

[16] It must not be imagined that Panaetius was different from earlier Stoics in being wealthy. Our evidence for their wealth is poorer, but most philosophers would tend to be from wealthy backgrounds and the Stoics seem to be no exception. Zeno's father was said to have been a merchant, D.L. 7.32, cf. 7.2, 7.4-5. Chrysippus' family was wealthy enough to contribute to Athens at the time of the liberation in 229. Cleanthes' background is much less clear. He is reported to have come to Athens with only four drachmae; his poverty was well-known and he is said to have done labouring jobs to subsist, D.L. 7.168-70.

[17] Cf. Seneca *Ep.* 120.18.

[18] FGH 87 F108c, Diod. 34/35.2.33, cf. Cic. *De Off.* 1.41, Seneca *Ep.* 47.

[19] Cic. *De Off.* 2.63, 2.78.

[20] Ibid. 2.26-7, cf. *Ad Q.F.* 1.1.

APPENDIX

Panaetius

Family

Panaetius, son of Nicagoras, was a member of a prominent Rhodian family, which played a part in the governing of Rhodes for generations (father: Panaetius F.2, 4). According to Strabo there were generals and athletes among his ancestors (Panaetius F.3, Strabo 14.2.13). It is probably Panaetius who is described in the *Index Herculanensis Stoicorum* as the eldest of three aristocratic brothers (Panaetius F.1, *Ind. Stoic.* col. 55, Van Straaten 1946: 236). As one might expect from this he possessed considerable wealth (Panaetius F.1, *Ind. Stoic.* col. 60; Traversa, following Susemihl, understands *hexis* here as wealth).

Inscriptions from Lindos in Rhodes reveal that a Panaetius, son of Nicagoras, was a hierothyte there in about 149 BC. Blinkenberg has no doubt that this is the philosopher himself (Blinkenberg 1941: no. 223, l. 17 and accompanying discussion). There are two main reasons for thinking that this is the philosopher. First, 'Panaetius' is a rare name on Rhodes and, therefore, 'Panaetius, son of Nicagoras', is rarer still (Blinkenberg 1941: 365). Secondly, the family background of this hierothyte is consistent with that of Panaetius the Stoic; the hierothyte's family is both important in Rhodian affairs and rich. As a result of this identification epigraphic evidence from Rhodes helps to fill out Strabo's rather brief statement about the philosopher's family. Since much of this comes from Lindos we know most about the priestly functions they performed. The philosopher's grandfather, Panaetius, son of Nicagoras, was a priest of Poseidon Hippios (Blinkenberg 1937: 29-30, no. 100; this appears as Panaetius F.4*, but Blinkenberg shows that it cannot be the philosopher as Hiller 1900: 21, Dittenberger SIG II, no. 725a, n. 6, believed) and in about 223 BC was the priest of Athene (Blinkenberg 1941: no. 129). He was at some point *grammateus boulas* in the city of Rhodes (*Clara Rhodos* II, p. 199, no. 31). His wealth is attested not only by his social position, but also by his large family monument with its seven statues, of himself, his wife and his five children (Blinkenberg 1941: no. 129). This monument helps to provide a basis for a family tree (for which see Blinkenberg 1941: 46). The philosopher's father, Nicagoras, son of Panaetius, was the priest of

Athene in about 184 (Blinkenberg 1941: no. 165, 166) and priest of Artemis Kekoia in about 182 (Blinkenberg 1941: no. 167). His uncle, Dionysius, son of Panaetius, was *stratêgos* in about 185 (SIG 619, 1.23; Blinkenberg 1941: no. 129), while his cousin, Panaetius, son of Dionysius, was archierothyte in about 138 (Blinkenberg 1941: no. 228, 1. 14).

Politics and Panaetius' family

Panaetius came from a state which had experienced considerable difficulties in its relationship with Rome since the beginning of the Third Macedonian War. At first sight, therefore, it may seem odd that he should be so intimate with leading Romans and especially that he should show support for their policies. As a fellow member of the upper classes he shared a similar ideology, which would embrace, for instance, concern for the protection of property rights. Nevertheless being an upper-class Greek did not necessarily entail support for Rome (cf. Briscoe 1967). At the time of the Third Macedonian War there had been serious conflict in Rhodes between those who favoured support for Rome and those who opposed it, the latter being led by Deinon and Polyaratus (Polyb. 27.7, 14, 28.2, Berthold 1984: 181-94, Deininger 1971: 184-91; the conflict is minimised by Gruen 1975: 58-81). It has already been noted that Panaetius' family had a lengthy tradition of office-holding. In such circumstances they could hardly have been indifferent to the dispute within the city. After Perseus' defeat the Rhodians at the suggestion of the Romans carried out a purge of all those who had opposed support for Rome. It was decreed that all those who were convicted of supporting Perseus in word or action would be condemned to death (Livy 45.10.4-15, Dio Cass. 20.68.1). Given Panaetius' staunchly pro-Roman position it is unlikely that his father suffered such a fate. At the same time those who did support Rome were likely to be even more demonstrative after the event in order to dissociate themselves from the anti-Roman group.

But is there any evidence for the stance adopted by Panaetius' father, Nicagoras, in this period? In 169 an embassy from Rhodes, consisting of Hagesilochos, son of Hegesias, a leading member of the pro-Roman group, Nicagoras and Nicander, was sent to Rome to acquire permission to export corn from Sicily (Polyb. 28.2.1-2, 28.16.5). Von Scala has argued that Nicagoras was the father of Panaetius, on the grounds that, if there were two prominent Rhodians called Nicagoras, Polybius would have added the father's name (Von Scala 1890: 252 n. 3, Schmekel 1892: 2 n. 1). Polybius is certainly well-informed on Rhodian names in this period, indicating a Rhodian source (Walbank 1979: 327). Moreover Panaetius' father came from that class of citizen which would tend to furnish the island with its ambassadors. If Berthold is correct to hold that Deinon and Polyaratus exercised their influence through the assembly while the pro-Roman group maintained control over the prytaneis and the council, then Nicagoras is likely to have favoured support for Rome; for embassies were appointed by the prytaneis (Berthold 1984: 186-7).

Early career

With such a background Panaetius had the time and the money to travel. He visited Pergamum, where he studied under Crates (Panaetius F.5, Strabo 14.5.16, C676), and Athens, where his teachers were the Stoics, Diogenes of Babylon and Antipater of Tarsus (Diogenes: Panaetius F.2; Antipater: Panaetius F.6, Cic. *De Div.* 1.3.6). It is an indication of his social importance that the Athenians honoured him with a crown and a *proxenia* (Panaetius F.1, *Ind. Stoic.* col. 68). This had nothing to do with his philosophical standing; for we are told that he was still young at the time. In the light of this it is probably the philosopher who appears as Panaitios Rhodios in the list of *hieropoioi* for the Athenian Ptolemaia in 148/7 (IG II^2 1938, line 25, Panaetius F.28, dated by Pritchett and Meritt 1940: xxx, Dinsmoor 1939: 193).

Panaetius and Rome

Much of what we know about Panaetius' life concerns his association with Rome, in particular with P. Scipio Aemilianus (Panaetius F.2, 8-26, 137-47). He may have come to know Scipio through C. Laelius, who was a pupil of his own teacher, Diogenes of Babylon (Panaetius F.141, Cic. *De Fin.* 2.24). As has been seen from his family history, his sympathies may already have inclined in the direction of Rome. In 140 he accompanied Scipio on an embassy to the East, visiting among other places, Rhodes and Pergamum (Panaetius F.24, 25; on the date, Astin 1959: 221-7). Whether they had met before this is unknown. Scipio would have benefited from the presence of an educated upper-class Greek who knew the area and was sympathetic to Rome. At some point, probably in the 130s, he stayed in Scipio's house in Rome (Panaetius F.8, 11, Cic. *Pro Mur.* 66, *Tusc. Disp.* 1.81), but he also must have spent some of this time in Athens, because he helped Antipater with the school (Panaetius F.31, *Ind. Stoic.* col. 60). Velleius writes that Polybius and Panaetius were with Scipio *domi militiaeque* (Panaetius F.15, Vel. Pat. 1.13.3). This has led some scholars to speculate about the campaign that Panaetius was present on; Cichorius, for instance, suggests that he was at Carthage in 146 (Cichorius 1908: 220-3, criticised by Tatakis 1931: 26). But it is unwise to press this phrase too far; Velleius may have been using it casually.

Polybius was certainly with Scipio at Carthage in 146 and Panaetius did accompany Scipio on the eastern embassy. These occasions alone may have been sufficient for Velleius to feel that the phrase was suitable. Thus it may merely confirm what we know rather than add anything new. At Rome Panaetius appears at ease. He understood Latin (Panaetius F.139, Cic. *Tusc. Disp.* 4.4) and knew a number of important Romans, apart from Scipio and Laelius, including C. Fannius and Q. Mucius Scaevola, both sons-in-law of Laelius, Q. Aelius Tubero and P. Rutilius Rufus (Panaetius F.137-47).

Bibliography

Abbreviations are those used by *L'Année Philologique.*

Aalders, H. *Political Thought in Hellenistic Times* (Amsterdam 1975)
——. *Plutarch's Political Thought* (Amsterdam 1981)
Africa, T.W. *Phylarchus and the Spartan Revolution* (Berkeley/Los Angeles 1961)
——. 'Aristonicus, Blossius and the city of the Sun', *International Review of Social History* 6 (1961), 110-24
Annas, J. 'Cicero on Stoic moral philosophy and private property' in Barnes, J. *Philosophia Togata* (forthcoming)
Arnheim, M.T.W. *Aristocracy in Greek Society* (Ithaca 1977)
Arnold, E.V. *Roman Stoicism* (London 1911)
Asheri, D. *Distribuzione di terre nell'antica Grecia* (Turin 1966)
——. 'Leggi Greche sul problema dei debiti', *SCO* 18 (1969), 5-122
——. 'La declamazione 261 di Quintilio' in *Studi in onore di Eduardo Volterra* (Milan 1971), vol. 1, 309-21
Astin, A.E. 'Diodorus and the date of the embassy to the East of Scipio Aemilianus', *CPh* 54 (1959), 221-7
——. *Scipio Aemilianus* (Oxford 1967)
——. *Cato the Censor* (Oxford 1978)
Babut, D. *Plutarque et le Stoïcisme* (Paris 1969)
Badian, E. 'Alexander the Great and the unity of mankind', *Historia* 7 (1958), 425-44
——. 'Tiberius Gracchus and the Roman revolution', *Aufstieg und Niedergang der röm. Welt*, vol. 1 (1972), 668-731
——. *Publicans and Sinners* (Oxford 1972)
Bagnall, R.S. *The Administration of the Ptolemaic Possessions outside Egypt* (Leiden 1976)
Baldry, H.C. 'Zeno's ideal state', *JHS* 79 (1959), 3-15
——. *The Unity of Mankind in Greek Thought* (Cambridge 1970)
Bauman, R.A. *Lawyers in Roman Republican Politics* (Munich 1983)
✳Baur, C. *John Chrysostom and his Time*, 2 vols (London/Glasgow 1959)
Bayer, E. *Demetrios Phalereus der Athener* (Berlin/Stuttgart 1942)
Beloch, K. *Griechische Geschichte*, 2nd ed. (Berlin/Leipzig, vol. 4.1, 1925, vol. 4.2, 1927)
Bernstein, A. *Tiberius Sempronius Gracchus – Tradition and Apostasy* (Cornell 1978)
Berthold, R. *Rhodes in the Hellenistic Age* (Ithaca 1984)
Bevan, E.R. *Stoics and Sceptics* (Oxford 1913)
Bidez, J. *La cité du monde et la cité du soleil chez les Stoïciens* (Paris 1932)
Bieber, M. *History of the Greek and Roman Theatre* (Princeton 1961)
Blinkenberg, C. *Les Prêtres de Poseidon Hippios* (Copenhagen 1937)

——. *Lindos Inscriptions*, vol. 1 (Berlin/Copenhagen 1941)

Boren, H.C. 'Tiberius Gracchus – the opposition view', *AJPh* 82 (1961), 358-69

Botsford, G.W. *Roman Assemblies* (New York 1909)

Bréhier, E. *Chrysippe et l'ancien Stoïcisme* (Paris 1951)

Brink, C.O. 'Oikeiôsis and oikeiotês – Theophrastus and Zeno on Nature in moral theory', *Phronesis* 1 (1956), 123-45

—— and Walbank, F.W. 'The construction of the sixth book of Polybius', *CQ* 4 (1954), 97-122

Briscoe, J. 'Rome and the class struggle in the Greek states, 200-146 BC', *Past and Present* 36 (1967), 3-20, also in Finley, M.I. *Studies in Ancient Society* (Cambridge 1974), 53-73

——. *A Commentary on Livy, Books 31-33* (Oxford 1973)

——. 'The Antigonids and the Greek states, 276-196 BC' in Garnsey, P. and Whittaker, C.R. *Imperialism in the Ancient World* (Cambridge 1978), 145-58

——. *A Commentary on Livy, Books 34-37* (Oxford 1981)

Brunt, P.A. 'Aspects of the social thought of Dio Chrysostom and the Stoics', *PCPhS* 19 (1973), 9-34

——. 'Stoicism and the Principate', *PBSR* 30 (1975), 7-35

——. 'From Epictetus to Arrian', *Athenaeum* 55 (1977), 19-48

——, 'Laus Imperii' in *Imperialism in the Ancient World*, ed. Garnsey, P. and Whittaker, C.R. (Cambridge 1978), 159-92

Burnyeat, M. 'Aristotle on learning to be good' in *Essays on Aristotle's Ethics*, ed. Rorty, A.O. (California 1980), 69-92

Bux, E. 'Zwei sozialistische Novellen bei Plutarch', *Klio* 19 (1925), 413-31

Cameron, A. 'Strato and Rufinus', *CQ* 32 (1982), 162-73

Capelle, W. 'Griechische Ethik und römischer Imperialismus', *Klio* 25 (1932), 86-113

Cartledge, P. *Sparta and Lakonia* (London 1979)

Chadwick, H. and Oulton, J.E.L. *Alexandrian Christianity* (London 1954)

Chrimes, K.M.T. *Ancient Sparta* (Manchester 1949)

Chroust, A-H. 'The ideal polity of the early Stoics: Zeno's *Republic*', *Review of Politics* 27 (1965), 173-83

——. *Aristotle* (London 1973)

Cichorius, C. 'Panaitios und die attische Stoikerinschrift', *RhM* NF 63 (1908), 197-223

Cloché, P. 'Remarques sur les règnes d'Agis IV et Cléomène III', *REG* 56 (1943), 53-71

Coleman-Norton, P. 'St. John Chrysostom and Greek philosophy', *CPh* 25 (1930), 305-17

Colish, M.L. *The Stoic Tradition from Antiquity to the Early Middle Ages*, 2 vols (Leiden 1985)

Cooper, J.M. 'Aristotle on the goods of fortune', *PhR* 94 (1985), 173-96

Cornford, F.M. *Before and After Socrates* (Cambridge 1932)

Crönert, W. 'Kolotes und Menedemus' in Wesseley, C. *Studien zur Palaeographie und Papyruskunde*, vol. 6 (1906)

Davidson, W. *The Stoic Creed* (Edinburgh 1907)

Davies, J.K. *Athenian Propertied Families* (Oxford 1971)

Deininger, J. *Der politische Widerstand gegen Rom in Griechenland 217-86 v. Chr* (Berlin 1971)

De Lacy, P. Review of Simon 1956 in *Gnomon* 30 (1958), 60-3

Delatte, A. *Les traités de la Royauté d'Ecphante, Diotogène et Sthénidas* (Paris/Liège 1942)

Derow, P.S. 'Rome, Polybius and the East', *JRS* 69 (1979), 1-15

——. Review of Walbank 1979, *JRS* 74 (1984), 231-5

De Ste Croix, G.E.M. *The Origins of the Peloponnesian War* (London 1972)

——. 'Early Christian attitudes to property and slavery' in *Studies in Church History* 12 (1975), 1-38

——. *Class Struggle in the Ancient Greek World* (London 1981)

Devine, F.E. 'Stoicism on the best regime', *Journal of the History of Ideas* 31 (1970), 323-36

De Vries, G.J. *Commentary on the 'Phaedrus' of Plato* (Amsterdam 1969)

De Witt, N.W. *Epicurus and his Philosophy* (Minneapolis 1954)

Dinsmoor, W.B. *The Athenian Archon List in the light of recent discoveries* (New York 1939)

Dorandi, T. 'Filodemo. Gli Stoici (P. Herc. 155 e 339)', *Cronache Ercolanesi* 12 (1982), 91-133

Dow, S. and Edson, C. 'Chryseis', *HSPh* 48 (1937), 127-80

Droysen, J.G. *Geschichte des Hellenismus* (Gotha 1877, 2nd ed.)

——. 'Der attische Volksbeschluss zu Ehren des Zenon', *Hermes* 16 (1881), 291-301

Dudley, D.R. *History of Cynicism* (London 1937)

——. 'Blossius of Cumae', *JRS* 31 (1941)

Dunn, J. 'The identity of the history of ideas', in *Philosophy, Politics and Society*, 4th series, ed. P. Laslett, W.G. Runciman, Q. Skinner (Oxford 1972), 158-73

Dyroff, A. *Die Ethik der alten Stoa* (Berlin 1897)

Earl, D. *Tiberius Gracchus – a study in politics* (Brussels 1963)

Edelstein, L. *The Meaning of Stoicism* (Cambridge, Mass. 1966)

Étienne, R. 'Le Koinon des Hellènes à Platées et Glaucon, fils d'Étéoclès', in *La Béotie Antique*, Actes de Colloque International, 16-20 May 1983 (Paris 1985), 259-63

—— and Piérart, M. 'Un décret du Koinon des Hellènes à Platées en l'honneur de Glaucon, fils d'Étéoclès, d'Athènes', *BCH* 99 (1975), 51-75

Farrington, B. *Science and Politics in the Ancient World* (London 1939)

——. *The Faith of Epicurus* (New York 1967)

Ferguson, J. *Utopias of the Ancient World* (London 1975)

Ferguson, W.S. *Hellenistic Athens* (London 1911)

Ferrabino, A. *Il problema dell'unità nazionale nella Grecia antica I: Arato di Sicione e l'idea nazionale* (Florence 1921)

Ferrary, J-L. 'Le Discours de Philus (Cicéron, *De Re Publica* III. 8-31)', *REL* 55 (1977), 128-56

Finley, M.I. (ed.) *Slavery in Classical Antiquity* (Cambridge 1960)

——. 'Inalienability of land in ancient Greece: a point of view', *Eirene* 7 (1968), 25-32

——. *Slavery and Modern Ideology* (London 1980)

Fisch, M.H. 'Alexander and the Stoics', *AJPh* 58 (1937), 59-82, 129-51

Flacelière, R. and Chambry, E. *Plutarques Vies – Agis/Cléomène, Les Gracques* (Paris 1976)

Forrest, W.G. 'The date of the Lycurgan reforms in Sparta', *Phoenix* 17 (1963), 157-79

——. *A History of Sparta* (London 1980, 2nd ed.)

Forte, B. *Rome and the Romans, as the Greeks saw them*, Papers and Monographs of the American Academy in Rome, vol. 24 (1972)

Fortenbaugh, W.W. (ed.) *On Stoic and Peripatetic Ethics: the work of Arius Didymus*, Rutgers University Studies in Classical Humanities, vol. 1 (1983)

Fraccaro, P. 'Studi nell'età graccana', *Studi storici* 5 (1912), 317-448, 6 (1913), 42-136

Fraser, P.M. Review of Habicht 1979, *CR* 31 (1981), 240-2

——. *Ptolemaic Alexandria*, 3 vols (Oxford 1972)

Fuchs, H. *Der geistige Widerstand gegen Rom* (Berlin 1964)

Fuks, A. 'Agis, Cleomenes and equality', *CPh* 57 (1962), 161-6

——. 'The Spartan citizen body in the mid third century and its enlargement proposed by Agis IV', *Athenaeum* 40 (1962), 244-63

——. 'Non-Phylarchean tradition of the programme of Agis IV', *CQ* 12 (1962) 118-21

——. 'Social revolution in Greece in the Hellenistic Age', *La Parola del Passato* 111 (1966), 437-48

——. 'Redistribution of land and houses in Syracuse in 356 BC and its ideological aspect', *CQ* 18 (1968) 207-23

——. 'Patterns and types of social-economic revolution in Greece from the 4th to the 2nd century BC', *Ancient Society* 5 (1974), 51-81

Gabba, E. 'Studi su Filarco', *Athenaeum* 35 (1957), 3-55, 193-239

——. Review of Africa 1961 in *RFIC* 91 (1963), 359-63

——. 'Studi su Dionigi d'Alicarnasso', *Athenaeum* 42 (1964), 29-41

Gehrke, H-J. 'Das Verhältnis von Politik und Philosophie in Wirken des Demetrius von Phalerum', *Chiron* 8 (1978), 149-93

Gill, C. 'Did Chrysippus understand Medea?', *Phronesis* 28 (1983), 136-49

Glucker, J. *Antiochus and the Late Academy* (Göttingen 1978)

Gould, J. *The Philosophy of Chrysippus* (Leiden 1970)

Graham, A.J. 'The colonial expansion of Greece', *Cambridge Ancient History* vol. 3 pt. 1 (Cambridge 1982)

Grant, R.M. *Early Christianity and Society* (London 1978)

Griffin, M. *Seneca, a Philosopher in Politics* (Oxford 1976)

Grilli, A. *Il problema della vita contemplativa nel mondo greco-romano* (Milan/Rome 1953)

——. 'Zenone e Antigono II', *RFIC* 91 (1963), 287-301

Grote, G. *History of Greece*, vol. 2 (London 1872, 4th ed.)

Gruen, E. *The Hellenistic World and the Coming of Rome*, 2 vols (Berkeley/Los Angeles 1984)

——. 'Rome and Rhodes in the second century BC; a historiographical inquiry' *CQ* 25 (1975), 58-81

Gullath, B. *Untersuchungen zur Geschichte Boiotiens in der Zeit Alexanders und der Diadochen* (Frankfurt/Bern 1972)

Guthrie, W.K.C. *A History of Greek Philosophy*, vol. 3 (Cambridge 1969)

Habicht, C. *Untersuchungen zur politischen Geschichte im 3. Jahrhundert v. Chr.* (Munich 1979)

——. *Studien zur Geschichte Athens in hellenistischer Zeit* (Göttingen 1982)

——. *Pausanias' Guide to Ancient Greece* (Berkeley/Los Angeles 1985)

Hadas, M. 'The social revolution in third-century Sparta', *Classical Weekly* 26 (1932), 65-8, 73-6

Hadot, I. 'Tradition stoïcienne et idées politiques au temps des Gracques', *REL* 48 (1970), 133-79

Haepke, N. *C. Sempronii Gracchi Romani Fragmenta Collecta et Illustrata* (Munich 1915)

Hagendahl, H. *Augustine and the Classics* (Göteborg 1967)

Hammond N.G.L. and Walbank, F.W. *A History of Macedonia*, vol. 3 (Oxford 1988)

Hansen, E.V. *The Attalids of Pergamum* (Ithaca/London 1971, 2nd ed.)

Harris, W.V. *War and Imperialism in Republican Rome 327-70 BC* (Oxford 1979)

Heinen, H. *Untersuchungen zur hellenistichen Geschichte des 3. Jahrhunderts v. Chr.* (Wiesbaden 1972)

Hill, H. *The Roman Middle Class in the Republican Period* (New York 1951)

Hiller, F. Review in *Berliner Philologische Wochenschrift* (1900), 16-22

Hirzel, R. *Untersuchungen zu Ciceros philosophischen Schriften*, vol. 2 (Leipzig 1882)

Holleaux, M. *Études d'épigraphie et d'histoire grecques*, vol. 3 (Paris 1942)

Hope, R. *The Book of Diogenes Laertius* (New York 1930)

Immerwahr, H.R. 'Five dedicatory inscriptions from the north wall of the Acropolis', *Hesperia* 11 (1942), 338-48

Ingholt, H. 'Aratus and Chrysippus on a lead medallion from a Beirut collection', *Berytus* 17 (1967-68), 143-77

Inwood, B. *Ethics and Human Action in Early Stoicism* (Oxford 1985)

——. Commentary on Striker 1987 in Cleary, J.J. *Proceedings of the Boston Area Colloquium in Ancient Philosophy*, vol. 2 (Lanham/London 1987), 95-101

Irwin, T. 'Stoic and Aristotelian conceptions of happiness' in Schofield, M. and Striker, G. *The Norms of Nature* (Cambridge 1986), 205-44

Jacoby, F. *Apollodors Chronik* (Berlin 1902)

Jones, A.H.M. *Sparta* (Oxford 1967)

Kaerst, J. *Studien zur Entwicklung und theoretische Begrundung der Monarchie im Altertum* (Munich 1898)

——. *Geschichte des Hellenismus*, vol. 2 (Leipzig/Berlin 1926, 2nd ed.)

Kagan, D. *The Great Dialogue – The History of Greek Political Thought* (New York 1965)

Kargl, J. *Die Lehre der Stoiker vom Staat* (Erlangen 1913)

Katz, S. 'The Gracchi – an essay in interpretation', *CJ* 38 (1942), 65ff

Kerferd, G.B. 'What does the wise man know?' in Rist 1978: 125-36

Kessler, E. *Plutarchs Leben des Lykurgos* (Berlin 1910)

Kidd, I.G. 'Stoic intermediates and the end for man' in Long 1971: 150-72

——. 'Posidonius on Emotions' in Long 1971: 200-15

——. 'Posidonian methodology and the self-sufficiency of virtue' in *Aspects de la Philosophie Hellénistique, Fondation Hardt*, vol. 32 (Geneva 1986)

Kirk, G.S., Raven, J.E and Schofield, M. *The Presocratic Philosophers* (Cambridge 1983, 2nd ed.)

Köhler, U. 'Exegetisch-kritische Ammerkungen zu den Fragmenten des Antigonos von Karystos', *RhM* 39 (1884), 292-300

Krämer, H. *Quid valeat homonoia in litteris Graecis* (Göttingen 1915)

Kroll, J.H. 'Early Athenian bronze coinage c. 350-250 BC' in *Essays in honour of M. Thompson*, ed. O. Morkholm and N. Waggoner (Wetteren, Belgium 1979)

Laffranque, M. *Poseidonios d'Apamée* (Paris 1964)

Legrand, P.E. 'Sur quelques épigrammes du IIIe siècle', *REA* 3 (1901), 185-95

Long, A.A. 'Carneades and the Stoic *telos*', *Phronesis* 12 (1967), 59-90
——. 'The Stoic concept of evil', *PhilosQ* 18 (1968), 329-43
✗—— (ed.). *Problems in Stoicism* (London 1971)
——. 'Language and thought in Stoicism' in Long 1971: 75-113
——. 'Freedom and Determinism in the Stoic theory of human action' in Long 1971: 173-99
✗——. *Hellenistic Philosophy* (London 1974, 2nd ed. 1986)
——. 'The Early Stoic concept of moral choice' in *Images of Man in Ancient and Medieval Thought – Studies for Gerado Verbeke* (Louvain 1976), 77-92
Luce, T.J. *Livy, the composition of his history* (Princeton 1977)
Lynch, J.P. *Aristotle's School* (California 1972)
Macdowell, D.M. *Spartan Law* (Edinburgh 1986)
Marrou, H. *History of Education in the Ancient World* (London 1956)
Marvin, F.S. *Western Races and the World* (Oxford 1922)
Martha, C. 'Le philosophe Carnéade à Rome', in *Études morales sur l'antiquité* (Paris 1896), 61-134
Mejer, J. *Diogenes Laertius and his Hellenistic Background*, Hermes Einzelschriften (Wiesbaden 1978)
Mendels, D. 'Sparta in Teles' *Peri Phugês*', *Eranos* 77 (1979), 111-15
——. 'Polybius and the socio-economic reforms of Cleomenes III re-examined', *Grazer Beiträge* 10 (1981 (1983)), 95-104
Merlan, P. 'Alexander the Great and Antiphon the Sophist', *CPh* 45 (1950), 161-6
Michell, H. *Sparta* (Cambridge 1952)
Milani, P. *La schiavitu nel pensiero politico: dai Greci al Basso Medio Evo* (Milan 1972)
Momigliano, A. *Alien Wisdom* (Cambridge 1975)
——. 'Athens in the third century BC and the discovery of Rome in the Histories of Timaeus of Tauromenium', in *Essays in Ancient and Modern Historiography* (Oxford 1977), 37-66
Mommsen, T. *Die römische Chronologie bis auf Caesar*, 2 vols (Berlin 1859)
——. *Römisches Staatsrecht*, vol. 3.2 (Leipzig 1888)
Müller, A. *Autonome Theorie und Interessedenken, Studien zur politische Philosophie bei Platon, Aristoteles und Cicero* (Wiesbaden 1971)
Müller, R. 'Zur Staatsauffassung der frühen Stoa' in *Proceedings of the 7th Congress of the International Federation of the Societies of Classical Studies*, ed. J. Harmatta, vol. 1 (Budapest 1984), 293-301
Murray, O. 'Philodemus and the Good King according to Homer', *JRS* 55 (1965), 161-82
——. Review of Baldry 1965 in *CR* 80 (1966), 368-71
——. *Peri Basileias – Studies in the Justification of Monarchic Power* (D. Phil. Oxford 1970)
Musti, D. 'Polibio e la democrazia', *Annali della Scuola Normale Superiore di Pisa* 36 (1967), 155-207
Nicolet, C. 'L'inspiration de Tiberius Gracchus', *REG* 67 (1965), 142-58
——. 'La polémique politique au IIe siècle' in *Demokratia et Aristokratia*, ed. C. Nicolet (Paris 1985), 37-50
Oliva, P. *Sparta and her Social Problems* (Prague 1971)
Ollier, F. 'Le philosophe stoïcien Sphairos et l'oeuvre réformatrice des rois de Sparte Agis IV et Cléomène III', *REG* 49 (1936), 536-70
——. *Le Mirage Spartiate*, vol. 1 (Paris 1933), vol. 2 (1943)

Osborne, M.J. 'Kallias, Phaedrus and the Revolt of Athens in 287 BC', *ZPE* 35 (1979), 181-94
——. *Naturalization in Athens* (Brussels, vol. 1, 1981; vol. 2, 1982; vol. 3/4, 1983)
Pearson, A.C. *The Fragments of Zeno and Cleanthes* (Cambridge 1891)
Pembroke, S.G. 'Oikeiosis' in Long 1971: 114-49
Pfister, F. *Die Reisebilder des Herakleides* (Vienna 1951)
Philippson, R. 'Panaetiana', *RhM* 78 (1929), 337-60
Piper, L.J. *Spartan Twilight* (New York 1986)
Pöhlmann, R. von *Geschichte der sozialen Frage und des Sozialismus in der antiken Welt* (Munich 1925)
Pohlenz, M. *Antikes Führertum: Cicero De Officiis und das Lebensideal des Panaitios* (Leipzig/Berlin 1934)
——. *Freedom in Greek Life and Thought* (Dordrecht 1966)
——. *Die Stoa: Geschichte einer geistigen Bewegung*, 2 vols (Göttingen 1970, 4th ed.)
Porter, W.H. *Plutarch's Life of Aratus* (Cork 1937)
Pouilloux, J. 'Glaucon, fils d'Étéoclès, d'Athènes' in *Le monde grec – hommage à C. Preaux*, ed. Bingen, Cambier, Nachtergael (Brussels 1975), 377-82
Powell, J.U. *Collectanea Alexandrina* (Oxford 1925)
Pritchett, W.K. and Meritt, B. *Chronology of Hellenistic Athens* (Cambridge, Mass. 1940)
Rawson, E. *Intellectual Life in the Late Roman Republic* (London 1985)
Reesor, M.E. *The Political Thought of the Old and Middle Stoa* (New York 1951)
Rhodes, P.J. *The Athenian Boule* (Oxford 1972)
Rich, J.W. 'The supposed Roman manpower shortage of the later second century BC', *Historia* 32 (1983), 287-331
——. *Declaring War in the Roman Republic* (Brussels 1976)
Richter, W. 'Seneca und die Sklaverei', *Gymnasium* 65 (1958), 196-218
Rist, J.M. *Stoic Philosophy* (Cambridge 1969)
——. *Epicurus: an introduction* (Cambridge 1972)
——. 'Zeno and Stoic consistency', *Phronesis* 22 (1977), 161-74
——— (ed.). *The Stoics* (California 1978)
——. 'The Stoic concept of detachment' in *Rist* 1978: 259-72
Robert, L. 'Sur des inscriptions d'Éphèse: 9', *RPh* 41 (1967), 1-84
Rohde, E. 'Die Chronologie des Zeno von Kition', *RhM* 33 (1878), 622-5
Rorty, R. 'The historiography of philosophy: four genres', in *Philosophy in History*, ed. R. Rorty, J.B. Schneewind, Q. Skinner (Cambridge 1984), 49-75
Rostovtzeff, M. *The Social and Economic History of the Hellenistic World* (Oxford 1941)
Samuel, A.E. *Ptolemaic Chronology* (Munich 1962)
Sanctis, G. de 'Atene dopo Ipso e un Papiro Fiorentino', *RFIC* 64 (1936), 134-52, 253-73
Sandbach, F.H. *The Stoics* (London 1975)
Sartori, F. 'Cremonide: un dissidio fra politica e filosofia' in *Miscellanea di studi Alessandrini in memoria di Augusti Rostagni* (Turin 1963), 118-51
Schäfer, M. *Ein frühmittelstoiches System der Ethik bei Cicero* (Munich 1934)
Schlaifer, R. 'Greek theories of slavery from Homer to Aristotle', *HSPh* 47 (1936), 165-204, and Finley 1960, 93-132
Schmekel, A. *Die Philosophie der mittleren Stoa in ihren geschichtlichen*

Zusammenhangen dargestellt (Berlin 1892)

Schulze, C.E. *Dionysius of Halicarnassus as an historian* (D.Phil. thesis Oxford 1980)

Scullard, H.H. 'Scipio Aemilianus and Roman Politics', *JRS* 50 (1960) 59-74

Seel, O. *Römisches Denken und römischer Staat* (Leipzig/Berlin 1937)

Shear, T.L. *Kallias of Sphettos and the revolt of Athens 286 BC* (Princeton 1978)

Shimron, B. 'Polybius and the reforms of Cleomenes III', *Historia* 13 (1964), 147-55

——. 'Some remarks on Phylarchos and Cleomenes III', *RFIC* 94 (1966), 452-9

——. *Late Sparta* (Buffalo 1972)

Shochat, Y. *Recruitment and the Programme of Tiberius Gracchus* (Brussels 1980)

Simon, H. and M. *Die alte Stoa und ihr Naturbegriff* (Berlin 1956)

Simpson, R.H. 'Antigonus the One-eyed and the Greeks', *Historia* 8 (1958), 385-409

Sinclair, T.A. *A History of Greek Political Thought* (London 1967²)

Sizoo, A. 'Paetus Thrasea et le stoïcisme', *REL* 4 (1926), 229-37; 5 (1927), 41-52

Skeat, T.C. 'The reigns of the Ptolemies', *Mizraim* 6 (1937), 7-40

Skinner, Q. 'Meaning and understanding in the history of ideas', *History and Theory* 8 (1969) 3-53

——. 'Some problems in the analysis of political thought and action', *Political Theory* 2 (1974) 277-303

Smith, R.E. *The Failure of the Roman Republic* (Cambridge 1955)

Smuts, F. 'Stoisyne invloed op Tiberius Gracchus', *Acta Classica* (1958), 106-16

Stalley, R.F. *An Introduction to Plato's Laws* (Oxford 1983)

Strasburger, H. 'Poseidonius on the problems of the Roman Empire', *JRS* 55 (1965), 40-53

Striker, G. 'Origins of the concept of Natural Law' in Cleary, J.J. *Proceedings of the Boston Area Colloquium in Ancient Philosophy*, vol. 2 (Lanham/London 1987), 79-94

Susemihl, F. *Geschichte der griechischen Literatur in der Alexanderzeit* (Leipzig 1891)

Swift, L.J. '*Iustitia* and *ius privatum*: Ambrose on private property', *AJPh* 100 (1979), 176-87

Taeger, F. *Tiberius Gracchus* (Stuttgart 1928)

Tarn, W.W. *Antigonus Gonatas* (Oxford 1913)

——. 'The social question in the third century' in *The Hellenistic Age*, J.B. Bury etc. (1923), 108-40

——. 'Macedon and Greece' in *Cambridge Ancient History*, vol. 7 (Cambridge 1928)

——. 'Alexander the Great and the unity of mankind', *PBA* 19 (1933), 123-66

——. 'Alexander, Cynics and Stoics', *AJPh* 60 (1939), 43ff

——. *Alexander the Great* (Cambridge 1948), 2 vols

——. *Hellenistic Civilisation* (London 1952, 3rd ed.)

Tatakis, B.N. *Panétius de Rhodes* (Paris 1931)

Taylor, L.R. 'The forerunners of the Gracchi', *JRS* 52 (1962), 19-27

Testard, M. *Saint Augustin et Cicéron*, 2 vols (Paris 1958)

Thomson, G. *The Oresteia of Aeschylus*, 2 vols (Cambridge 1938)

Tigerstedt, E.N. *The Legend of Sparta in Classical Antiquity*, vol. 2 (Uppsala 1974)

Toynbee, A. *Hannibal's Legacy*, 2 vols (London 1965)

Urban, R. *Wachstum und Krise des Achäische Bunde* (Wiesbaden 1979)

Van Straaten, M. *Panétius, sa vie, ses écrits et sa doctrine* (Amsterdam 1946)

Vatai, F.L. *Intellectuals in Politics in the Greek World* (London 1984)

Vernant, J-P. 'Marriage' in *Myth and Society in Ancient Greece* (Brighton 1980), 45-70

Vlastos, G. 'Slavery in Plato's Republic', *PhR* 50 (1941), 289-304, and Finley 1960, 133-49

——. 'Isonomia', *AJP* 74 (1953), 337-66

——. 'Does slavery exist in Plato's Republic?', *CPh* 63 (1968), 291-5

Von Fritz, K. *Quellen-Untersuchungen zu Leben und Philosophie d. Diogenes von Sinope*, Philologus Suppl. 18 (Leipzig 1926)

——. *The Mixed Constitution in Antiquity* (New York 1954)

Von Scala, R. *Studien des Polybios*, vol. 1 (Stuttgart 1890)

Walbank, F.W. *Aratus of Sicyon* (Cambridge 1933)

——. 'Alcaeus of Messene, Philip V and Rome', *CQ* 37 (1943), 1-13

——. *Historical Commentary on Polybius*, vol. 1 (Oxford 1957), vol. 2 (1967), vol. 3 (1979)

——. 'Political morality and the friends of Scipio', *JRS* (1965), 1-16

——. *Polybius* (Berkeley/Los Angeles/London 1972)

——. in *Cambridge Ancient History*, vol. 7.1 (Cambridge 1984, 2nd ed.)

Watson, G. *The Stoic Theory of Knowledge* (Belfast 1966)

——. 'The Natural Law and Stoicism' in Long 1971: 216-38

Weil, R. *Aristote et l'histoire: essai sur la 'Politique'* (Paris 1960)

Welles, C.B. *Royal Correspondence in the Hellenistic Period. A Study in Greek Epigraphy* (New Haven 1934)

West, W.C. 'Hellenic Homonoia and the new decree from Plataea', *GRBS* 18 (1977), 307-19

Westerink, L.G. *The Greek Commentaries on Plato's Phaedo*, vol. 2: *Damascius* (Amsterdam/Oxford/New York 1977)

Wilamowitz, U. von *Antigonos von Karystos* (Berlin 1881)

Wilamowitz, U. von 'Die griechische Literatur des Altertums' in P. Hinneberg, *Die Kultur der Gegenwart*, I.VIII, (Berlin/Leipzig 1912), 3-318

Wilkes, K.V. 'Aspects of Stoicism: from revisionary to reactionary ethics', *Concilium Eirene XVI, Proceedings of the 16th International Eirene Conference*, ed. P. Oliva, A. Trolikova (Prague 1983), vol. 1, 183-8

Will, E. *Histoire politique du monde hellénistique*, vol. 1, (Nancy 1979, 2nd ed.)

Wiseman, T.P. 'The definition of the *Eques Romanus*', *Historia* 19 (1970), 67-83

Wood, E. and N. *Class Ideology and Ancient Political Thought* (Oxford 1978)

Wycherley, R.E. 'The Painted Stoa', *Phoenix* 7 (1953), 20-35

——. *The Athenian Agora*, vol. 3, *Literary and Epigraphical Testimonia*, (Princeton 1957)

Young, F. *From Nicaea to Chalcedon* (London 1983)

Zeller, E. *Die Philosophie der Griechen in ihrer geschichtlichen Entwicklung*, vol. 3.1: *Die nacharistotelische Philosophie* (Leipzig 1923)

Index

All dates of Roman magistracies are BC.